KEVIN F. McMURRAY

DARK DESCENT

Diving and the Deadly Allure of the
Empress of Ireland

International Marine / McGraw-Hill

Camden, Maine • New York • Chicago • San Francisco
Lisbon • London • Madrid • Mexico City • Milan • New Delhi
San Juan • Seoul • Singapore • Sydney • Toronto

The **McGraw·Hill** Companies

1 2 3 4 5 6 7 8 9 10 DOCDOC 0 9 8 7 6 5 4

Library of Congress Cataloging-in-Publication Data

McMurray, Kevin F.
  Dark descent : diving and the deadly allure of the Empress of Ireland
/ Kevin F. McMurray.— 1st US ed.
     p.   cm.
Includes bibliographical references.
  ISBN 0-07-141634-X (hardcover)
  1. Empress of Ireland (Steamship) 2. Scuba diving—Quebec
(Province)—Saint Lawrence River Estuary. 3. Shipwrecks—Quebec
(Province)—Saint Lawrence River Estuary. I. Title: Diving and the
deadly allure of the Empress of Ireland. II. Title.
  GV838.673.Q84M36 2004
  797.2'3—dc22   2003025917

Photographs © by Kevin F. McMurray unless otherwise indicated
Illustration on pages VIII-IX by Jim Sollers
Map on pages VI-VII by David Norton

In memory of divers
Edward Cossaboom, Hector Moissan,
Dr. Lise Parent, Xavier Roblain,
Pierre Lepage, and Serge Cournoyer,
who died exploring the wreck
of the *Empress of Ireland*.

"Tasting real fear sharpens the senses."

— Dany St-Cyr, *Empress of Ireland* diver

Contents

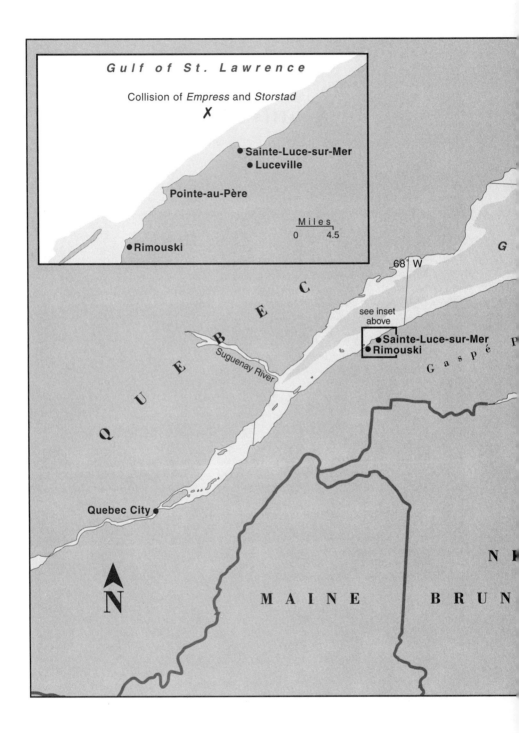

Gulf of St. Lawrence

Collision of *Empress* and *Storstad*
X

● **Sainte-Luce-sur-Mer**
● **Luceville**

Pointe-au-Père

Miles
0   4.5

● **Rimouski**

68° W

see inset
above

● **Sainte-Luce-sur-Mer**
● **Rimouski**

Suguenay River

G

QUEBEC

Gaspé P

● **Quebec City**

N

MAINE   BRUN

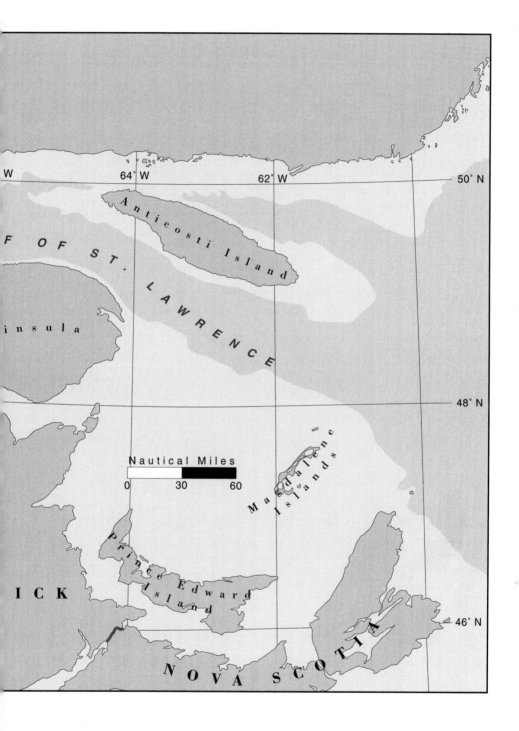

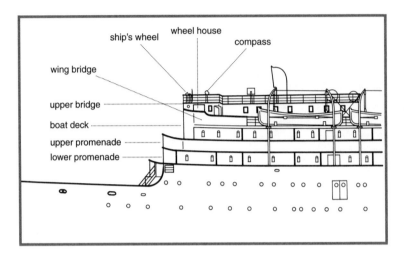

wing bridge

ship's wheel

wheel house

compass

upper bridge

boat deck

upper promenade

lower promenade

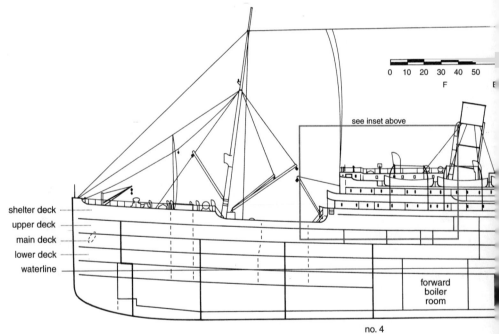

0 10 20 30 40 50

F

see inset above

shelter deck

upper deck

main deck

lower deck

waterline

forward
boiler
room

no. 4
bulkhead

The *Empress of Ireland* (from original deck plans)

Length: 548 feet
Displacement: 26,000 tons
Owner: Canadian Pacific Railway
Year of Building: 1905–6
Passenger Capacity: 1,550
Crew: 420

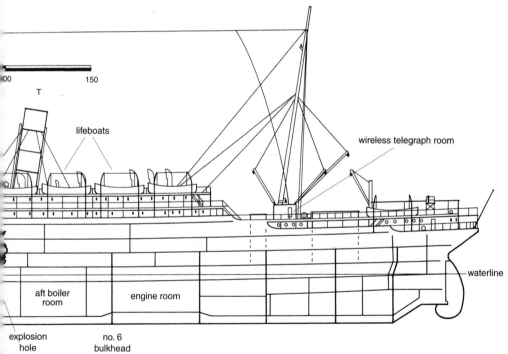

Preface

"The Empress of Ireland," Pitt said quietly. "It's the ship the
world forgot. A tomb of a thousand souls. God only knows
what we'll find when we get inside her."

—CLIVE CUSSLER, *Night Probe!*

I was in my junior year at Syracuse University when I first heard the
dramatic story of the *Empress of Ireland*. I had been a diver for a little
over three years, and like other new arrivals to the sport, I was obsessed with it. From my parents' home on Long Island, I regularly made
underwater forays into the ocean off the Island's South Shore. Being en-
sconced in central New York State during the school year, I found, was
not a hindrance to my diving ambitions. Central and upstate New York
held a wealth of diving locales.

I had joined the Syracuse Scuba Society, a group of local divers who
traveled throughout the northeastern United States to pursue their common passion. The Finger Lakes, Lake Ontario, and the Thousand Islands region of the St. Lawrence River were among the popular dive des-
tinations our club explored. It was on one such weekend trip in 1970 that
I learned of the mysterious *Empress of Ireland*.

Peter Perrault was president of the club. The forty-something engineer
was well suited to the position. He already had decades of diving experience and a contagious quest for adventure and discovery. An excellent
diver and leader, he was held in awe by the dive club members, including
me.

On that long-ago weekend, Pete Perrault regaled us with stories of his
exploits on a sunken Canadian ship somewhere in the remote Quebec
Maritimes. I don't recall the details of his story, but I clearly remember

that the sunken ship he described was one I wanted to see firsthand. To a twenty-year-old kid, such a dive had all the ingredients of an unforgettable adventure.

Perrault was planning another trip to the ship, and a few other members were planning to dive with him. I didn't have the time, the income, or the experience needed to join them; in any case, they never invited me. But I didn't let go of the idea of making the trip to distant Quebec and diving the wreck. Sure enough, almost a year later, in 1971 I found myself ready to descend to the remains of the great ocean liner.

In the early 1970s the sport of scuba diving was still new. Diving technology hadn't progressed much past the 1940s, when the Frenchmen Jacques Cousteau and Émile Gagnan conceived and built the first self-contained underwater breathing apparatus (scuba).

Sitting on a boat's gunwale waiting to enter the thirty-six-degree water of the St. Lawrence off Rimouski, Quebec, I wore a quarter-inch-thick wetsuit, a single seventy-two-cubic-foot tank with a basic regulator, fins, mask, snorkel, knife, and little else. Years later, the thin wetsuit would be replaced by a snug drysuit, the single small-volume tank upgraded to twin high-volume cylinders. My buoyancy would be controlled by a

The *Empress of Ireland*, 1906.

The author diving in California, 1970.

buoyancy compensating device, my stay on the bottom lengthened by oxygen-enriched air, my ascent determined by a dive computer, and I'd carry backups for all my equipment to ensure a safe dive.

My memory of that first dive is as murky as the frigid water I slid into. Back then most dive lights were little more than underwater penlights, not the high-candlepower floodlights available today. Consequently the meager beam hardly penetrated the forbidding darkness.

It was like swimming down into a black hole. I couldn't see the bottom, and when I looked up I couldn't see the boat sitting on the surface. The incredibly cold water rushed into my inadequate wetsuit, chilling me to the bone. As I pulled myself down the anchor line, I felt the river's herculean drag as the tidal waters rushed out to the waiting ocean—intent, it seemed, on taking me with them. My already exhausted breath bubbled out of my regulator and escaped to the surface, leaving me to stubbornly pull myself deeper.

The massive steel hull below me materialized just moments before I alighted on it. It was covered with bizarre-looking creatures I had never seen before. They looked like mutant bulbous flowers, a field of poppies stretching endlessly beyond my limited vision.

I clutched the anchor line in my neoprene-encased fist for fear of being swept away by the current into the surrounding darkness. As I surveyed my steel perch, I realized the crushing weight of the water had rendered my thin wetsuit useless against the cold and had also stripped it of its buoyancy. The fabric was sucked hard against my skin, displacing any thermal layer of warm water.

Still, I made some tentative, shivering probes into the porthole-pocked hulk. But fear was getting the best of me, as if my worst nightmare had become reality. Escaping to the surface was my only thought. Fighting the current back to the anchor line, I pulled and kicked upward until warm air and sunshine flooded my senses. It was as welcome a feeling as I had ever experienced.

I recall that on the trip back to the harbor in Rimouski (as exotic and foreign a place as I had yet visited in my young life), I thought, "God, was that stupid." I was thankful that my life had been spared and resolved to be more careful about how I spent my time underwater. Still, as the years passed, I thought often of that brief dive and of what lay beneath the waters of the St. Lawrence. It was unfinished business.

I had met the mysterious *Empress of Ireland*. The hook had been set. I wanted to learn more about her and understand why she now rested forgotten on the barren bottom of the Gulf of St. Lawrence. I wanted to swim along her corridors where passengers once strolled and peer out the windows of the bridge as her master had done. I wanted to touch the lifeboats still tethered to their davits, the same lifeboats that never received the panicky hordes who sought deliverance. I wanted to touch the raised letters that spelled out her name on the bow. I wanted to see her anchor, which would never again be weighed for distant ports. I wanted to make the *Empress* part of my life.

It took me decades, but I finally went back and wrestled with the story of the *Empress of Ireland*. My understanding would begin by learning its place in history and why it held such fascination for so many. That is why I found myself listening to a master storyteller and *Empress* expert, author Clive Cussler, as he gave me his take on the Canadian ocean liner some thirty years after my first dive on her.

Clive Cussler was a tough interview to land. In 2002, after several phone calls, I finally cajoled him into a meeting. Two years earlier, he had written some kind words about my first book, *Deep Descent*, which chronicled diving the wreck of the *Andrea Doria*, but it was our shared passion for shipwreck research that finally won him over.

I flew out to Arizona to visit him at his winter home, a fitting place for a best-selling author. I found him in the courtyard of his expansive adobe house, painting his front door. He was dressed in a polo shirt and khakis and welcomed me as if I were a neighbor dropping by. Tall and lanky and sporting a rakish goatee, the seventy-three-year-old author shuffled through the living room with me in tow. He opened a glass door to the Spanish colonial veranda and ushered me back out into the Arizona sun. A lavish, custom-designed pool lay outside the door of his library, which served as his writing space.

Cussler's two-story library would make any researcher, writer, or mariner envious. The walls hold oil paintings of famous ships, and ship models crowd the tables. All of them represent conquests of sorts for Cussler.

His two books on searches for lost shipwrecks, *The Sea Hunters* and *The Sea Hunters II*, written with coauthor Craig Dirgo, have sold millions of copies. But it is his Dirk Pitt® adventure novels such as *Raise the Titanic!*, *Inca Gold*, *Sahara*, and *Deep Six* that have financed his true passion: solving the great mysteries of ships that disappeared. Cussler himself was a deep-wreck hunter who discovered several lost ships.

I found it curious that Cussler kept only two artifacts recovered from sunken ships whose stories he had used as plots or had investigated for his nonfiction books. Both mementos were from the *Empress of Ireland*.

Cussler's philosophy about treasure hunting on shipwrecks is clear: his goal has never been lifting artifacts from famous shipwrecks for his own aggrandizement. Integrating the ship's history into his novels and solving the mysteries of lost vessels gave satisfaction enough. The famous ghost ship *Mary Celeste*, the tragic *Lexington*, the historic CSS *Hunley*,

Clive Cussler at his Arizona home.

and the torpedoed *Carpathia* were proof of that. Yet here were a soup plate and a champagne bottle from an obscure Canadian ocean liner, treasured gifts from Canadian diver Mark Reynolds.

He proudly lifted the items from a bookshelf so I could examine them. After nearly a century on the bottom of a river, the bottle was unevenly worn by the constant buffeting of water and sand. The soup plate's glaze was cracked and discolored by the salt water and mud that had entombed it. But both felt smooth in my hands and spoke of a time long past.

Cussler had never dived the wreck or even visited the remote shores of the Quebec Maritimes. Still, the vessel had inspired him; hence his reverence toward the ship's artifacts he now cradled. They were a tangible connection to the wreck, the links he needed to connect to the story of her demise. These trinkets must have made the wreck, and therefore the story, more real to him.

Before putting the story together for his novel *Night Probe!* he had briefly considered using the torpedoed ship *Lusitania* as his plot vehicle, but that wreck was simply too famous, and the story would have seemed contrived. Cussler cast about for another shipwreck that could carry the book and decided on the *Empress of Ireland*. It was a ship, he said, "that no one has ever heard of but that nonetheless was a compelling story."

A compelling story indeed. Understanding its place in history became a quest that drove me across more than three decades. Cussler, as both a shipwreck authority and a best-selling author, confirmed for me the mystery, tragedy, and intrigue of the *Empress of Ireland*.

When I returned to the *Empress* in the summers of 2002 and 2003, even though I was physically less fit than I was in 1971, I was better equipped mentally to deal with the dangers and challenges the wreck presented. And there were many.

IN THE YEARS after my first visit to the *Empress*, I had made over two thousand dives, mainly in California, the Pacific Northwest, the Caribbean, and Hawaii. But it was the northeastern United States that was to become the focus of my most dramatic dives.

The northern latitudes of this country are not blessed with warm or gin-clear waters. Surface conditions are affected by the North Atlantic's frequent storms. It's always a crapshoot whether a dive will be canceled owing to bad weather at sea. Usually you don't find out until you arrive at the dock with a gear-laden truck after a several-hour drive. The underwater world often mirrors surface conditions. In northern seas unexpected currents and thermoclines stir up silt in the nutrient-thick waters and impair visibility.

Northeast wreck diving compares to an underwater swim through a Caribbean reef system as scaling an ice-coated peak does to a stroll through a tropical garden. As you plunge through dark, freezing water, strong currents and poor visibility often render the dive an exercise in blindman's bluff. Abandoned fishing nets, monofilament, razor-sharp corroded steel, and the collapsed remains of sunken ships can trap and sometimes kill an exploring diver. Deep-wreck diving is never easy and never completely safe.

Despite the latest innovations in computing algorithms to ward off an attack, decompression sickness still plagues deep divers. Nitrogen bubbles compressed in blood and soft tissue can expand upon ascent to cripple or kill a diver. Too rich an oxygen mix can be toxic at depth, sending the diver into convulsions that often result in drowning. These dangers plague cold-water wreck divers more than others. On average there are eighty scuba-related deaths a year in the United States; a disproportionate number come from the small group of deep-wreck divers. According to the Divers Alert Network (DAN), a nonprofit organization that provides medical information and advice to the diving public, in 2001 the average incidence of decompression sickness was about 10 in 10,000 dives and 1.3 per 100 divers, but in the cold-water wreck group the average was 37 in 10,000 dives and nearly 3 per 100 divers—almost three times the overall average. Life insurance companies place divers like me in the same actuarial category as professional race car drivers. Consequently I have no life insurance. This extreme diving is not for everyone, but for those who accept the challenge and the physical risk, the rewards are plentiful. Over five hundred years of history lie hidden beneath the Atlantic off the coast of the northeastern United States and Canada. Most of this history goes unexplored, its artifacts unrecovered. The few of us who venture below are spared being overrun by theme-park masses.

The sea bottom off the northeastern United States is probably the least known. The challenging conditions there help explain why. Paradoxically, for many of us in the dive community who call the Atlantic coast our home, the difficult environment has only made us more eager to probe its mysteries. A unique creativity is required in diving there, in learning how to adapt and survive.

Warmer but bulkier drysuits have mostly replaced the old wetsuits, so we no longer have to shiver in waters that rarely rise above fifty degrees Fahrenheit on the bottom. Carrying duplicates of each piece of critical equipment has become our guard against catastrophic system failures. High-intensity lights can now better pierce the blackness of the depths, while advances in breathing-gas mixtures, such as the oxygen-enriched air called nitrox, and trimix, a helium-rich mixture, allow longer and safer stays on the bottom and reduce the chance of nitrogen narcosis.

Dive computers and software programs now take the guesswork out of decompression planning, so you know how long you have to hover at various depths as you ascend after a dive to "off-gas" the accumulated inert gas in your blood and soft tissues and decrease the chance of the dreaded "bends." Wreck-diving techniques borrowed from cave divers have made penetrating a sunken ship an experience one is more likely to return from. Such techniques as penetration lines and slimmed-down gear configurations were all pioneered by "cavers."

The advances in diving technology that make divers safer in the world's oceans made it possible for me to dive the fabled *Andrea Doria* in 1990. But descending to "the Mount Everest of diving" back then was not my culminating achievement; it was only the beginning of a renewed quest.

There was still that memory of my first bungled attempt to experience another great ocean liner that had tragically succumbed to the depths: the *Empress of Ireland*. The siren call that emanated from the cold reaches of the St. Lawrence had remained strong for many years. I suppose a lot of the appeal of diving the *Empress* versus the *Andrea Doria* was that the Canadian Pacific ship was from an era long before my time, whereas I remembered the *Andrea Doria* and its dramatic sinking. A dive to the *Empress* was a trip further back in time.

The lure of the wreck was tempered by the knowledge that more experienced divers had paid for the encounter with their lives. Researching those accidents and their causes would help protect me on my three returns in 2002 and 2003. My recounting them in these pages may also warn other divers that the *Empress* should not be taken lightly.

Exploring the *Empress of Ireland* is a pinnacle dive, a highlight of a career, much as summiting the tallest peak is for a mountaineer. And like the mountaineer entranced with his "Everest," returning again and again to relive the experience, I would return to the *Empress*. I told myself it was because the ship was so large that to know her would take a whole career of diving.

Yet there was more to it than physically experiencing the lost ocean liner. I believe it's like visiting a loved one's grave. Some things you just can't let go of—or don't want to. But why did this ship have such a hold on me?

There were the technical and physical challenges I loved, but each dive also had the potential to forge a stronger connection to a great story—a story of loss, heroism, and hubris. I wanted to be part of that story and to make the story a part of me.

I would not be alone in my journey. In August 2003 my return to the *Empress of Ireland* would be particularly poignant. I would be joining Ronni Gilligan, a pioneering diver of the *Empress*, returning to the wreck after thirty-two years. Ronni's quest to reconnect to the old ship would give me a better understanding of my own as I tried to analyze the appeal of this sunken vessel that had slipped beneath the waves ninety years ago.

CHAPTER ONE

Fourteen Minutes

Our concern for those in danger seems to turn
especially to those in peril on the sea.

—LOGAN MARSHALL, *The Tragic Story of the "Empress of Ireland"* (1914)

T hroughout Canada, winter releases its frigid grip only reluctantly.
In the Quebec Maritimes, ice floes still choke the St. Lawrence
River well into May. Abetting the freezing chokehold on this eastern Canadian province, the Labrador Current continues to chill the waters
into summer, a clear reminder that in these northern latitudes intemperate
weather reigns supreme.

The Labrador Current streams down from the Davis Strait, off the west
coast of Greenland, southward along the coast of Labrador. Colder than
the surrounding waters and laden with nutrients, the main stem of the
current continues south past Newfoundland and over the Grand Banks,
contributing to the productive groundfishery for which the Banks are
famous. But an offshoot of the Labrador Current squeezes through the
Strait of Belle Isle between Labrador and Newfoundland, then flows west-
ward along the northern shore of the Gulf of St. Lawrence. Plunging
below the outflowing surface waters, this cold, deep-running current pen-
etrates far into the gulf to the Suguenay River where a steep-walled sill
forces the frigid waters to the surface. The surrounding wind-whipped
shores bear mute witness to these forces of nature.

Loosening winter's fierce grasp, warm southern winds frequently blow
across the rolling Quebec countryside and spill out onto the river. The
meeting of cold water and warm air produces a dense concentration of water particles called advection fog as the air cools to the dew point. The

resulting phantom fog banks on the St. Lawrence are as inevitable as the tides, though not as predictable.

During the early morning hours of May 29, 1914, two ship captains, one on the bridge of an opulent ocean liner and the other on an unglamorous collier, or coal-carrying cargo ship, were speeding to their home ports, traveling in opposite directions.

Both men were intent on making their scheduled arrival times. The ocean liner's precise landfall at her destination would avoid disrupting passengers' travel plans. A timely port arrival for the collier meant fulfilling her contract for delivering a valuable cargo. But both captains had on their minds the fog regularly produced by the forces of nature along this busy waterway. Visibility could be poor to nonexistent on the St. Lawrence, and conditions had been known to change without warning.

The *Empress of Ireland*

The *Empress of Ireland*, built and operated by the Canadian Pacific Railway, was making ready for departure from Quebec City on Thursday, May 28, 1914. Aboard were 420 crew members and 1,060 passengers. The *Empress's* destination, despite her Canadian ownership, was her homeport of Liverpool, England, with her landfall projected for six days hence.

The *Empress of Ireland* was about to make her first Quebec City–Liverpool round-trip of the 1914 summer season. The ice on the St. Lawrence had finally broken up on April 25, freeing the river for transatlantic service. In Canada it was always big news when the massive steel leviathans of both shipping and passenger traffic could finally make ports of call deep in the heart of the province. During winter and spring, when the river was frozen over, ships were forced to make their landfalls in Canada at the ports of Halifax, Nova Scotia, and St. John, New Brunswick. Although fine deepwater ports, these two oceanfront cities lay hundreds of miles and many hours by train from Quebec City and Montreal, the inland hubs of Canadian commerce and the points where immigrants from Europe wanted to disembark.

By 1914 the *Empress of Ireland* had proudly flown the checkered red-and-white banner of the Canadian Pacific Railway for eight years. Along

The *Empress of Ireland*. Courtesy of P. Beaudry Collection.

with her sister ship the *Empress of Britain*, the *Empress of Ireland* had made ninety-five transatlantic crossings for the giant Canadian transportation company without major problems. The two vessels were the pride of the railway line, and the line had much to be proud of.

At the time, the Canadian Pacific Railway was one of the largest and wealthiest companies in Canada, an all-encompassing monopoly. Not only did it own the transcontinental Railway line, it also owned a fleet of ships that crossed the Pacific as well as the Atlantic. The company boasted of being able to pick up passengers in such faraway ports as Hong Kong and Yokohama, connect them with one of its famous trains for transcontinental passage across North America, with stopovers at its grand hotels in the interior of Canada, and then deliver them to another luxurious ocean liner for service to Europe.

In the first few years of the twentieth century, the Canadian Pacific Railway had been reluctant to enter the transatlantic trade, preferring to focus on its land-based operations. But it could not ignore the booming market of hordes of immigrants seeking passage to the New World. For decades the company had sat by as steamship giants Cunard and White Star amassed fortunes by transporting immigrants. It was not until a Railway rival, the Canadian Northern, threatened to leap into the business of ocean shipping that the Canadian Pacific Railway's hand was forced.

After purchasing the Elder Dempster Line and its fleet of ships in 1903 and hiring some of its experienced mariners, the company further raised the competitive stakes by ordering two new ocean liners from the renowned Fairfield Shipbuilding and Engineering Company of Glasgow, Scotland. Construction started on hull numbers 442 and 443 on Glasgow's Clyde River on April 10, 1905. The two identical vessels were the epitome of modern design. The *Empress of Britain* was launched in 1905, and the *Empress of Ireland* followed on Saturday, January 27, 1906.

Both ships were fittingly referred to as the "Empresses of the Atlantic." From stem to stern, each measured 548 feet 9 inches. From port to starboard rail they stretched 65 feet 7 inches; from the keel to the uppermost deck they soared 87 feet. The vessels drew just 27 feet fully laden, a relatively shallow draft ideal for river travel. Their gross register, or carrying capacity, was 14,191 tons, and they displaced 26,000 tons.

Two state-of-the-art quadruple-expansion reciprocating steam engines cranked out 18,000 horsepower and spun twin propellers. The *Empress of Ireland* could steam across the seas at an average cruising speed of 18 knots (21 mph), an astonishing feat for that era. The vessel also had a double bottom that ran from stem to stern, which prevented flooding should she run aground. Twin two-hundred-foot bilge keels projected from the hull below the waterline on each side, reducing the ship's tendency to roll. Ten transverse bulkheads divided the *Empress* into eleven watertight compartments, making her unsinkable—at least on the drawing board.

The helmsman steered the huge vessel by means of a telemotor, a hydraulic mechanism that transmitted the wheel's movement from the bridge to a distant steam engine in the stern through five hundred feet of copper piping to operate the rudder. The reliability of the rudder would later be called into question.

Compartments four and six in the middle of the ship were the largest, since they contained the engine room and boiler room; they took up 175 feet of the ship. In case of catastrophe, thirty-two stewards were assigned to manually close the horizontally sliding watertight doors. Operating the compartment doors was a laborious task under the best of conditions, a design flaw that would prove to be the ship's Achilles' heel.

The *Empress of Ireland* could accommodate 300 first-class passengers, 450 second-class (or cabin-class), and 800 third-class, all in a style that the *Times* of London called "delightful and cheerful."

The Canadian Pacific Railway had no desire to compete head-to-head with Cunard or White Star on sheer luxury. Those two lines served the more lucrative New York to Southampton market. The Canadian Pacific would hammer home a different marketing angle in advertisements liberally circulated throughout Europe: passage aboard one of their ships required only four days on the open sea, a powerful selling point after the recent *Titanic* disaster in 1912. Many passengers saw world travel as a dangerous endeavor, as that "unsinkable" White Star liner had proved. As a further selling point, the ocean route to Canada on the *Empress of Ireland* was considerably shorter than the New York route, with two of the journey's six days spent on the inland waterway of the St. Lawrence. Many jittery immigrants traveling in

Empress of Ireland postcard, about 1912.

third-class steerage found solace in this idea—most had never experienced ocean travel, and even fewer could swim.

Although not in the class of White Star's *Titanic, Britannic,* or *Olympic* in luxurious trappings, the *Empress of Ireland* held her own. The first-class rooms, adorned with cherry and mahogany and featuring private baths, were in the ship's airy superstructure of the upper and lower promenade decks.

A grand staircase swept down from the promenade decks under a central skylight and spilled into the shelter deck, which housed the spacious first-class dining room. The dining room accommodated families in its snug alcoves or served large parties in Edwardian splendor at banquet-sized tables. A music room, smoking room, library, open fireplaces, and children's playrooms all were much admired features on the Canadian Pacific ship. First-class trappings were lavish by today's standards and harked back to a time when travelers expected fine craftsmanship in public transportation.

If not elegant, second-class accommodations were certainly comfortable and up to snuff for travelers who were more frugal but still relatively well-off. Most of the 450 second-class passengers were either businessmen

The first-class dining room.
Courtesy of P. Beaudry Collection.

A first-class cabin.
Courtesy of P. Beaudry Collection.

The grand staircase.
Courtesy of P. Beaudry Collection.

who traveled back and forth between North America and Europe or middle-class Canadians and Americans traveling on holiday. Berthed in the main and upper decks at the rear of the ship, they too were serenaded by the ship's string quintet in the sumptuous public rooms.

Although lacking the amenities of first and second class, third-class passengers still found themselves in reasonable quarters. The Canadian Pacific adhered to government travel standards, and at the time the public considered the company to be "enlightened," and not only because of national pride. Third-class passage was highly profitable for the company. On their way to populating the open spaces of the Canadian Commonwealth, third-class passengers enriched the railway with their meager earnings (in 1914 fares for steerage were under twenty dollars, equivalent to a bit over three hundred in 2004 dollars). In 1913 alone, almost half a million immigrants crossed the Atlantic to populate the vast Canadian territories, many of them aboard the railway's two new liners. To the Canadian Pacific, there seemed no end to the traffic.

In addition to nautical engineering designed to ensure a smooth, safe passage, the *Empress of Ireland* bore sixteen steel lifeboats suspended from davits on the boat deck, as well as twenty collapsible lifeboats and twenty Berthon wood-and-canvas lifeboats, for a total of fifty-six with a total capacity for 1,948 people. The lifeboats provided a space for every passenger and crew member, as dictated by the new regulations for safety at sea after the *Titanic* disaster.

Commanding the *Empress of Ireland* was a man well suited for the job, Captain Henry George Kendall. Kendall had the kind of career that might have inspired the adventure writer Joseph Conrad. Leaving his home in Liverpool at age fifteen, Kendall signed on to a merchant marine training ship, a square-rigger named the *Iolanthe*. The *Iolanthe* and her harsh skipper were tough initiations into the mariner's life. Jumping ship in Australia to avoid a murderous shipmate, Kendall drifted from one adventure to another, having a go at panning for gold in the Australian outback, pearling in the Arafura Sea, and crewing aboard a Norwegian bark hauling nitrogen-rich guano to the United Kingdom.

Kendall finally achieved the rank of first mate aboard another square-rigged sailing vessel, the *Liverpool*, the largest British sailing ship of its time. Kendall stayed on after the Canadian Pacific Railway bought the line and continued to rise in rank for eleven years, until he acquired his own well-deserved command. Kendall was forty years old when he assumed command of the *Empress of Ireland* in April 1914. As master, or captain, on May 28 he was overseeing the loading—of coal for the ship's furnaces, of passengers, and of cargo—for only his third time, in the shadow of Quebec's Lower Town.

Captain Henry George Kendall.
Courtesy of V. Gilligan Collection.

Even though he had been with the ship a scant four weeks, Kendall was highly regarded by his crew of seasoned sailors. Joining him on the bridge were six officers, four of whom carried "master's tickets," the same captain's credentials that Kendall had. Thirty-six able-bodied seamen and a total of 130 coal stokers, firemen, engineers, and trimmers (crewmen detailed to rake, or "trim," the burning coal in the furnaces for maximum heat production and complete combustion) labored under his keen eye. The rest of the ship's crew consisted of kitchen and dining staff and stewards who catered to the passengers' other needs. With 2,600 tons of coal in her belly, the *Empress of Ireland* cast off at 4:27 P.M. on that warm, sunny May afternoon.

Among those aboard were 170 Salvation Army members. The Salvationists were off to London to attend their Third International Congress, overseen by the organization's founder, General William Booth. The contingent was led by Commissioner David Rees, head of the Salvation Army in Canada and its thirty-nine-member Territorial Staff Band. Also getting settled in their second-class cabin were fifty-year-old Major David Creighton and his wife, Bertha. David Creighton had labored long for the Salvation Army, and this trip to London was a reward for his diligent service. The couple must have been excited, looking forward to their trip across the ocean on the opulent ship; the hard life they lived with their five children among the immigrant and working class in Toronto could be put aside for a few precious weeks.

The *Empress* was not without her complement of celebrities. Foremost among them was the famous English actor Laurence Irving and his equally renowned actress wife, Mabel Hackney. The pair had just finished a triumphant tour of Canada with their acting troupe and were returning home. Also bound for England was the wealthy sportsman Sir Henry Seton-Karr, who had managed to fit in some hunting and fishing between various North American business ventures. Socialite Ethel Paton of Sherbrooke, Quebec, was to visit family in Europe, while Montreal millionaire Major Henry Lyman, fifty-nine years old, was embarking on a romantic tour of the Continent with his young bride. Filling out the first-class cabins were dozens of the moneyed elite of Canada, many traveling with nannies and maids.

Despite the prominent presence of celebrities, wealthy capitalists, and old-money aristocrats, the *Empress* passenger manifest was still representative of broad Canadian society. Berthed in the lower levels of the ship were hundreds of hardworking immigrant families, many going home to the Old World for the first time. Some were returning to reestablish links with their roots or to show off children or grandchildren. Many, no doubt, went home to spread their largesse among their less-fortunate relatives. Still others were returning home for good, broke and soured by their failed North American ventures.

That day on the *Empress*, hundreds of passengers also hailed from the American Midwest, including three hundred immigrant workers from Detroit's Ford Motor Company. The auto workers had recently been laid off and were returning to Europe until the production lines would hum once again in the fall. Passengers from the British Commonwealth countries of Australia, New Zealand, and South Africa were also among the shipboard community.

As the great ocean liner cast off from Quebec's quayside, the Salvation Army Band, assembled on the ship's promenade deck, played "O Canada" and "Auld Lang Syne" for the throngs that lined the rails. As the *Empress of Ireland* steamed out onto the river, the band ended the impromptu concert with a Salvation Army favorite: the bittersweet "God Be with You Till We Meet Again."

The *Storstad*

On May 27, 1914, after taking on 7,500 tons of coal, the steam-powered collier *Storstad* weighed anchor in Sydney, on Cape Breton Island, and began her routine run to Montreal, four days up the St. Lawrence River. The *Storstad*, a newer vessel than the *Empress of Ireland* built in 1911, was a workhorse compared with the racehorse *Empress*. She was also considerably smaller, 440 feet long and 58 feet wide. She displaced a mere 6,028 tons, and her maximum speed was 18 knots. She was built in Newcastle, England, but flew the Norwegian flag of her owner, the Klavenes line. Her single black smokestack was emblazoned with a large white *K*. The *Storstad* was an ugly, squat vessel, devoid of color. Manned by Norwegian sailors, the ship was on a charter run for the Dominion Coal Company of Canada. The *Storstad* was as suited for the unglamorous work of transporting coal as the *Empress* was for quality passenger service. The *Storstad* was designed for utility, not comfort. There was no fine wood paneling, artwork, carpeting, or grand rooms on this ship. She was a floating coal bin with engines.

The advantage the Norwegian ship had over the Canadian ocean liner was strength in design. She was a heavy cargo hauler. During the winter months she transported iron ore, and since she often called on icebound ports in Nordic countries, she had an Isherwood design system. Unlike the traditional design of vertical ribbing for hull strength used in most vessels of the time, the Isherwood system employed horizontal beams that ran from stem to stern for reinforcement. With a sharply raked, or slanted, bow designed for breaking ice, the *Storstad* was a formidable weapon against ice floes—and other ships—in the unlikely event of a collision. She was built like a chisel and could cut through another ship like a dagger.

The captain of the *Storstad*, Thomas Andersen, was a no-nonsense bull of a man with thirty years of experience on the sea. He had commanded the *Storstad* and a crew of thirty-six for the past three years without incident. Described as modest and unassuming, Captain Andersen was not a man to brag because just weeks before his ship had rescued a crew of six from a fishing boat who had been cast adrift off the coast of New Jersey.

The St. Lawrence

The St. Lawrence Seaway was still a work in progress in 1914 and would remain so for another forty years. The then-existing locks between the river and Lake Ontario would not accommodate ships longer than 250 feet. Nevertheless, the St. Lawrence was the pride of Canada. As one citizen wrote in 1914, the waterway was "a fitting entrance to a great country, an adequate environment for the history of a romantic people, a natural stage-setting for great events and gallant deeds."

When the Lachine Canal, which bypassed the Lachine Rapids in Montreal, opened up the American Midwest's Great Lakes to commercial shipping in 1825, it gave impetus for the widening and deepening of the 750-mile long St. Lawrence River to accommodate large commercial ships. By 1844, vessels over five hundred tons could navigate the entire river to Lake Ontario. The massive effort to make the St. Lawrence an economically vital waterway continued. In 1914, noted maritime historian Logan Marshall put it this way:

> The deepening of the channel, the straightening of curves and the removal of obstructions—these things have been but the beginning of measures taken for the safety of the St. Lawrence route by the Canadian government. The waterways had to be charted. The tides had to be measured. The darkness had to be lighted and beacons erected to throw a warning or a welcoming flash across the waters. Fog alarms have been installed. Wireless and other signal stations have been erected, and a system of marine intelligence has been built up to warn the mariner of coming storms. Science has been enlisted in the cause and the Dominion has in several directions been a pioneer in the world-wide work of providing for the safety of those who go down to the sea in ships.

One such safety improvement was the construction of the Pointe-au-Père (Father Point) Lighthouse, just four miles downriver from the commercial center of Rimouski near the remote Gaspé Peninsula. The lighthouse was originally built in 1859, then rebuilt in 1867 after a fire. It was replaced with still another tower of more modern design in 1909. The Pointe-au-Père Lighthouse cast a beam that could be seen for twenty miles on a clear evening, but of course it had little effect in fog.

The lighthouse was also where ships took on, and dispatched, their government-mandated river pilots. River pilots were expert navigators of the river temporarily put in charge of a ship's bridge to guide the vessel safely up and down the river. Pointe-au-Père was also the point where the river arguably became the Gulf of St. Lawrence.

Despite the efforts of the Canadian government to portray the St. Lawrence River as a safe, navigable waterway, experienced mariners were wary of its charms. In addition to weather-induced hazards common on the St. Lawrence, the river and the Gulf were both notorious for precipitous drop-offs, making depth soundings guesswork at best. The Imperial Merchant Service Guild calculated that in 1912 and 1913 "it had spent more money on Canadian lawyers to represent its members after St.

Pointe-au-Père Lighthouse, about 1914. *Courtesy of V. Gilligan Collection.*

Lawrence accidents than it had spent on legal fees in any other part of the world."

The portion of the Gulf of St. Lawrence just east of Rimouski was devoid of marked channels for vessels making their way up or down the Seaway. The channels today provide a defined two-lane waterway for ship traffic, but in 1914 defenders of the Seaway argued that none were needed, since at Pointe-au-Père the Gulf was over thirty miles wide. Surely, they said, that was enough room for oceangoing ships to maneuver.

The Collision

At his small desk in his cabin amidships, Major David Creighton wrote a letter to his oldest son, eighteen-year-old Wilfred.

My Dear Son:

We were so pleased to get your wire and to learn that all were well. May the dear Lord, whom I humbly endeavour to serve and whom you also strive to follow, abundantly bless you & Edith & Willie & Arthur & Cyrus & give us in due time the pleasure of meeting again with good news & all well.

I do believe you will all honestly strive to be helpful to each other & do your best during our absence. It was really brave of you all.

I had a frightfully busy trip down and right up to this minute. We are now sailing down along the St. Lawrence & I hope to mail this from Rimouski. Everything is going very nicely and the day has been beautiful. . . . We will have a good budget of news to mail you when we land at Liverpool.

Our very best affection & love for all. Let the others read this letter.

Papa & Mama

David Creighton signed the letter along with his wife, Bertha, and posted it in time for the bagging of mail to be shipped ashore at Rimouski. He then climbed into bed with Bertha and turned off his bedside electric lamp, sure that he and his wife would get a good night's sleep.

As David Creighton wrote, it had been a "frightfully busy" day. Long train rides and the rush of boarding a ship for Europe had exhausted the excited travelers. Few people were awake as the *Empress of Ireland* loaded her last bags of mail onto the waiting *Lady Evelyn*, a postal tender sent

The Creighton family, 1914. *Courtesy of David Creighton.*

out from Rimouski. At 1:30 A.M. the river pilot transferred to the tug *Eureka*, based at Pointe-au-Père. The tide was running in, and the temperature had dropped precipitously. The night air was well below freezing.

The *Empress*, laboring forward under the constant hum of her steam engines, slipped farther into the Gulf of St. Lawrence, glittering like a Christmas tree in the darkness. The tireless Captain Henry Kendall was still in command as the ship left the southern shore in her wake and took a northeast heading. It was customary for the captain of a vessel to stay on the bridge as long as the river pilot was aboard. Kendall was now due for relief from his next in command, Chief Officer Mansfield Steede, but Kendall was new to this ship. He wanted to remain on deck for his first trip on the *Empress* from the inland waterway to the open sea.

After the river pilot left, Kendall had his helmsman steer a course of 50 degrees, which would take him a comfortable six miles offshore from the Gaspé Peninsula. Once there, he would head east-southeast to the Cabot Strait and then east for the seas of the Atlantic, 250 miles away.

At 1:38 A.M. Seaman John Carroll, huddled in the crow's nest on the forward mast, notified the bridge that the lights of an unknown vessel were an estimated eight miles off her starboard bow. There was no cause for alarm. Ship traffic along the vital river was to be expected.

Gauging the heading of the mystery ship was a fairly straightforward affair, even in 1914. According to the Rules of the Road, the internationally accepted set of maritime standards, every ship had to have prominent range lights mounted on the forward masts and navigation lights on the starboard and port bridge beams (at the widest part of the ship).

The starboard (right) side carried a green light, the port (left) side, red. On the fore topmast was a white light, and at least fifteen feet behind it, mounted higher, was another white light. The navigation lights were screened so they could be viewed by an oncoming ship only from the angles between dead ahead and ninety degrees abeam (to the side). Thus a captain could determine an approaching ship's heading in relation to his own by reading its navigation and range lights. If the approaching ship was headed directly at him, officers on the bridge would see both the starboard and port lights and the two range lights, one above the other. If the oncoming ship slowly showed just the red light, exposing its port side, it was turning to its right, and the degree of separation between its two range lights would widen at the same time. Since the white range lights were visible from a greater distance than the red and green navigation lights, a lookout often had to guess another vessel's heading from these alone. If both range lights were visible, the vessel was heading toward the observer. (The lower, forward light could not be seen from astern.) If the forward, lower light was to the right of the higher, the other ship was angling to the observer's right, and vice versa.

Because the other ship was on his starboard bow and its forward range light was to the right of its aft one, Captain Kendall determined that the inbound ship would pass the *Empress* on her inshore side, starboard to starboard. The Rules of the Road generally called for two ships approaching each other on roughly parallel courses to pass portside to portside, but with over six miles of deep water between the *Empress*'s starboard side and the southern shores of the St. Lawrence, as well as over twenty miles to her port side, Kendall was not worried. Having put the desired distance between his ship and the southern shore, he calmly ordered his helmsman to turn the *Empress* twenty-six degrees to the right. The new heading would carry the *Empress* down through the gulf. It would also put the *Empress* on a course more parallel to that of the other ship, but still with a safe separation on a clear night.

With his binoculars locked on the oncoming ship, Kendall observed its movements. Even though the other ship was still miles away, because of the closing speed of both vessels they would pass each other in minutes. He went out onto the navigational bridge to get a bearing on the other ship from a binnacle-mounted prismatic compass that would allow him to view simultaneously the object being sighted and its magnetic heading. Before returning to the bridge, he saw the other ship's green navigation light, confirming that it would be passing the *Empress* starboard to starboard. Then Kendall noticed something else.

With his ship still under a full head of steam, he watched in consternation as a dreaded blanket of fog crept toward him from the southern shore like a slow-motion avalanche. In moments his visibility could all but disappear. Now Captain Kendall had something to worry about.

As the drama was unfolding, Chief Officer Alfred Toftenes was the officer in charge of the *Storstad*'s bridge. Captain Andersen had retired to his cabin four hours earlier to take his place in bed beside his wife (it was relatively common then for captains' wives to sail with their husbands). Toftenes, thirty-three years old, had a master's certificate and had been aboard the *Storstad* for three years. Captain Andersen had the highest regard for his seamanship. Toftenes was under orders to awaken the captain when the ship neared Pointe-au-Père to pick up the river pilot.

Toftenes had been alerted to the presence of the other ship by two clangs of the lookout's bell from the bow. Toftenes and Third Mate Jakob Saxe quickly picked up the lights of the approaching vessel at approximately the same time the *Storstad* was sighted by the *Empress*. The chief officer and Saxe later said they saw the other ship's lights off their port bow, and as they watched, the ship swung slowly toward the *Storstad*'s port side. Since the unknown ship was to his left, he decided that the Rules of the Road called for a port-to-port passing, and he maintained his course of 245 degrees (S65W).

In 1914 fog was mariners' most feared adversary. In a time before ship-to-ship radio communication and radar, fog rendered them almost clueless about the location of other ships. Ship whistles were notoriously unreliable, since fog could play tricks with sound waves. Nevertheless, mariners were required to signal their intentions: one long whistle blast for making way on a steady course; one short blast for a turn to starboard; two short blasts for a turn to port; three short blasts for slowing down; and two long blasts to signify dead in the water.

Chief Officer Toftenes was under further orders to notify Captain Andersen if fog arose. It was a duty he neglected. Perhaps Toftenes felt that the captain, who was to be awakened soon enough upon approaching Pointe-au-Père, could use the extra minutes of sleep before his long watch. Or perhaps Toftenes simply felt capable of captaining the ship through the adverse conditions.

On the bridge of the *Empress*, Captain Kendall had determined that the other vessel was holding its course. Then the fog swallowed up his ship. Though he didn't think a collision was imminent, Kendall, ordered his ship "full astern," reversing the engines. He was still confident there was no real danger; nevertheless, he took the precaution of halting his forward progress.

His decision was transmitted down to the engine room through the ship's internal telegraph and signaled to the other captain by three short blasts of the whistle. Kendall walked to the wing bridge and looked over the side to make sure his ship had stopped moving forward. Satisfied, he returned to the bridge and further ordered "stop engines." Kendall then gave the whistle two long blasts, signaling that his ship was now dead in the water. Kendall assumed the other ship would hold its course for a starboard-to-starboard passing. Although a port-to-port passing was generally preferred, every captain had the discretion to make passing decisions with the safety of his ship in mind. All Kendall could do now was wait.

Toftenes would later state that he believed the *Empress* was still off his port bow when the fog engulfed them. To be safe, Toftenes slammed the ship's telegraph indicator to "stop." The engine room responded by decoupling the shaft of the single propeller, effectively putting it in neutral. The *Storstad* couldn't come to an immediate stop and continued to plow through the seas, propelled by her forward momentum. Toftenes gave one long blast of the whistle, indicating to the other ship that he was holding his course even though the *Storstad* was no longer under power.

An event two years earlier must have been spinning through Henry Kendall's head. The *Empress of Britain*, the *Empress of Ireland*'s sister ship, had encountered heavy fog off the Magdalen Islands and had struck and sunk the British cargo ship *Helvitia*. Despite heroic action by both ships' crews, reputations and careers had been destroyed. The captain of the *Empress of Britain*, accused of excessive speed in the fog but not completely to blame, had been given a desk job in Quebec City. Kendall didn't want that to happen to him.

On the bridge of the *Storstad*, Alfred Toftenes feared that his ship, no longer under power, was losing steering control, since no water was moving against the plane of the rudder. There was also the incoming current to consider. To hold his course, Toftenes reluctantly ordered "ahead slow."

To correct the drift of the ship in the current, Toftenes then ordered his helmsman to steer her a bit to starboard and signaled his intent with a single long blast of the whistle. Toftenes then alerted Captain Andersen, in his cabin, of the fog, using the bridge's voice tube, which communicated with various parts of the ship. In the meantime Third Officer Saxe, noticing that the ship had not responded well to the corrective steering order, grabbed the wheel from the helmsman and spun it hard, turning the ship sharply to starboard.

The Fatal Embrace

Captain Kendall, still nervously waiting for the other ship to pass, slipped into the chart room directly aft of the bridge to check the time. It was 1:53 A.M. He returned to the bridge and peered apprehensively into the sepulchral fog. No more than two further minutes had passed when suddenly

Kendall saw the range lights and both navigation lights of the mystery ship appear out of the dense mist, not passing but bearing down on him. With the ship dead in the water, the starboard flank of the *Empress of Ireland* was totally vulnerable, perpendicular to the *Storstad*'s chisel-like bow. At that moment he knew the worst had come to pass: his ship was about to be rammed.

Captain Andersen had just arrived on the bridge of the *Storstad* at 1:55 A.M. He stared along his bow, shocked at what he saw. Dead ahead, shrouded in the fog but now visible, was the glittering hull of the festively lit ocean liner. Without hesitating, Andersen ordered full speed astern, trying to put his vessel in reverse, his only evasive option once he saw the ocean liner. All he could do then was brace for the impact.

Kendall ordered his engines "full ahead" and turned his huge ship hard to starboard. He hoped this desperate action would kick the starboard rear quarter out of harm's way so that his ship would suffer only a glancing blow.

Kendall grabbed the megaphone and tried to hail the other ship's bridge. But it was too late. The noise of steel crushing steel never thundered around him. There was no jarring crash, no sailors knocked from their feet. Kendall felt just a bumping sensation, barely noticed by some of the passengers belowdecks. The surprised captain of the *Empress* quickly realized why. The invading ship had penetrated as smoothly as a scalpel through the *Empress*'s most vulnerable place, between the hull's ribs in the expansive engine room, the heart of the ship.

Kendall shouted through his megaphone to the other captain to "go ahead full," hoping that the gaping wound in his ship's flank could be temporarily plugged by the bow of the invasive ship. If the *Storstad* maintained forward motion, the wound might stay closed long enough to keep the sea from pouring into his ship's engine room. Kendall desperately needed time for his crew to close the bulkhead doors in the damaged compartment or the *Empress* would sink.

Andersen had every reason to comply with the command shouted from the *Empress*'s bridge. His own crushed bow made his ship equally susceptible to the waters of the St. Lawrence, and holding the ships locked in their embrace could save them both. But Andersen could not keep the ship in place. The bigger ship was still moving forward, and seconds later his smaller vessel was swept aside.

Frigid water poured into the gash in the *Empress of Ireland*. The great ocean liner immediately began to list to starboard. Kendall's only hope for saving his ship was to run her aground on the distant south shore of the St. Lawrence, some five miles away. He ordered the engines "full speed ahead." Captain Andersen, on the bridge of the *Storstad*, watched as the black hull of the wounded ship disappeared into the fog.

Andersen's wife had rushed from their cabin and joined her husband as the *Empress* faded from view. She asked if they were going to sink. Andersen replied quietly, "I think so." If the ship was going down, then she would go down with her husband. She moved closer to his side.

Both the senior and junior wireless operators aboard the *Empress* were awakened by the ship's shrill whistles moments before the collision. Both felt the gentle bumping coming from the starboard side of the ship and ran in their pajamas to see what had happened. Peering over the side of the ocean liner, they were shocked to see the *Storstad* brushing alongside them, having just been torn from their ship's side. Senior wireless operator Norman Ferguson acted quickly, without waiting for orders. In the wireless room he cranked up the transmitter and tapped out a message to the Pointe-au-Père station saying that they had been hit by another ship and might need assistance—to stand by. Assistant operator Crawford Leslie at the Marconi wireless office at Pointe-au-Père received the message and acknowledged it.

Suddenly awakened, the Pointe-au-Père senior wireless operator William Whiteside then took over the wireless headset. Moments later he heard the SOS signal and learned that the *Empress of Ireland* was "listing terribly." But back on board the injured ship, Ferguson could not transmit the ship's coordinates; no one up on the bridge had called down with their location, and Ferguson couldn't leave his post to ask. The senior wireless operator rightly surmised that the ship's officers were occupied with saving the ship.

Ferguson could only estimate their distance from Rimouski—about twenty miles out. Whiteside tapped back that he was dispatching two rescue ships, the tender *Lady Evelyn* and the pilot boat *Eureka*. That was the last message the *Empress* received. Within seconds of Whiteside's message, the ship lost all power. By the time the captains of the *Lady Evelyn* and the *Eureka* were notified, their crews assembled, and a head of steam generated by their coal-burning engines, forty-five crucial minutes had passed.

Belowdecks on the *Empress*, most of the passengers who were awakened by the collision would later report that they hadn't thought much of it. One survivor described the noise as being "like two dishpans clashed together in the distance." Other sleep-fogged passengers thought the ship had simply brushed against the dock at Rimouski.

Second-class passenger Will Measures was awakened in his cabin on the forward main deck. He later remembered that the collision was "a gentle bump like the starting of a train." He glanced out his porthole, saw nothing but the blackness of night, and tried to go back to sleep.

Salvation Army band member Stanley Bigland, also in second class, was jarred from his slumber by the impact. Scrambling out of bed, he woke his cabin mates and told them, "Something struck us." Fellow band member Alfred Keith threw open their door to see water already pouring into the corridor. He yelled to his fellow Salvationists, "We've struck an iceberg." The men quickly pulled on their trousers.

James Duncan of London, England, would remember being awakened in his first-class cabin by the ship's whistle signals. Duncan's cabin was just above the point of impact. After dressing and grabbing his life belt, a canvas vest filled with cork, Duncan made his way up to the promenade deck to find the ship listing horribly to starboard: "It was pretty rotten on deck. We simply stood there, we knew we were going down, there was no question about that from the first, and it was no good struggling. The poor women were hysterical, but there was no chance to do anything for them."

Chief Steward Augustus Gaade was jolted from his sleep by the sound of crunching metal two decks below him. After dressing quickly, he encountered night watchman William Morl, who said they'd been hit by something. The chief steward told Morl to start waking the sleeping passengers and to have them put on their life belts and go up to the open decks. Gaade, suppressing his rising panic, rushed back to his cabin to finish dressing, then sprinted up to the boat deck to help launch the number one lifeboat.

By that time the ship had listed so badly that getting the boat in the water was almost impossible. Panicky passengers scrambled for space. Once free of its holding chucks, the boat swung wildly out over the water, pitching the occupants into the water while the six who had been trying to free it clung to the gunwales, as one observer would later say, "like so many monkeys." Gaade decided it was his duty to report to the bridge for orders.

Shutting down the bulkheads to lock off a compartment was a practiced procedure that thirty-two of the ship stewards were assigned to do in an emergency. It was a task that required a good deal of muscle. The team of stewards had to use a lever to move the horizontally sliding steel bulkhead doors, which divided each of the lower three decks into even-sized sections of passenger accommodations. Working in pitch blackness since the ship's electric power had been snuffed out, the stewards also had to overcome gravity, deep inside the ship, while fighting what must have been a strong instinct to flee for their lives, given the frightening pitch of the vessel. Standing in seawater fouled by debris and with screams of panic ringing in their ears, the stewards attempted to do the impossible.

As the team set to work, the ship listed even more sharply to starboard. Of the thirty-two stewards who manned the bulkhead doors, only thirteen would survive, and of those only five were from the wounded starboard side of the ship.

Then there was the matter of closing the portholes. Many of them were open to the cool air of the night. Many passengers had apparently ignored the stewards' earlier orders to shut them when retiring for the night. No doubt the travelers preferred sea spray to the stagnant air that aggravated seasickness. The portholes pocked the ship, some just five feet above the waterline. With the ship listing, those portholes were all submerged, and water poured through them.

After slamming the ship's telegraph indicator to "full ahead," Kendall, trying to control his fear, grabbed the bridge telephone and called down to Chief Engineer William Sampson. He ordered Sampson to give him full power, but the engineer could not restart the engines. It was easy to understand why.

The knifelike bow of the *Storstad*, over forty-six feet high, had opened a gaping wound fourteen feet wide that extended twenty-five feet below the *Empress*'s waterline. Worse than the size of the hole was its location. The watertight bulkhead between the two boiler rooms had been crushed, and the two compartments, together 175 feet long, were now open to the sea. Water poured in at sixty thousand gallons a second, extinguishing the boiler fires. The *Empress of Ireland* had lost all power and floundered helplessly in the frigid black water.

Not only was all propulsion lost, but the flooded generators meant that the *Empress* had no lights in the cabins and corridors. It was a moonless night; panic raged below in the dark, flooded passageways. Cries for help echoed down the rapidly filling corridors as people slogged through waist-deep water. There was little to be done, it seemed, but try to save oneself and one's immediate family.

The Passengers

Since it was the first night out at sea, passengers—already weary from the strain of reaching the ship via early twentieth-century transportation—would not be expected to run safety drills. The first drill was scheduled for the second day out.

Most of the passengers were not yet familiar with the layout of the ship or the location of escape routes to the boat deck. Adding to the pandemonium, the listing staircases were slanted and disorienting. The cascades of icy water quickly numbed the few lower-decks passengers who were able to escape from their cabins. It was every ocean traveler's nightmare: being trapped inside a sinking ship in freezing water in the black of night.

Second-class passenger John Black of Ottawa was one of the lucky few. Awakened by the collision, Black thought at first he had simply been having a vivid nightmare. But he stumbled to his door and looked out to see frantic passengers rushing past. Then he noticed the sharp leaning of the ship. Black shook his wife awake. The pair fled for the open deck, with his wife crying and the panic nearly consuming him. By the time they reached a railing, the *Empress* was angled so steeply that both husband and wife slipped down the deck and were pitched into the water.

The plunge sent Black deep into the St. Lawrence. He desperately struggled upward in the black water. As he burst to the surface, air filling his grateful lungs, he found his wife bobbing beside him. That was not the only miracle. A lifeboat that had broken free from its davits was just a few strokes away. Black was able to boost his wife over the boat's side, but he could not then muster the strength to climb in himself. The freezing water was robbing his extremities of all feeling and power. He told his wife to be brave, then struggled off toward another nearby lifeboat full of people. Surely, he thought, they would be able to pull him aboard.

Before he could reach the lifeboat, part of the ship's superstructure broke free and fell onto it with a terrible crash. Black shut his eyes in horror. When he opened them, he was stunned to see the lifeboat reduced to a pile of flotsam. There was no sign of survivors. At least, Black thought, their deaths were "sudden and merciful." Minutes later, a lifeboat from the *Storstad* picked him up.

Many survivors would later tell how they had slipped into the sea. Some said it felt surreal, like walking down the beach and into the water. Others reported that the deck suddenly lurched beneath them, spilling them, grasping and clawing, into the St. Lawrence. Still other passengers simply stepped off the *Empress* as if they were entering a pool. Few reported leaping from up high.

First-class passenger James Duncan of London was one of those who stepped into the sea; he was wrapped in an overcoat. He immediately began swimming for the distant *Storstad*, which appeared out of the slowly dissipating fog, not knowing that she too was wounded. Duncan's frigid swim lasted almost an hour, "a jolly long time" he later recalled with aplomb.

There was little time for heroics aboard the sinking *Empress*, as passengers and crew were overcome by the rapid deterioration of the vessel, the blackness of night, and the fast-encroaching waters. But Merton Darling of Shanghai encountered one act of selflessness. The renowned English sportsman Sir Henry Seton-Karr came upon Darling in a first-class

This chilling illustration depicting the disgorging of the *Empress*'s passengers into the sea appeared in *Colliers* magazine.

corridor full of panicking people. Darling had forgotten his life belt but had no intention of retreating to his cabin to find it. Seton-Karr thrust his own into Darling's arms. Darling tried to give it back, telling him to save himself, but the English gentleman would hear none of it. He shoved the life belt back, telling his astounded fellow passenger that he would find another. Seton-Karr rushed off before Darling could protest further. Sir Henry never found another life belt. He perished in the freezing waters.

Frederick Abbott of Toronto was the last person to see the actor Laurence Irving and his wife, Mabel Hackney, alive. He encountered them just outside their cabin in the passageway. Irving quietly asked Abbott if the ship was sinking. Told that it appeared so, Irving turned to his crying wife, telling her there was no time to lose. He moved to grab a life belt. Just at that moment the ship lurched, throwing Irving against his cabin door. His face was bloodied, and Mabel went into hysterics. Irving wrapped his wife in his arms and tried to calm her. He put the life belt on her and carried her up the leaning staircase to the boat deck. Abbott shouted after the couple, offering to help, but the English actor replied, "Look after yourself, old man, but God bless you all the same."

Abbott did just that. Jumping into the sea, he quickly found a piece of floating wood to hold on to. He could still see Irving and his wife on board the sinking *Empress*, locked in an embrace. Abbott continued to watch the couple helplessly. Just before the ship slipped away beneath their feet, they kissed one last time. Both Laurence Irving and Mabel Hackney drowned.

Third-class passenger John Fowler of Vancouver was one of the few survivors who actually saw the *Storstad* strike the *Empress of Ireland*. He too had been awakened by the two ships' warning whistles. Curious, he poked his head out his porthole on the starboard side, shocked to see another ship's bow moving rapidly toward the *Empress*'s flank. He quickly retreated inside his cabin, thinking he would be crushed. Fowler was spared the blow because he was just forward of the collision point, yet he could still see the crash by peering out his porthole. But to the Canadian, the impact didn't seem fatal.

Fowler immediately tried to close his porthole, but his cabin was so close to the waterline that the inrush of water made it almost impossible. Struggling desperately, he finally managed to wrestle it closed as the numbing water reached his shoulders. Once out in the passageway, he saw that madness had taken hold. Panic-stricken passengers were climbing

British actress and *Empress of Ireland* victim Mabel Hackney. *Courtesy of V. Gilligan Collection.*

over one another to escape from the sinking ship. Fowler came across a woman carrying two small children. He tried to reassure the frightened woman and fastened life belts on her and the children as others rushed past. Fowler was able to escort them up the slippery staircases to the open deck but quickly lost them in the chaos. There was little else to do but to save himself. He jumped into the St. Lawrence and swam until a lifeboat from the *Storstad* picked him up. John Fowler would never learn whether the mother and children survived—he didn't know their names.

Fowler and Black were not the only passengers the *Storstad* picked up. After the collision Captain Andersen quickly ordered his four lifeboats away to help rescue passengers from the sinking ship. In the fog, Andersen could not see the struggling mass of people in the freezing water below, but he certainly could hear their screams.

Like so many of the passengers aboard the *Empress of Ireland*, Salvation Army Major George Attwell and his wife barely stirred at the collision. Attwell told his wife the *Empress* must be dropping off the pilot in Rimouski, but his wife was not convinced. Finding bedlam outside their cabin, the Attwells collected themselves and rushed for the boat deck in their nightclothes. Attwell found fellow Salvationist Major Hugh Findlay trying to help his wife up the steeply angled staircase. Mrs. Findlay cried out that she couldn't make it, so her husband asked Attwell to help, but the two men together couldn't pull the older woman up. Attwell had to abandon the Findlays to save himself and his wife. It was a harrowing three minutes before the Attwells emerged into the chill air. The Findlays were not so lucky; both went down with the ship.

The Attwells climbed to the port side boat deck, but because of the pitch of the ship, the lifeboats swung inward over the boat beck and could not be launched. Knowing of no other option, the couple sat down and slid to the other side of the ocean liner and into the water.

Both Attwells had had the presence of mind to put on their life belts, which kept them afloat until they were picked up by a lifeboat from the *Storstad*. The *Empress* life belts could easily keep a grown adult afloat for days, but in the frigid water of the St. Lawrence, rescues were measured in minutes, not hours.

Before escaping, the Attwells had seen Alice Foord at the rail of the *Empress* next to her husband, Ernest, clutching their small daughter. They had no life belts. They thrust the little girl into the Attwells' arms, telling them, "We'll take our own chances." But another Salvationist, Kenneth McIntyre, came along and gave Mrs. Foord a life belt. She reached for her daughter, telling Attwell, "I'll take the baby myself now." George Attwell watched as the woman hugged the little girl and turned to find a lifeboat. The Foords never made it to safety.

It was estimated later that only those passengers who emerged from inside the ship within five minutes had any chance of survival; the others were all doomed. Within those first few minutes, water was already lapping at the boat-deck level, normally forty-five feet above the water. The dramatic list of the ship made all the boats on the port side unusable, since they were swinging from their davits over the deck instead of the sea. Falling debris made launching the starboard lifeboats a dangerous endeavor. Only six of the sixteen lifeboats were successfully put to sea.

What little hope there was for those still entombed below evaporated altogether within ten minutes of the collision, when the *Empress of Ireland* suddenly lurched to starboard, leaving just the port side of the great ship barely above water.

No survivor ever caught sight of David and Bertha Creighton among the crowd of passengers struggling to survive the calamity. The Creightons were berthed in the second-class section, two decks below the promenade deck. No one knows whether they were on the starboard or port side, since the Canadian Pacific Railway kept no such records. If they were in the starboard section, in all likelihood they were crushed or drowned quickly. If their quarters were on the port side, it may have been an agonizing wait for the encroaching waters. Their fellow Salvationists could only pray that the Crieghtons' faith eased them in their final moments.

The Heroic Captain

Before the last sudden lurch to starboard, Chief Steward Gaade found Captain Kendall on the port wing bridge issuing orders to his junior officers who were deploying the lifeboats. It had become harder and harder to stand without holding onto something. Gaade asked his captain if he could run the ship aground. Kendall, exhausted from only minimally successful attempts to save passengers and crew, said in a barely audible voice that it was not possible since they had lost all steam. Gaade then commented that it looked as if they were finished. Kendall replied, "Yes, and a terrible finish it is too."

The final violent lurch of the ship, caused by the water's filling the starboard side, catapulted Captain Kendall from the wing bridge into the water. The two large black-and-yellow smokestacks crashed into the sea, crushing many bobbing passengers. The St. Lawrence swirled down into the gaping smokestack holes, further overwhelming the ship with tons of water. The vast port side, however, was still afloat. Over seven hundred passengers clung to the black steel hull, which was slowly descending into the sea. Some of the survivors later described it as like sitting on the beach anxiously watching the tide come in: "The waves came splashing up the slope of the steel, and then retired one after the other. But each came a little higher than the last."

Just minutes later, Captain Henry Kendall, treading water in the freezing St. Lawrence, watched in shock as the *Empress of Ireland* slipped silently to the bottom, taking with her eight hundred passengers and crew still trapped inside. In her frothy wake she left a trail of bubbles, deck furniture, shattered lifeboats, and a wailing mass of humanity, many of whom would quickly perish from the cold. It was 2:09 A.M., just fourteen minutes after the collision.

Second-class passenger Robert Crellin was wearing only a nightshirt when he collected in his arms an eight-year-old child named Florence Barbour, the daughter of his neighbor back in British Columbia. She had been separated from her mother in the panic of abandoning ship. Crellin swam off in search of a lifeboat with the child clinging to his back. He later remembered that the air and water were "as cold as winter." "The child was pluckier than a stout man. She never even whimpered, and complaint was out of the question. Time and time again I feared Florence would lose her hold, and I would speak to her when my mouth and eyes were clear. Each time her little hands would clutch me tighter, until it seemed she'd stop my breath, but I welcomed the hold because it showed she had the pluck and courage needed." Crellin and the girl made it to one of the lifeboats. Florence's three-year-old sister, Evelyn, and their mother, Sabena, did not have the good fortune of encountering a man like Robert Crellin. Both drowned.

Kenneth McIntyre, one of the Salvation Army Band members who had serenaded the ship's company when leaving Quebec City just ten hours earlier, swam off in the direction of the *Storstad*. Minutes into his swim, when his arms became so numb from the cold that he lost control of them, McIntyre flipped over onto his back and began to kick. When the fog finally lifted, minutes after the *Empress* sank, the Salvationist was able to navigate to the distant *Storstad*, where he was safely pulled aboard.

Captain Andersen had been quick in getting the *Storstad*'s lifeboats into the water. After the collision the Norwegian collier had drifted just a short distance from the *Empress*. Andersen was worried that his own ship might still sink, but he could not ignore the cries for help coming from where the big ocean liner had been.

The crew from the *Storstad* made multiple trips in their lifeboats to the floating mass of terrified and crying survivors. On one such trip, a lifeboat picked up Captain Henry Kendall. Kendall then took charge of the *Storstad* lifeboat and picked up sixty survivors before returning to the collier. Kendall remained with the lifeboat and with a small crew rowed back to the site of the sinking to rescue more survivors; but time was running out for those left behind.

Nearly four hundred *Empress* survivors were eventually taken aboard the Norwegian ship *Storstad*, where Captain Andersen and his crew were overwhelmed by the crush of desperate people. All of the survivors had been ill prepared for the freezing waters of the St. Lawrence. Many had fled their berths and jumped into the water naked. The captain and crew, without hesitation, distributed their clothing to those suffering from hypothermia. Captain Andersen's wife pulled down the draperies in their cabin, which she had painstakingly sewn just days before, and distributed them to shivering survivors. Circulating among them, she poured coffee and whiskey. The generous woman even gave away her shoes. Dr. James

Grant, the *Empress*'s surgeon, had escaped from his cabin by squeezing through his porthole. He almost hadn't made it, but a passenger standing on the capsized hull noticed the doctor trying to pull himself out, grabbed him under the arms, and hauled him out. Grant suffered severe lacerations, but once free of the steel ship's embrace, he leaped into the sea. His experience among terror-crazed clusters of floating survivors was harrowing: "There were several hundred souls swimming around in the water screaming for help, shrieking as they felt themselves being carried under, and uttering strange, weird moans of terror."

Grant was scooped from the sea by a *Storstad* lifeboat. What he found aboard the Norwegian ship was equally horrifying. Wrapped in blankets and borrowed clothing, Grant did his best to attend to the survivors. Many were beyond help. Women and children died in his arms, victims of exposure. As the surgeon later put it, for many of them "the last spark of energy had been exhausted." Of the four hundred *Empress* passengers aboard the *Storstad*, twenty-two died before they could reach shore at Rimouski, less than an hour away.

Though the *Storstad*'s lifeboats arrived within minutes of the collision, they came too late for many of the desperate *Empress* passengers. The mass of screaming survivors was quickly reduced to a quiet grave of bobbing cadavers. The thirty-two-degree Fahrenheit water took a horrible toll. Over two hundred passengers who managed to flee the sinking ship lived only long enough to die from hypothermia while waiting for rescue. Gordon Davidson, however, did not give up.

Davidson, a history professor from San Francisco, managed not only the most remarkable *Empress* survival story but also one of the greatest of all time. In just his pajamas and life belt, Davidson swam all the way to land, over four miles distant, in water temperatures that killed most people in just minutes. Scrambling up the rocky shore at Sainte-Luce, Davidson headed for the church rectory's door and knocked. One can only imagine the housekeeper's shock when she opened that door in the early morning hours of May 29, 1914.

When Captain Kendall finally succumbed to fatigue, and to the realization that there were no more survivors to rescue from the now-silent waters around the tomb of his ship, he steered the lifeboat back to the *Storstad* and wearily climbed aboard. He reportedly confronted Captain Andersen on the bridge of his ship. "Sir," he said, "you have sunk my ship. You were going full speed in a dense fog."

The offended and equally spent Norwegian captain replied, "I was not going full speed. You were going full speed." Thus began the recriminations that would bedevil both Canada and Norway for months to come.

What was immediately certain was the huge loss of life in the collision. The sinking of the *Empress of Ireland* remains one of the greatest maritime disasters in the history of peacetime North America, and the most devastating in Canada. The numbers are staggering. The *Empress of Ireland* lost 840 passengers, or almost 80 percent of the paying clientele. Of the 87 passengers in first class, 36 were saved, just 41 percent. Only 48 of the 253 in second class (19 percent) lived to recount their ordeal, and just 133 of 717 (18 percent) in third class made it to shore in Rimouski.

Sadly, the statistics mock the idea of "women and children first," making the sinking an even greater tragedy. Only 41 of the 310 women (13 percent) aboard would survive, and just 4 of the 138 children (3 percent). The lucky Florence Barbour, rescued by Robert Crellin, was one of them.

Fate did not spare many of the celebrities aboard the Canadian Pacific ship. The body of Sir Henry Seton-Karr was found forty miles downriver from Sainte-Luce, days later, without a life belt. He was identified by the monogrammed handkerchief stuffed in his pocket. Sir Laurence Irving's corpse, floating among the other dead above the sunken ship, was identified by a signet ring. At least he would receive a tombstone; his wife was either trapped in the *Empress* or later buried with other unidentified bodies in a mass grave at Pointe-au-Père. The body of David Reese, the commissioner of the Salvation Army, was found days later and returned to Toronto for burial.

Although the couple were "promoted to glory" in the parlance of the Salvation Army, the bodies of David and Bertha Creighton still are entombed inside the *Empress of Ireland*. What had been planned as a reward for service had become a terrifying ordeal that ended their lives. Perhaps their only consolation was in experiencing those last moments of life to-

Empress dead at a makeshift morgue in Rimouski. *Courtesy of P. Beaudry Collection.*

gether. Their sad, untimely, and tortured deaths, like the deaths of so many of the *Empress* victims, would give inspiration to the quest of many survivors, family members, and authors to understand the *Empress of Ireland* tragedy.

The Devastating Aftermath

Although more people perished aboard the *Titanic* just two years earlier—1,503 total lives had been lost in 1912—the *Empress* disaster claimed a larger number of passengers: 840 passengers died on the *Empress* to 807 passengers aboard the *Titanic*. Of the 420 crew employed on the *Empress*, 248 survived, a disproportionate 59 percent compared with just 20 percent of passengers. Newspapers made much of this telling statistic in the weeks that followed. The crew and owners of the vessel contended that it was the time factor and new passengers' unfamiliarity with the ship, rather than cowardice or irresponsibility on the part of the crew, that explained the crew's disproportionate survival rate. It was the first night out, they explained, the collision happened late at night, and the

Empress sank in just fourteen minutes. It was a crisis situation, ultimately, of "every man, woman, and child for themselves," although the crew members, by most accounts, reacted to the accident in a professional and brave manner and did their best in the worst of circumstances. The crew of the *Empress* was not legally bound to help passengers off the ship once the abandon ship order was given or the ship was in imminent danger of sinking.

There was another connection to the *Titanic* that the press made much of. A coal stoker named William Clarke had amazingly escaped the flooding engine room of the *Empress*; the plucky Irishman had also been feeding the *Titanic*'s engines on that April night in 1912 when it went down. When asked by reporters to compare the two sinkings, Clarke replied, "Waiting around for the end was the hard part on *Titanic*. There was no waiting with the *Empress* . . . she rolled over like a hog in a ditch."

Legal Wrangling

After dropping off survivors of the collision in Rimouski, the *Storstad* arrived in Montreal two days later under her own power. Amid the mangled steel of her battered bow, newspaper reporters and the curious public could still spot the paint from the hull of the *Empress*. Officers from the High Court's Admiralty Marshal stood by, waiting to board the ship and begin the investigation of the disaster.

The Canadian Pacific Railway's lawyers had already filed a claim of $2,000,000 ($30,000,000 in 2004 dollars) against the Norwegian vessel for the loss of the company's ship. As condolences poured into Canada from all over the world and as services for the dead were headlining newspapers in North America and Europe, lawyers for the two shipping lines began to point fingers at each other. The legal maneuverings, however, actually had begun the day after the sinking near Rimouski.

The local coroner called for an inquest, which was held in a schoolhouse in the small riverside community. Captain Kendall, still haggard and exhausted from the ordeal, rose from his hospital bed and fired the first shot in the legal battle that would determine who was responsible for one of the greatest maritime disasters in history.

Storstad's battered bow in Quebec City. *George Scott Railton Heritage Centre.*

Kendall accused the *Storstad*'s captain not only of negligently ramming his stopped ship but also of backing out of the gash he created instead of continuing under forward power to minimize the flooding of the damaged compartments. Kendall also took the position that the *Storstad*'s rescue efforts were insufficient and vigorously insisted that it was not the Norwegian boats but the *Empress*'s lifeboats that had delivered most of the survivors to the *Storstad*. Kendall no doubt spoke under the emotional and physical strain of surviving the disaster himself. As it was later established in the official inquiry, Andersen and his crew acted selflessly and heroically in the rescue of the *Empress* survivors.

The Canadian, American, and British press immediately began a media war for justice, falling in squarely behind the English sea captain and the *Empress*. One story appearing in the *Toronto Globe* was fairly typical of the media's sentiment when it spoke of how the *Storstad* was "driving throughout the dangerous night, reckless of the consequences."

In his 1978 book *Fourteen Minutes*, then widely thought of as the definitive book on the accident, James Croall wrote that underneath the accusations against the *Storstad* lay a thinly disguised resentment of the Norwegian monopoly of coal and iron ore transport up and down the St.

Lawrence. The Norwegians maintained their monopoly, this public sentiment went on, by "cutting corners, both metaphorically and literally."

The *Storstad*'s management company, the Maritime S.S. Company, countered with a press conference in Montreal on June 2, 1914. They claimed that the *Storstad*, despite having the right of way, had slowed and then stopped her engines while maintaining the same heading in the fog. It was the *Empress of Ireland*, they claimed, that had changed course by turning to port and exposing her flank to the *Storstad*.

After the collision, Captain Andersen said, he had ordered "full ahead" to keep the gash plugged, but the *Empress*'s forward momentum had swept aside the much smaller *Storstad*. The crew of the Norwegian collier was blameless, the *Storstad*'s lawyers claimed. The Maritime S.S. Company countersued for $50,000 ($750,000 in 2004 dollars) to cover the damage to the *Storstad*.

The Canadian government wanted a public inquiry, and it wanted one fast. No such procedure existed in Canadian maritime law, so legislation was quickly proposed and passed in just three days. Since the Canadians had no experience in these matters, they turned to England, which sent John Charles Bigham, widely known by his title of Lord Mersey, to Quebec to preside over the inquiry. The Norwegian government was not consulted about its choice of who was to preside.

Lord Mersey had been a member of Parliament, a high court judge, and finally president of the Probate, Divorce and Admiralty Division. It was in this division of English law that he had become known. In 1912 he had sat as chairman of the court of inquiry that had looked into the sinking of the *Titanic*. Two distinguished Canadian judges would sit with Lord Mersey in the inquest of the *Empress* accident.

The Canadian Pacific Railway found the best legal counsel money could buy. It engaged Butler Aspinall, a London attorney who was known for his expertise in Admiralty Court and who, like Lord Mersey, had served during the *Titanic* inquiry.

The Norwegians, not to be outdone by some canny English Admiralty lawyer, turned to New Yorker Charles Sherman Haight, who was acknowledged as the best that the United States Admiralty Bar could offer.

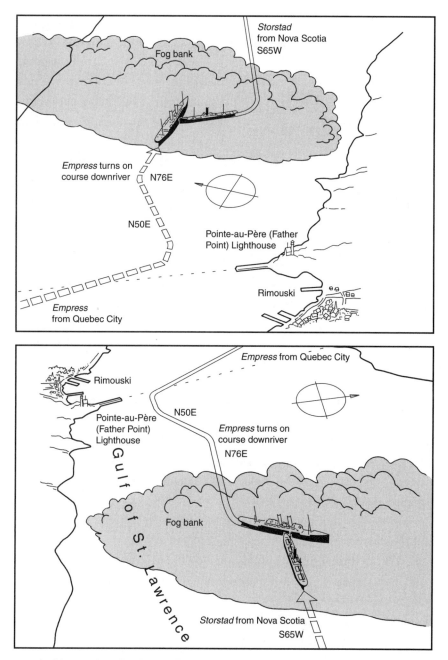

Incident as described by the *Empress of Ireland* (top) and the *Storstad* (bottom).
Drawn by Jim Sollers.

"Canada mourns." *Halifax Herald*, June 2, 1914.

On June 16, 1914, the inquest into the loss of the *Empress of Ireland* opened in Quebec City to a great deal of media coverage that crowded out news of the growing conflict in Europe that would soon snowball into World War I.

Lord Mersey, not surprisingly, turned out to be a no-nonsense judge. One legal obstacle after another, proposed as stalling tactics by attorneys from both sides, was rejected by his gavel, leaving some of them, in the own words of the media, "gasping."

When the inquest began, Captain Henry Kendall was the first witness. He stated unequivocally that both ships were on a heading that would have permitted them to pass each other starboard-to-starboard, or green running light to green light, at a safe distance. The only explanation for the collision, he contended, was that the *Storstad* had altered her course in the fog by turning sharply to starboard, which carried the Norwegian ship into the *Empress*. But Charles Haight, in his cross-examination of Kendall, suggested that the *Empress* had actually intended a port-to-port passing.

Haight pressed by contending that the *Storstad* had stopped her engines and then later turned to starboard enough to hold her course in the current. The starboard turn would have given the *Empress* more room in the port-to-port passing. Haight stated that since the *Storstad* had lost her steering ability (because she had stopped, so no water was flowing across the rudder plane), Chief Officer Toftenes had telegraphed down to the engine room a "slow ahead" in an effort to hold her heading.

Haight focused his questioning on several issues. One was the speed of the *Storstad* on impact, as estimated by Kendall, and why he had felt the need to stop his ship if he believed it was on a course that would have them passing safely starboard-to-starboard. Haight also questioned Kendall's assertion that the *Storstad* had turned to starboard in the fog, as if the collier had been on a deliberate course to ram the *Empress*.

Haight also brought up the *Empress*'s rumored steering problems. He called on the *Empress*'s quartermaster, James Galway, to reiterate his claim that the steering mechanism that operated the rudder was malfunctioning at the time of the accident. As it turned out, Galway didn't make a convincing witness. He appeared to be a disgruntled employee, and the evidence he gave, as reported by the attending press, was often "unintelligible."

The *Storstad*'s chief officer, Alfred Toftenes, also underwent a grueling interrogation by Canadian Pacific Railway's counsel Butler Aspinall. Toftenes stuck to the story as outlined by Charles Haight and acquitted himself well. It was Captain Andersen, questioned next, who began to poke holes in the story of how his ship had been handled during the last few minutes before the collision.

Andersen admitted that Toftenes was supposed to wake him if there was fog, which he did not do. The *Storstad*'s captain also admitted that Toftenes had altered the course of the *Storstad* in the fog by ordering the helmsman to turn slightly to starboard, thus ignoring standing orders. Toftenes and Third Officer Saxe also admitted under questioning that they had initiated the crucial turn without orders. Andersen also had no explanation for, among other things, why the *Empress* would dangerously change course and cross the *Storstad*'s bow in the fog.

In their decision issued on July 11, 1914, Lord Mersey and his two colleagues determined that the two ships' stories were "irreconcilable." They wrote, "Times, distances and bearings vary so much even in the evidence from witnesses from the same ship, that it is impossible to rely or to base conclusions on them. We have, therefore, thought it advisable to found our conclusions almost entirely upon other events spoken to by the witnesses and upon their probable sequence in order to arrive at a solution of the difficulty."

It all came down to this: if those on the *Storstad*'s bridge, as testified, had seen the *Empress*'s port red light, then only a highly dangerous turn hard to port in the fog by the *Empress* would have brought the ocean liner in front of the collier's bow. But if the officers aboard the *Empress* were correct in stating that they were on a starboard-to-starboard passing track, then only an equally dangerous starboard turn in the fog by the Norwegian ship would have taken her off her heading toward the starboard flank of the Canadian Pacific Railway ship.

The inquest also examined why the ship sank so fast. After questioning the engineer from the Fairfield Shipbuilding Company, the court determined that, theoretically, the ship should have stayed afloat if all the watertight bulk-

"He is the pilot in a fog." The Canadian press was quick to lay blame on the Norwegian ship *Storstad* for the disaster.

heads and portholes had been shut down. This was never done. Haight continued to hammer at the purported steering problems aboard the *Empress* and went on to attack Captain Kendall's credibility. Haight suggested that Kendall was lying about the ship's heading to avoid admitting that the terrible tragedy resulted from his rash decision to change course. But these arguments did not sway the court.

Conceding that the case was a "very peculiar" one, the three presiding judges concluded that one of the ships must have been mistaken about the position of the other one. The judges also believed that both ships' bridge officers were honest in their recollections of the accident but that they had both been wrong in estimating how close they were to each other when entering the fog bank. Ultimately the court ruled that the *Storstad* had misread the *Empress*'s heading and had responded in an incorrect manner, causing the collision.

The court, however, faulted Kendall for stopping his engines when he should have proceeded "ahead slow" as dictated by the Rules of the Road. The court also believed that Captain Kendall was "mistaken in supposing that the way [momentum] had been entirely taken off his ship," and that the movement of his ship had contributed to "the force of the impact."

After eleven days and sixty-one witnesses, the inquest decision was read by Lord Mersey on a blistering hot Saturday in July 1914. It took Lord Mersey one hour to read the sixty-five-page report aloud. Sifting through the fine points of marine navigation, both ships' seaworthiness, and the Rules of the Road, the ruling came down to which ship had altered its course in the fog. That, the report concluded, had been the *Storstad*.

Although the scales tipped against the crew of the *Storstad*, they did have the small satisfaction of knowing that not all blame could be laid on them. The court concluded that both ships had made mistakes that contributed to the sinking. Said the court's final decision:

> We regret to have to impute blame to anyone in connection with this lamentable disaster, and we should not do so if we felt that any reasonable alternative was left to us. We can, however, come to no other conclusion than that Mr. Toftenes was wrong and negligent in keeping the navigation of the vessel in his own hands and in failing to call the captain when he saw the fog coming on.

To the relief of the Canadian government, the court of inquiry also absolved the St. Lawrence waterway, stating: "It was a disaster which might have occurred in the Thames, in the Clyde, in the Mersey or elsewhere in similar circumstances." A great symbol of Canadian ingenuity and pride remained untarnished.

The Canadian Pacific Railway quickly seized the *Storstad* and later sold it at auction for $175,000 ($2,625,000 in 2004 dollars). Buoyed by its success in convincing the inquest judges that the *Storstad* was at fault, the Canadian Pacific Railway filed suit a year later in the Canadian Supreme Court. The court duly found the *Storstad* solely to blame for the disaster in this unique case. In the meantime the owners of the *Storstad* and their lawyers had effectively vanished. Claims of over $300 million ($4.5 billion in 2004 dollars) by passengers, crew members, and cargo owners were settled by the Canadian Pacific Railway, dividing up the meager $175,000 received for the *Storstad*.

The Norwegians held a court of inquiry in August 1914 of their own at their consulate in Montreal, where the *Storstad* officers gave testimony without a public audience or press present. Afterward, they presented all evidence to the Norwegian Maritime Court in Oslo. To the surprise of no one, the Norwegian court absolved the *Storstad*'s crew of all blame for the disaster in Quebec.

THROUGH A TANGLE of legal maneuvers and quietly executed sales, the *Storstad* appears to have been later repurchased by the Norwegian Klavenes Line at a sum well below its value. The workhorse ship went on to serve its new owners for three more years.

On March 8, 1917, somewhere off the southwest coast of Ireland, the *Storstad* was torpedoed by a German U-boat. Heavily laden with relief supplies for Belgium, the ship resisted the inevitable sinking long enough for Captain Thomas Andersen and his crew to abandon ship safely. What happened to Captain Thomas Andersen after the sinking of the *Storstad* remains a mystery.

At the outbreak of the Great War, Henry Kendall was the marine superintendent managing shipping traffic for the Canadian Pacific Railway in Antwerp. Kendall managed to escape the Belgian seaport before the German army arrived by piloting the ship *Montreal* to England, with his old command the *Montrose* in tow. Kendall later had a ship torpedoed out from under him during the war but survived to work once again for the Canadian Pacific Railway after the war ended. He retired in 1939 to live a quiet life of a pensioned mariner in London. In November 1965, at ninety-one, he succumbed to old age, unlike so many of his shipmates who had died prematurely. His obituary did not mention that he had been the captain of the ill-fated *Empress of Ireland*, still resting at the bottom of the Gulf of St. Lawrence.

CHAPTER TWO

Brave Pioneers

From Initial Salvage to Jacques Cousteau

Nothing that the ingenuity of man has permitted him to do is more unnatural
than working as a diver in deep water.

—COMMANDER EDWARD ELLSBERG, U.S. NAVY

The *Empress of Ireland* had barely settled into the muddy bottom of
the St. Lawrence River when lead-weighted commercial divers
hired by the Canadian Pacific Railway began to make their first
probes in June 1914. Ostensibly, the goal of the commercial dive operation
was to recover bodies trapped inside the hull. The Canadian Pacific Railway was anxious to demonstrate to the grieving public that it would make
every effort to do so. More than six hundred victims of the ships' collision were still unaccounted for.

The daunting task of attempting to recover the bodies was initiated by
the famous American salvor William Wotherspoon. Wotherspoon had
established a reputation as the foremost salvor of sunken ships when he
successfully recovered the remains of sailors entombed in the American
battleship *Maine*, sunk in Havana Harbor on the eve of the Spanish-
American War.

Recovery operations, however, would be far more difficult for the *Empress of Ireland* than for the warship sixteen years before. The *Maine* had
settled onto the rocky, shallow bottom of a protected warm-water port.
The *Empress* had sunk 140 feet to muddy depths swept by frigid currents
in an active seaway. Salvaging the *Empress* would test the technical strate-
gies of commercial diving as no operation had done before.

The Canadian Pacific Railway had other reasons for being quick to hire Wotherspoon and his complement of brass-helmeted divers—called, in the vernacular of salvors, "hard hats." The offices of the shipping and rail giant in Toronto were being inundated with lawsuits brought by those wishing compensation for losses suffered in the sinking. Only the retrieval of the purser's safe—the repository of most of the ship's valuables—would prove or disprove the size of the losses. There were also thousands of pieces of mail stuffed in hundreds of sacks still aboard the vessel, as well as 212 bars of silver destined for banks in England, valued at over $1 million in 1914.

The Canadian navy warship HMCS *Essex* had located the sunken remains of the *Empress*. It was not a difficult task. The shipwreck was still leaking air bubbles, and clouds of yellow mud mushroomed up from the still-shifting ship. At low tide the tip of the forward mast poked out from the depths. A Canadian navy diver, Wilfred Whitehead, was the first to descend to the wreck. Whitehead trudged the length of the ship's hull, tracing the layout of the wreck by the trail of his air bubbles. Locating and mapping the wreck was the extent of the Canadian navy's expertise. The rest of the job was left to the American salvage experts.

Wotherspoon had outfitted an obsolete schooner, the *Marie Josephine*, for the salvage operations. With the ship anchored above the *Empress* less than a month after she had gone down, Wotherspoon was ready to send his divers down to the wreck.

Edward Cossaboom's End

Commercial diving equipment in 1914 hadn't changed much from 1837, when the gear was patented by German-born Englishman August Siebe. The diving suit consisted of a brass or copper helmet with heavy glass view ports, connections for air supplied by surface pumps, and an exhaust valve. A full-length waterproof canvas suit enclosed the diver except for his hands. Rubber seals flush to the wrists made the suit watertight, and divers wore protective gloves that allowed them to use tools. A large yokelike rubber collar, attached to a metal breastplate, was fitted on the top of the suit to ease the weight of the fifty-five-pound helmet on the diver's shoul-

Divers preparing to enter the water from the *Marie Josephine* and proceed with salvage operations on the *Empress*, June 1914. *Courtesy of P. Beaudry Collection.*

ders. The diving paraphernalia weighed over two hundred pounds, including weight belts and each seventeen-pound lead-weighted boot. Each diver had a "tender" who monitored his air supply and fed out the lifeline and air hose as the diver worked underwater. The tender communicated with the diver via a telephone system whose cable was part of the "umbilical"—the lifeline to the diver.

The hard hats on the *Empress* job, burdened with all the heavy gear, trailing the long umbilical, and working alone, had little mobility and rarely could see much farther than ten feet on the wreck. Violently shifting currents also stalked the unwary diver, as they did on June 21, 1914.

Edward Cossaboom was an experienced professional diver from New York who, day after day, descended to the wreck for Wotherspoon's joint American-Canadian salvage effort. On that morning the hardworking Cossaboom had already retrieved two bodies from inside the ship and returned them to the surface. Then, on another dive, Cossaboom apparently decided to move forward along the flank of the sloping hull, which was exposed to the faint sunlight from above.

Cossaboom's tender aboard the *Marie Josephine* had been lax in keeping taut his charge's umbilical containing his air supply and tether. Unknown to Cossaboom, his lifeline slackened in a lazy arc behind him as he plodded along the hull in his lead-weighted boots. Suddenly a strong current began to buffet the wreck. Before he could scream his predicament over the phone to his tender, Cossaboom lost his footing and slipped over the side of the hull, plummeting another 65 feet to the bottom, at 140 feet.

Cossaboom knew the real dangers that deep diving presented. For every foot farther he descended, an added load of almost half a ton pressed on the surface of his body. At 140 feet down, on the bottom of the St. Lawrence, that load would exert over sixty tons of pressure on him. Commander Edward Ellsberg described this dangerous situation best in *On the Bottom*, his 1929 classic on commercial diving:

> To prevent the diver from being crushed into jelly by this weight, it is necessary for him to breathe air under pressure slightly exceeding that of the water; this internal air pressure is transmitted by his lungs to his blood, and enables him to balance the external water pressure. The diver is then in a condition similar to that of a pneumatic tire on a heavy automobile; the tire stays rounded out in spite of the weight of the car on it because it is inflated with air under sufficient pressure to balance the load. If, however, the inner tube is ruptured and the air escapes, down comes the weight of the car and flattens out the tire. In the same way, the diver, inflated with compressed air, stands the weight of the sea pressing on him; but if through any accident, he loses the air pressure, like a hammer down comes the weight of the sea and crushes him as flat as any blown-out tire.

This knowledge surely must have flashed through Cossaboom's mind, along with the fate that awaited him as he plummeted to the bottom, frantically trying to stop his fall. But the pressure differential was too sudden and too great. It sent blood flooding into his heart and lungs, quickly exploding these organs before he could stop his plunge or receive an increase of pressure from his tender to compensate for the crushing depths. By the time he hit the bottom, the invading sea pressure had stripped the flesh from his bones. His skin and organs were pile-driven into the only part of his suit that was resistant to the pressure, his copper diving helmet.

Cossaboom's tender signaled the alarm when he lost communication with his diver. By the time the crew and tenders aboard the *Marie Josephine* realized what had happened, there was little to do but send down a search team for his body. Evidently the rescue divers lost the trail of the umbilical line in the dark depths and couldn't find him. No fresh divers were available on the salvage vessel to continue the search. A Canadian diver aboard HMCS *Essex*, anchored nearby, volunteered to take a look around the wreck. On his first dive, he found what was left of Edward Cossaboom. His body was returned to the *Marie Josephine*. The crew later reported that all that remained of the unfortunate diver was "a jellyfish with a copper mantle and dangling canvas tentacles."

Commercial diver fully equipped at Musée de la Mer. © *Edie Summey.*

Despite the gruesome end of Edward Cossaboom, the grim work on the bottom of the St. Lawrence proceeded. The removal of waterlogged bodies continued on a scale unparalleled in diving history at that time. Crabs and lobster were drawn to the bounty of the wreck, feeding on the dead and making it impossible to identify many of the remains. Divers came across nightmarish horrors. Progressing deeper into the holds of the ship, down dark corridors, they would often be surprised by hideously decomposed corpses illuminated by their beams. Many of the dead faces had frozen into a look of horror brought on by their terrible last moments of life when the sea replaced the air in their lungs. One diver reported that "the faces of the dead seemed to dart for the diver's helmet as though to plant a kiss in gratitude for their release to the surface."

Some of the dead had to be dislodged from portholes. Apparently many of the passengers in the lower steerage decks had been trapped trying to squeeze through the narrow openings. The divers told of underwater scenes they could never have imagined in their worst nightmares. Despite their best efforts, the divers recovered fewer than two hundred bodies from inside the *Empress*. Weather conditions and technology simply did not allow for extensive penetration into the lower holds of the ship, where most of the third-class passengers had been accommodated. The divers were more successful with their economic priority—the recovery of the mail, silver, and purser's safe.

The recovery of 318 intact sacks of mail and all 212 silver ingots was routine. The purser's safe, which was the size of a phone booth and weighed several hundred pounds, proved more challenging. The Canadian Pacific Railway was facing serious litigation for losses and insisted that the integrity of the safe not be compromised during its retrieval; it feared further lawsuits from passengers claiming their valuables had been lost or stolen in the effort.

Studying blueprints of the ship and visiting her sister ship the *Empress of Britain*, the salvage divers planned their effort to raise the valuables-laden safe. Once underwater they quickly found the safe in the upper deck near the port side of the ship. Because of the size of the safe and its location, it was too difficult to cut a hole from existing hatch openings and lift it out. The team resorted to dynamite.

In 1914 there were only two options in choosing an explosive for underwater demolition: nitroglycerine or stick dynamite. "Nitro" was far too unstable to be used at these depths, so divers had to descend to the *Empress* with the safer, but still volatile, dynamite sticks carried in canvas bags. The explosives were fitted with blasting caps and placed in holes drilled in the steel hull around the safe. They ran a fuse up to the *Marie Josephine* and detonated the dynamite from the boat by an electrical charge when the divers were safely out of the water.

Once the "explosion hole" was created, divers could descend directly to the purser's office in the upper deck. In 1914 an effective underwater torch had yet to be developed. Divers had to loosen the safe from the bulkhead mounts with wrenches and then demolish with sledgehammers any obstructions that might hinder its removal. It was a grueling, tedious job done in the worst of conditions, but the divers, wielding crowbars, slowly extricated the safe through the explosion hole. A steam-powered winch aboard the *Marie Josephine* lifted the safe into the sunlight on August 20, 1914.

The *Lady Evelyn* transported the safe upriver to Quebec City, where it was deposited in the Bank of Montreal. Before a crowd of lawyers, claimants, Canadian Pacific Railway officers, government officials, and members of the press, the safe was opened in dramatic fashion. A locksmith known for his safe-cracking skills was employed for the job. With the flair of a show-

The purser's safe is lifted from the waters of the St. Lawrence after divers successfully extricate it from the wreck. *Courtesy of V. Gilligan Collection.*

man, pausing for effect at crucial moments, the locksmith took his time in performing his exacting task.

The contents hardly justified all the hoopla. After opening all three compartments, he found little in the way of cash, negotiable stocks, cashier's checks, or jewelry. Much to the amusement of the curious public, the value of the recovered riches amounted to less than 1 percent of the losses litigants had claimed. The Canadian Pacific Railway quickly dispensed with spurious claims, and newspaper editors slowly relegated *Empress* stories to the back pages.

Within days, dispatches from Europe began to squeeze news relating to the *Empress* out of the newspapers altogether. Headlines about the assassination of Archduke Ferdinand in Sarajevo, the invasion of the Belgian lowlands by the Imperial German Army, and the siege of Paris took priority. World War I had made the tragic loss of the *Empress of Ireland* a footnote in history. The stories surrounding one of the greatest losses of life in a North American maritime accident slipped into oblivion. It would take fifty years and five divers from Quebec to resurrect the story of the *Empress of Ireland*.

The Fiftieth Anniversary: 1964

In May 1964 the Toronto *Star Weekly*, the newspaper's Sunday magazine supplement, ran an article on the *Empress of Ireland* to mark the fiftieth anniversary of the tragedy. It came to the attention of five friends: André Ménard, forty; Jean-Paul Fournier, forty-six; Fernand Bergeron, thirty-four; Claude Villeneuve, twenty-six; and Robert Villeneuve, twenty-eight. Ménard and Fournier were government workers in Ottawa, Bergeron was a salesman in Hull, Quebec, and the Villeneuve brothers were factory workers in Montreal. All were avid divers.

In 1964 scuba diving was still relatively new, particularly in the bitter cold waters of Canada; but it was a passion the five men shared. The French Canadian men had explored the freshwater Ottawa and Lièvre rivers and Lake Simon in Quebec. Ménard had also done some diving in the North American mecca of scuba, the coral reefs off the coast of Florida. But it was the article in the Toronto magazine that fired their imaginations.

The five had never heard of the Canadian Pacific Railway's ocean liner *Empress of Ireland*. They were surprised to learn that more passengers had been lost on her than on the famous *Titanic*. They were amazed to hear that the ship had carried more than 500,000 immigrants to Canada just after the turn of the century and that almost one in ten Canadians could trace their lineage to an ancestor who had crossed the ocean on one of the two *Empress* ships. That the *Empress of Ireland* lay somewhere in the river that flowed through their homeland tantalized them all. The only information they had about the location of the wreck came from the court of inquiry on the disaster. But after fifty years, the once-visible mast had long since collapsed, and the wreck would have settled deeper into the spongy bottom. Her location, like her memory in the collective consciousness of Canada, had been forgotten. All the divers from

Wotherspoon's initial salvage of the wreck in 1914 were long dead.

But there was a current personal connection. One of André Ménard's government colleagues in Ottawa was John David Ferguson, the son of Ronald Ferguson, the wireless operator aboard the *Empress of Ireland* on the night of the accident. Ménard was able to obtain a copy of the ship's plans, sent from England by the long-retired Ronald Ferguson. In England, Ferguson was still a minor celebrity among ocean liner enthusiasts for his role in the drama. He had kept the plans out of nostalgia and also to educate those who wanted to learn more about the lost liner.

André Ménard formulated a plan with his four friends to locate the wreck. But first they would need to raise some money and find a dive boat. Ménard approached Aubert Brillant, a wealthy eccentric who owned Quebec Telephone and lived in Rimouski, just ten miles from where the wreck was likely to be. Brillant was immediately taken with the prospect of locating the fabled ocean liner. Along with financing the entire expedition, Brillant also gave the divers the use of his yacht, *La Canadienne*, captained by nondiver Mario Lavoie.

For three days the men aboard *La Canadienne* scanned the river bottom off Sainte-Luce with a depth sounder. After so much fruitless searching, they were at a loss how to proceed. But word of their search in Rimouski brought Donal Tremblay down to the docks. Tremblay, a professor of navigation at Rimouski's Marine Institute, told the men they were going about the search wrong. The key to locating the *Empress* was to line up prominent landmarks, such as church bell towers and mountain peaks, as described by the salvors in 1914 and then make their watery probes.

Late one evening Jean-Paul Fournier dutifully marched up the stairs of the steeple of the church in Sainte-Luce, clutching a lantern. Back aboard *La Canadienne*, Mario Lavoie calculated the probable *Empress* location by plotting a triangle using the Sainte-Luce beacon, Sainte-Flavie steeple, and Pointe-au-Père Lighthouse as landmarks, as described by the 1914 team. He marked the spot in the rocking waters with a shot line and buoy and motored back to Rimouski. They would return the next morning with their depth sounder, ready to dive.

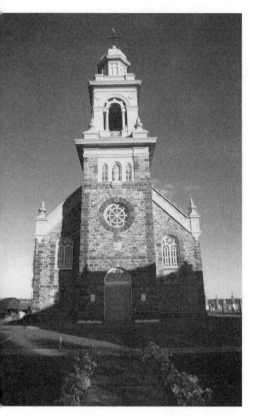

Sainte-Luce church steeple, another landmark used in triangulating the position of the wreck of the *Empress*.

On July 17, 1964, Captain Mario Lavoie began his search around the bobbing buoy the men had left the night before. After just minutes of taking soundings and dragging a grappling hook, he thought he'd hooked onto the wreck on the river bottom more than a hundred feet below. Claude Villeneuve, Fournier, and Ménard geared up and splashed in. None of the men had ever attempted so deep a dive, having never gone deeper than sixty feet. The fresh water of lower Quebec was much more hospitable than the briny, turbid, fast-moving water of the Gulf of St. Lawrence.

Compounding their problems and increasing the deadly risks was their equipment. Their recreational gear was designed for use in warmer, subtropical waters such as Florida—not for the frigid waters of these far-northern latitudes. Freeze-ups of the breathing regulators or free-flow problems, when the regulators expelled air uncontrollably, were a significant danger.

The French Canadian divers wore single tanks with only "Mae West" inflation vests for buoyancy control. The vests were virtually useless underwater but did give them some flotation on the surface. The divers still wore rubber wetsuits, since in 1964 drysuits were used only by commercial divers and the military. Wetsuits provided little protection from the relentless cold of the near-freezing water. Hypothermia would set in even after relatively brief stays underwater. Dives longer than fifteen to twenty minutes dangerously tested the men's ability to function underwater.

The dive lights the team employed were inadequate for the dark, turbid waters of the Gulf of St. Lawrence. Their beams barely illuminated what lay just an arm's length away. The enveloping frigid darkness was a claustrophobic experience that none of the divers had ever experienced before.

Escaping from a problem down below wasn't as simple as bolting for the surface, as if they were on a shallow reef dive off the Florida coast. Divers in 1964 knew they had to consider accumulated nitrogen gas in the blood and soft tissues brought on by the crushing pressure of the deep water. Still, the five Quebecois had only a rudimentary knowledge of this physiological process. There were no dive computers to formulate their decompression schedule. They had the time-tested U.S. Navy Dive Tables to rely on, but the bitterly cold water is not factored into the tables, and a hypothermic diver is at increased risk of taking a decompression "hit."

Inching down the lead-weighted shot line, the divers that day encountered a fierce running tide, but it dissipated once they dropped below eighty feet. Perhaps they were in the lee of some obstruction. Then the object of their quest materialized out of the murky darkness. As described by a Toronto *Star Weekly* reporter, "on the floor of the river, towering in the murky gloom like an ancient castle, they found the *Empress of Ireland*."

The men were surprised at the remarkably good condition of the fifty-year-old shipwreck. Lying on a sharp angle on her starboard side, the *Empress* was as noble a ship as they had ever seen. Barely containing their excitement over their find, they managed to pluck a deadeye, or wooden pulley, from the main deck and bring it to the surface as proof that they had indeed found the lost ship.

Poor weather prevented the men from diving the wreck again for another two days; the men were left to idle away the time by fiddling with their dive gear waiting for the weather to break. No word was spoken of their find in Rimouski for fear of inviting a horde of treasure seekers to the wreck location. On the return dive, the same three divers, along with Fernand Bergeron, managed to wrestle the stern ramp from the wreck. There was so much to see and retrieve; but their vacation time from their jobs was running out. They agreed to return in August and spend three weeks diving the wreck. Brillant was thrilled with the discovery and enthusiastically provided his boat and funds for additional dives to the wreck.

Unfortunately, bad weather again plagued the team in August. They managed only seven dives. In their modestly funded and grossly ill-equipped second expedition, these men successfully raised the ship's telegraph and compass as well as various brass fittings and plaques. Most important, they raised a small ship's bell from an entrance to the bridge, etched with the ship's name, dispelling any doubt as to the vessel's identity. The men accomplished all this using equipment that was not designed for use in such a hostile environment.

Toronto's *Star Weekly* breathlessly recounted the team's adventure in a July 1965 edition of the magazine, which heightened the public's interest in the divers' quest to explore the long lost shipwreck. Plans were quickly made to return to Rimouski the following summer to pick up where the five divers had left off. But André Ménard had grander ideas about what they hoped to accomplish the next time.

Sixties Diving and the First Woman Down

The following year, 1965, the five divers returned to Rimouski, this time to document their dives on film. Once again they had the support of Aubert Brillant, and this time no expense was spared. This time they hired a film crew, extra divers, and two support boats and purchased a four-ton diving bell that had to be shipped over from Italy. The diving bell, anchored to the wreck underwater, would be the platform from which all the diving would be done. Air would be supplied to divers from tanks on the bell through an umbilical hose. The expedition would eventually cost roughly $250,000, a large sum for a project of this type in 1965.

The divers now wore constant-volume suits, forerunners of today's drysuits. The suits were made of rubber, and divers could keep the air pressure inside constant with a valve connected to the air supply from the bell. They also wore full-face masks generally not employed by sport divers. Full-face masks also meant less skin was exposed to the frigid water (30 percent of body heat is lost through the head) and easier breathing through the nose and mouth. Communication among divers was also easier because of a two-way radio rigged inside the mask. This was all cutting-edge diving technology in 1965. Making it all the more impressive

was that the five French Canadian divers were basically "weekend war-
riors" on vacation, as were most divers then in this small, relatively unknown sport.

What they accomplished cinematically was astonishing. Canadian cameraman and commercial diver Harold Smyth braved the challenging ele-
ments in his quest to document the expedition. Although the black-and-
white film was somewhat melodramatic, starkly lit, and accompanied by a
horror-film score, he still produced a compelling underwater documentary
long before the world had ever heard of Jacques Cousteau. The film aired
on the Canadian Broadcasting Corporation (CBC) intermittently through
the late 1960s and the early 1970s. Today the twenty-eight-minute film
The "Empress of Ireland" certainly belongs in an underwater film hall of
fame for what it accomplished: successfully bringing the audience down
into the dark, frightening, alien, but exciting world of deep-wreck diving.

Little was done on the wreck for the next three years, but the *Empress*
continued to conjure up visions of treasure in the minds of at least a few
individuals. One of them was boat captain Brian Erb. Along with Donal
Tremblay, Erb hatched a plan to salvage the port-side propeller—twenty
feet in diameter and twenty tons—in September 1968. With the success of
the earlier film, they thought, certainly some museum would want this
part of local history on display. There would, of course, be a price for
such a precious artifact.

With surface support from the ninety-foot *Morrisburgh*, the divers
managed to secure the propeller to a cable and then blast through its
shaft. Since the support boat was not stable enough or big enough to
bring the mammoth propeller aboard, they towed it back to Rimouski,
dangling several feet under the boat's keel, at the agonizingly slow speed
of one knot.

But between Pointe-au-Père and Rimouski lie hazardous ledges that the
Morrisburgh crew apparently was unaware of. Striking one of these underwater obstructions, the priceless propeller lost one of its four blades.
Before a huge crowd at the Rimouski dock on September 28, 1968, the now
three-bladed propeller was successfully landed. Unfortunately for the
salvors, sudden riches never materialized. There were no takers for the

artifact, and it was eventually sold as scrap metal for the paltry sum of $5,000, barely enough to cover expenses.

What seemed to ship and sea historians a valuable tangible artifact from Canada's past was lost forever to a scrap dealer's furnace. Ironically, and no doubt due to the lack of interest in the preservation of the ship's propeller, Donal Tremblay would go on to become the first director of the Musée de la Mer, dedicated to preserving the memory of the *Empress* at Pointe-au-Père. The skipper of the salvage vessel *Morrisburgh*, Brian Erb, was later convicted of stealing a boat in Quebec and steaming out to sea from the Gulf of St. Lawrence. He was captured and incarcerated for piracy.

EARLY IN 1968 the pioneering *Empress* diver André Ménard drove from Ottawa down to Syracuse, New York, in search of experienced wreck divers. Curiously, Syracuse was a center of diving in North America, despite its landlocked location. The city's proximity to the St. Lawrence River, Lake Ontario, and various inland lakes fostered a rabid desire for underwater exploration among a sizable, tight-knit group of divers.

When the professorial-looking Ménard—pipe-smoking and owlish—approached the owners of a Syracuse dive shop for contacts in the local community, they gave him the name of Peter Perrault, an engineer by trade and a diver by passionate avocation. Perrault could have passed as a Marine drill sergeant, with his crew cut and taut physique. But Perrault was also cerebral: he was a scuba instructor who wrote about diving in several publications and lectured extensively on diving and shipwreck research. He was president of the Syracuse Scuba Society, a dive club whose members regularly dived the wrecks in the nearby St. Lawrence River, Lake Ontario, Lake George, and Lake Champlain.

The skeptical Perrault met with Ménard at a roadside café off the New York interstate near the Thousand Islands region of the St. Lawrence and listened to his story. Ménard, in his halting English, told him about the *Empress* and his two dive expeditions to the wreck with his "ship of fools," Ménard's self-effacing way of describing his crew of divers. Ménard showed him the *Star Weekly* article describing their expeditions and pictures of the ship, then unrolled the ultimate tease for a wreck diver: the ship's building plans.

Perrault's interest was piqued. Ménard told him he wanted divers who could penetrate the sunken ship, something the Canadian divers were ill prepared to do. It was not just lack of equipment, Ménard explained, but also lack of experience. Perrault was flattered. The clincher for Pete Perrault was that Ménard didn't ask for any money, so Perrault figured he was not talking to some schemer. Ménard was a diver on a mission, a unique mission that Perrault could help execute.

André Ménard asked Perrault if he could interest any other local divers. Perrault said he could and asked if Ménard had a problem with women divers. Surprised, Ménard replied that he didn't. Perrault made a phone call.

Veronica "Ronni" Gilligan still remembers getting that call. Gilligan, then twenty-eight, worked as a peripathologist, a rehabilitator of the blind, at the Upstate Medical Center in Syracuse. She had been a regular dive buddy of Perrault's since 1963. At five foot ten, tipping the scales at 180 pounds, she was as strong as any diver who shouldered the burdensome double tanks that had become the choice for deep-wreck divers in the northeastern United States. Ronni Gilligan was one of the top wreck divers in the world.

Perrault wasted no time in getting to the point. "You interested in diving a virgin ocean liner?" At first Gilligan thought he was pulling her leg. When she realized he wasn't, she said yes without asking the details, and there were a lot of them. She'd have to travel up to Rimouski, Quebec, and spend most of July and August diving the six-hundred-foot-long shipwreck. Perrault also told Gilligan she'd better brush up her high-school French.

Peter Perrault and Ronni Gilligan were joined for the expedition by diver Fred Zeller from Rochester, New York. Ménard would also dive, and Fernand Bergeron, his old friend and dive buddy from the 1964 and 1965 expeditions, would provide the boat, the forty-five-foot *Lyson L.* Zeller and Perrault took their families on an extended vacation to remote Quebec and found accommodations at a local campground. Ronni Gilligan was left to her own devices.

Gilligan thought she might find housing by asking the local priest if he knew of a farm family in the area that would give her room and board in exchange for help around their farm. She was promptly chased out of the rectory by the angry priest. She realized later that in her broken French she had asked the priest if he knew of anyone she could "sleep with." Gilligan ended up spending her nights dozing in her car or on Bergeron's *Lyson L.*, washing up on surreptitious visits to the ladies' room at Rimouski's Normandy Hotel.

The two French Canadians and three Americans spent their first three days trying to find the sunken ship. The marking buoys from Ménard's 1964 and 1965 expeditions had disappeared, no doubt succumbing to the Gulf's strong currents, ice floes, and the propellers of the huge ships that steamed by overhead.

Ménard carried a piece of wood with two screws and an *X* scratched in it, which he used as a sighting device. Ménard would line up the device with church steeples and roads on the Gulf's southern shore, which he had plotted four years earlier when he first found the wreck of the *Empress*. Relocating the wreck, he reasoned, was simply a matter of realigning landmarks and again marking the spot with a weighted shot line. For three days Ménard took sightings, dropped shot lines, and hunted for the wreck without success. Finally, on the fourth day, the grappling hook caught something.

Ronni Gilligan had tremendous respect for Perrault and felt honored to be with him on this dangerous, pioneering effort. She only hoped that as his dive buddy she wouldn't screw up and kill them both.

Pete Perrault and Ronni Gilligan made that first dive together as planned. Gilligan remembers the seemingly endless eighty-foot descent and then seeing "tulip-looking white things" waving in the current. Those were truncates, a close relative of the sea anemone, also called sea potatoes.

Though the condition was still little understood, divers did know that nitrogen under pressure was narcotic and affected individuals differently, commonly with a euphoria akin to drunkenness. Much like driving under the influence of alcohol, diving when "narc'd" can have dire consequences a hundred feet underwater. Many divers learn from experience how to function while slightly narc'd, but the risk of making fatal mistakes and

André Ménard, pioneering *Empress* sport diver, 1968. *Courtesy of V. Gilligan Collection.*

miscalculations always looms.

Gilligan was quickly "zonked" from nitrogen narcosis. She felt she was about to die yet, as she would later relate, that "that would be OK." Ronni Gilligan was entering a strangely beautiful world that in her narcosis-addled mind was drawing her in more deeply, perhaps fatally. The pair went right to the bottom in a matter of minutes. The icy water of the St. Lawrence invaded their wetsuits. Even with their body heat warming the thin layer of water in their rubber suits, they still shivered uncontrollably in the dark depths.

Gilligan was in awe of what she saw before her, despite the freezing cold, her narcosis-addled mind, and the murky water. The wreck of the *Empress* materialized out of the gloom like an apparition. The massive decking sheathed in teak, the porthole-pocked hull, and the looming, angled superstructure indeed looked like a ghostly castle of the deep. Ronni Gilligan had never seen anything like it; she couldn't get over how large and imposing it looked. Despite its forbidding appearance, she couldn't wait to probe the ship's hidden secrets. She remembers eagerly thinking, "We're at the bottom and there's the ship; let's go." But Perrault was overweighted with all his wreck-diving tools and wanted to ditch some gear. He aborted the dive.

It was an inauspicious first dive, although they had finally laid eyes on the mysterious shipwreck. They quickly set mooring lines from the *Lyson L.* and dug in, logging over fifty dives for each diver.

Wearing wetsuits, double tanks, and back-mounted pony tanks containing an emergency supply of air, Ménard, Perrault, Zeller, and Gilligan would make two dives a day. By the time the diving was done, the tanks off-loaded and refilled, and everything readied for the next day, eighteen grueling hours would have passed. The four divers had just enough time for dinner before collapsing onto their beds, only to rise and do it all over again for seven weeks running.

Perrault and Gilligan, continuing to dive as a team, made extensive surveys of the ship and were able to explore deep inside the *Empress*. Using a penetration line (a reel with a thin line laid out behind the diver) to help find the way back, Perrault would enter the ship while Gilligan, dive light in hand, acted as his beacon and safety backup outside the entry hole. They had a system of communication; the most critical signal was three tugs on the line. That meant Perrault was in trouble and Gilligan would have to swim in and help, which usually entailed freeing him or his line from the fallen electrical cables that crisscrossed the inside of the ship like spiderwebs.

Gilligan continued to be enthralled with the wreck. The history of the ship and the great loss of life made it seem like an underwater shrine. There were times when she could see the bones of victims poking out from the muck. She would say a prayer for them and cross herself, then move on. A poignant moment underwater occurred when she found a man's shirt still hanging limply, seemingly undisturbed, from a hook in the third-class quarters. She found it a bit unnerving; perhaps it was too close an encounter with the human reality of what had happened that night fifty-four years earlier. She left it untouched.

On their last dive, Perrault made an exciting discovery in the captain's quarters that would have the team itching to dive the wreck again. He found a safe. But since careers and family beckoned, Perrault and Gilligan had to put the dreamed-of contents on hold for another year before they could return to liberate the safe from the dark interior of the wreck. The same five divers would return again in July 1969 with visions of finding riches in the rotting hull. Their main goal would be to retrieve the captain's safe.

Over the winter Peter Perrault, ever the engineer, designed and built a contraption he teasingly dubbed "Gilligan's douche bag." The contraption was a rigid rubber diving bell, an open-bottomed container measuring six by four feet, which Perrault had persuaded the Goodyear Rubber Company to produce. Perrault mounted two scuba tanks on it that would provide independent ballast to the system and a lifting capacity of 3,500 pounds, making it considerably easier to carry the heavy safe to the surface. But the team also had to extricate the safe from inside the ship, two decks down from where the underwater douche bag hung waiting. Perrault devised an elaborate block-and-tackle system that he thought would make removing the safe from the dark holds possible.

Debris had since covered the safe, and the team needed several dives simply to expose it. When the safe was cleared of the muck, Fred Zeller, Ronni Gilligan, and Pete Perrault discovered they would not need the douche bag after all. They found they could open the safe underwater with just their dive knives. The corrosive seawater had already done most of the work for them.

On the much-anticipated dive, Fred Zeller did the puncturing and Perrault the cutting. Gilligan hovered over the pair shining a light on the operation, holding a "goody bag" ready to receive the booty. Through the billowing clouds of silt, Perrault began to hand her things from the safe, including a small, locked, metal box. Gilligan was thrilled, as visions of travels to exotic lands filled her nitrogen-narc'd brain. At the decompres-

Gilligan's douche bag, the lifting device built by Peter Perrault, 1969. *Courtesy of V. Gilligan Collection.*

sion stops, the threesome were giving each other "handshakes and doing somersaults." The moment they had all waited a year for had arrived.

Aboard Bergeron's boat, still wearing their tanks, they dumped out the contents of Gilligan's goody bag. They couldn't believe what they saw. There was absolutely nothing of value. A stack of tickets for a Liverpool

ferry and a *McClure's* magazine
from April 1914 were all they recovered, a terrible disappointment
as Gilligan later described it. Thus
ended the three-week expedition of
1969.

IN 1970 THE three upstate New
Yorkers—Gilligan, Perrault, and
Zeller—and the Canadians Ménard and Bergeron were joined by
more Syracuse Scuba Society
members. Ron and Diane Strong,
Ron Kenyon, Bill Robinson, Walt
Palmieri, and Diane Martiny
signed on, as did a French Canadian from Montreal, Philippe
Beaudry. This time the expedition
would be only two weeks long.

Peter Perrault and Ronni Gilligan celebrating
another successful dive on the *Empress*,
1970. *Courtesy of Diane Strong.*

Diane Strong remembers vividly
her first dive on the *Empress*. Diane
and her husband, Ron, "froze their asses off," since they all dived in wetsuits. In 1970 drysuits were still a luxury hard to come by and prohibitively
expensive, costing over $1,500. The pair also had to battle horrendous
currents. They splashed in with the job of checking to see if the group
had been successful in hooking the wreck with the grapple. They hurried
right to the muddy bottom at 140 feet, a depth below today's recreational
limit of 130 feet. Piercing the blackness with their lights, they slowly did
a ninety-degree turn.

Diane Strong later told me more about her and her husband's first dive.
"Suddenly," she said, "a wall of teak decking appeared out of the gloom,
going up like a skyscraper in front of us. All I can think of was *wow!* We
didn't bother to surface to tell them we'd hooked the wreck. We went right
to plan B and began to explore. Just over the gunwale, lying there, was a

whole wad of portholes, loose and off their mounts. It was just the coolest."

Besides dozens of dinner plates, portholes, and wine bottles—many still full of their valuable vintages—the Syracuse crew also recovered the much-prized shipbuilder's plaque, the bridge compass and binnacle (the tall housing of brass supporting the ship's compass), and the ship's helm, or steering wheel. But the booty taken from the ship would cause Gilligan and Perrault some legal problems, which they later would suspect started with Philippe Beaudry.

Philippe Beaudry:
The Self-Appointed Guardian

Philippe Beaudry grew up in the small French Canadian farming community of Eastman, in Eastern Township, a province of Quebec, sixty miles east of Montreal. Leaving the family farm at sixteen, he worked at a well-paying explosives factory near Montreal while attending night school to earn a degree in business. At twenty-one, Beaudry married. His wife, Diane, had a brother in legal difficulty in Florida, and when Diane bailed him out, he paid his sister back in part by giving her his scuba gear, acquired in the Sunshine State.

Intrigued with the exotic, new-fangled apparatus, Beaudry decided to see for himself what it was like on the bottom. Like a lot of kids growing up in the 1950s and 1960s, he'd watched the character Mike Nelson on American TV's *Sea Hunt* and was intrigued. With no training and technically unable to swim, Beaudry made his first dives in the Richelieu River in the hand-me-down gear. Despite a wetsuit that didn't fit his thick-set frame and painful "ear squeeze"—inadequate equalization between the inner ear and water pressure—Beaudry was hooked.

In 1968, after one year of diving by the seat of his pants and learning what he could from the few diving books then available, he'd become a regular at a Montreal dive shop. There he first heard about the *Empress of Ireland*. In the small but tight diving community in Quebec, the *Empress* had become a mecca for the passionate *plongeurs*, in large part owing to Ménard and Smyth's 1965 film *The "Empress of Ireland."*

Beaudry had family ties near Rimouski; his father had worked in the thriving logging business sixty miles south of Rimouski years before. So in 1969 he traveled to the region with his father on a supposed family visit to their old homeland. But Beaudry had things other than family on his mind. Leaving his father at a motel, he made a side trip to the Rimouski waterfront with his dive gear. Beaudry couldn't find anyone to dive with and he couldn't afford to hire a boat to take him out to the wreck site, which was jealously guarded by local boat captains. Wrecks were potential salvage jobs and lucrative recreational spots, and boat captains on both sides of the border, as is still true, were notorious for defending wreck locations. They didn't want competition. The wrecks were also magnets for fish, and a hot fishing spot was information they preferred not to share. Beaudry had to content himself with making some shallow-water dives off the pier in Rimouski. Undeterred by his lack of success in diving the *Empress*, he returned to Montreal even more determined to dive the wreck.

When Beaudry returned to the pier at Rimouski in 1970, he met the group of divers from Syracuse, New York, led by the determined Peter Perrault. Perrault had again enlisted Fernand Bergeron and his forty-five-foot boat to take them to the wreck of the *Empress*. Beaudry ingratiated himself by acting as a translator and arbiter in a dispute over some damage done to the boat by one of the Syracuse divers. By the time all the feathers were smoothed, Beaudry and his dive buddy, Michel Brunet, paid their share to the captain and joined the American divers. His goal of diving the *Empress* was about to be realized.

On the trip out to the wreck site, the more experienced Bergeron told Beaudry to follow the rope down to the hull, keeping the sloping decks to his right, then swim straight, and he'd come upon the bridge of the ship. Twenty-five-year-old Philippe Beaudry splashed in wearing a wetsuit, a single small-volume seventy-two-cubic-foot tank with a simple two-stage regulator, a Mae West inflation device useful mainly for surface flotation, an underwater flashlight, mask, fins, and snorkel. Beaudry planned to dive alone, a practice frowned on then as well as now but still practiced by more independent—some would say reckless—divers to this day.

On his first exploration of the partially exposed bridge, he quickly found the marine telephone hanging from what he thought was the ceiling but was really the wall. Beaudry's heart raced as he cut at the wires securing the phone, hacking away with his knife. The exhausting work of ripping the phone out, Beaudry knew, was rapidly depleting his air supply. He thought he would surely exhaust it and drown, but he had to have that phone. With barely any air remaining, Beaudry was ready to head for the surface with his first *Empress* artifact, a twenty-pound marine phone. It was the same phone that Captain Kendall had used to communicate with the engine room, along with the mechanical ship's telegraph, on that tragic night so long ago, issuing the last orders ever given on the doomed vessel.

After fifteen minutes on the bottom, Beaudry made his ascent, as he later said in a mixed metaphor, "frozen like hell," but already anticipating his next dive down to the grand old vessel. That next dive too was almost his last.

Beaudry again headed for the bridge of the ship, but instead of entering through the door as he had the first time, he decided to go in from the front, through one of the now paneless bridge windows facing forward. Trying to squeeze through, Beaudry got stuck between the two window ribs, unable to move. Dangerously wedged between the steel ribs, Beaudry desperately tried pushing and pulling himself free. The effort increased his air consumption. He glanced at his pressure gauge. He was almost out of air. With over a hundred feet of swirling river water above him, he felt panic slowly consume him. Was this how he was going to die? In frustration he began to cry, the tears burning his eyes and further obscuring his vision. Perhaps another diver would happen by and help him, but Beaudry knew that this was unlikely given the size of the ship and the limited visibility.

In a last-ditch effort to save himself, he stopped all his efforts to free his body from the steel grip of the *Empress*. Forcing himself to remain calm, he expelled all the air from his lungs, reducing his girth by a precious inch or two. With a burst of strength he pushed himself free and kicked furiously for the surface. The rush of fresh, warm air he sucked in as he burst from the depths was the most wonderful thing he'd ever experienced. Luckily, his relatively short bottom time and shallow depth on the wreck spared him a decompression hit.

The near-death experience did not dissuade the French Canadian. He had artifact fever. He would make several more dives that week, surviving yet another close call.

Once again on the *Empress*'s bridge, Beaudry found two navy phones and removed the telemotor needle, which he tore from its base with a crowbar and saw. On his way up the line, he knocked his face mask loose against a tensioning line, flooding it with freezing water. He couldn't find it in himself to drop the artifacts to right his mask. Instead he sprinted for the surface with his mask flooded, clutching the precious booty.

He had enough sense to slowly expel the increasing volume of air that was expanding his lungs and thereby avoided a fatal embolism, a deadly obstruction in an artery caused by a blood clot or by air bubbles from the suddenly expanding volume of gases in the lungs, which can lead to paralysis, heart attack, or stroke. Again Beaudry had not been down long enough to absorb a concentration of the dangerous nitrogen that would have required decompression stops. He knew he had cheated death a second time as he floated to the surface to face the warming sun. He then cried out for help and waited for Bergeron and the Americans to pull him from the water.

Divers from the States were well versed in the layout of the wreck and had a propensity for poring over deck plans of the ship and planning their dives accordingly. Their research methods and dive plans impressed him, so Beaudry next dived with Ron Strong to the third-class dining room, where the Americans had recovered some plates. Strong found a few but Beaudry did not. He would later trade one of his marine phones for a coveted third-class plate. It was a trade he would later regret, since the phones would be worth thousands of dollars as opposed to a few hundred for a common third-class plate.

Even though Philippe Beaudry himself had been removing artifacts from the *Empress*, he would come to believe that the wreck had to be protected. There were many reasons, he would explain to me in 2002, more than thirty years after his first dive. He firmly believed that the *Empress* was a part of Canada's heritage, which little by little was being spirited away south to the States. As early as 1970, he was already formulating a way to

Philippe Beaudry and Ron Strong with
marine phones recovered from the wreck.
Courtesy of Diane Strong.

Ron Strong with the *Empress*'s compass,
1970. *Courtesy of Diane Strong.*

house his collection in a local museum. According to Beaudry, no one
else in Rimouski shared his aspiration. He became convinced that only
he could save what was left of the *Empress of Ireland*.

It wasn't easy for a twenty-five-year-old with little worldly knowledge
to appreciate the magnitude of the job he decided to assume. Nevertheless,
he was sure he was the one to make the world aware of the great sunken
ship and to save her from complete dismantling. He took his first action
toward this goal on the last weekend of the 1970 expedition, with the same
Syracuse divers who had invited him along on their dives. Upon their
departure, Beaudry made a phone call to the Royal Canadian Mounted
Police, Canada's national police force. He was outraged when he learned
that the Americans were taking the recovered artifacts back to New York
with them.

Ronni Gilligan was in Rimouski gassing up her Chevy convertible,
packed with dive gear and luggage, when she was approached by what

Peter Perrault securing the *Empress*'s helm to the dive boat's stern after recovery from the wreck. *Courtesy of Diane Strong.*

she later called a "cute, English-speaking guy." He asked if she was one of the American divers who had been out to the *Empress*. Flattered to be recognized, Gilligan proudly said yes, she was, with a flirtatious smile. The man then produced a badge and announced that he was an officer in the Royal Canadian Mounted Police and asked if she would please accompany him to the local police station.

At the station the police searched her car for artifacts taken from the *Empress*. They kept her there for an hour, asking the whereabouts of the other American divers. They didn't find any artifacts, and she could only tell them that the rest of the Americans were on the way home to New York. Gilligan was released with an apology for the inconvenience, and she quietly slipped out of town. The 1970 expedition to the *Empress of Ireland* was Ronni Gilligan's last, or so she thought. Career and other dive interests beckoned.

Peter Perrault had indeed left for home with several artifacts in his possession, including the prized telemotor. Besides the Royal Canadian Mounted Police, Beaudry had also alerted the border patrol. But Peter Perrault had crossed at a small customs checkpoint without an inspection, making it through with the artifacts.

Although unsuccessful in preventing the Perrault group from taking *Empress* artifacts back to the United States, Beaudry continued to act as the self-appointed protector of the ship. He had learned enough about maritime law pertaining to salvage to cause problems for future divers searching the wreck. He cited obscure laws and positions such as the "receiver of wreck," a federal government official charged with cataloging all goods taken from shipwrecks. The position dates back hundreds of years to a time when ships often ran aground. The rights of the ship, cargo owners, and insurance companies were protected by the receiver of wreck. But the receiver also encouraged salvage by awarding salvors part of the value of the cargo, as an incentive to recover property. In the case of unclaimed property, if after a year no legitimate claim had been made by owners or insurers of the vessel, the salvor could take possession of the goods. Beaudry believed that the receiver of wreck could prevent valuable artifacts from being spirited out of the country. Beaudry was never reluctant to enter the fray and was publicly and privately vilified for his seeming double standard about artifact removal—he had a large collection of ship artifacts in his own possession. He now claims he immediately saw the possibility of opening a museum in Rimouski, dedicated to the memory of his beloved *Empress*, and he moved to Rimouski in 1976 to see it through. Beaudry planned for his private collection to become part of that display. Subsequently he insisted that all divers, himself included, who removed artifacts must report their finds to the receiver of wreck.

Mark Reynolds (left) and Philippe Beaudry with their recovered artifacts at the Sainte-Luce breakwater. *Courtesy of P. Beaudry Collection.*

One diver who ignored the requirements was Beaudry's friend and dive buddy Michel Brunet. The collection, which Brunet had not declared to the receiver of wreck, was worth thousands of dollars. Ultimately, this collection was reported and seized and the friendship forged by dangerous forays into the wreck was forever broken. Beaudry was becoming deeply embedded in his self-appointed role as the *Empress*'s guardian.

Even decades later, Beaudry never has apologized for his self-righteousness, particularly when it came to American divers. He has justified his protective stance by saying he knew of Canadians who had lost their diving gear and cars simply for taking lobsters from American waters. "There was no equity," Beaudry explained to me. "In the States we [Canadian divers] couldn't take anything, so why should we let Americans come here and strip our wrecks? Our rules would have to be respected, too." Beaudry candidly admitted that jealousy also played a part in his hard-line stance against American divers: "These American guys had the best equipment and training, and because we were poor and couldn't afford the equipment, we couldn't do the things they were doing. It wasn't fair."

In 1979, Beaudry realized part of his goal. A traveling exhibition of his artifacts titled *Empress: The Train of Discovery* opened at the Marine Cadet Training Center in Rimouski. In Rimouski alone, over eight thousand visitors saw the artifacts, 90 percent of which were his. But, again, problems and controversy would dog Philippe Beaudry. According to Beaudry the powers that be in Rimouski treated him like a *ti-cul*, a pejorative French Canadian term meaning a "small ass" or a nobody. Beaudry was an outsider in Rimouski; he was not part of the clique. He was forced to go through people like Donal Tremblay at the Institut Maritime du Québec à Rimouski, also called the Marine Institute, to find space for his exhibits.

Beaudry began warehousing the artifact collection at the Institute in June 1980. In March 1982 he brought journalist Michael Soegtrop from *Diver* magazine to see the artifacts as part of a story the magazine was planning to run on the wreck. What Beaudry discovered shocked him. Everything was stored in the basement. And, to his dismay, artifacts had been left in front of a window and had been adversely affected by sunlight.

Beaudry informed the board of the museum about the poor conditions and demanded better treatment for his collection. Several months later, Beaudry found that nothing had been done to rectify the situation and informed Tremblay that he was going to repossess the collection. Tremblay told him he'd have to go to court first, saying that Beaudry would never get his hands on the artifacts. Tremblay believed the collection was safe and, after being underwater for over half a century, unharmed by a little dust and sunlight. In 1982 the Musée de la Mer opened at Pointe-au-Père, and Beaudry's collection was to be part of it—or so Donal Tremblay thought.

The coast guard had finally closed the lighthouse at Pointe-au-Père in 1981 after 122 years of service. Parks Canada, the national parks service, took possession of the old lighthouse and its grounds. Tremblay, along with others, had negotiated with the park service for a permanent place to display *Empress* artifacts. Parks Canada would provide the building, and a nonprofit organization put together by Tremblay would provide the displays and the upkeep of the museum. But after losing the three-year legal battle over possession of Beaudry's collection, the museum would have to make do without his artifacts, which had made up the bulk of the exhibition.

Beaudry had shown up at the Musée de la Mer with a court order declaring that the collection was his to do with as he pleased. He wasted no time. That same day he personally loaded the artifacts onto a rented truck and sped out of Rimouski.

The museum survived Beaudry's removal of his collection, but Beaudry's thin support from the Rimouski community did not. Not that he cared anymore. He had decided that "his" dream for the museum was not to be, as long as men like Donal Tremblay were in charge. Beaudry thought it was time he profited from all his years of diving the *Empress*. He showed the collection in a traveling exhibition and put out feelers about selling all or part of it. As far as he was concerned, Rimouski and the museum be damned. Donal Tremblay quickly augmented his now sparse display with other loans and donations and over the years continued to add to it, and he didn't at all miss Phil Beaudry and the exasperation he'd caused.

Jacques Cousteau and the *Calypso*

In 1980, when Philippe Beaudry was teaching a diving course in Halifax, Nova Scotia, he learned that Jacques Cousteau and his world-renowned research vessel *Calypso* would be passing through the Cabot Strait. Cousteau had planned a stopover in Halifax and then would proceed up the St. Lawrence to the Great Lakes to do one of his much-ballyhooed diving expeditions. Beaudry went to meet Albert Falco, Cousteau's dive-master, and told him about the *Empress of Ireland*. Falco and Cousteau—respectfully called "the Captain"—had apparently never heard of it, but their curiosity went into overdrive.

Back in Rimouski, over the next few days Beaudry sent a steady stream of telexes to the *Calypso*, talking up the *Empress*. Beaudry also promised he could get Ronald Ferguson, the wireless operator who had sent out the last distress calls from the stricken ship and one of the last survivors of the sinking, to fly over from England to be interviewed for the film. It was the kind of story Cousteau loved, one that put a human face on a dramatic tragedy. It made for great television.

Beaudry had met Ronald Ferguson before on a tour in England and had interviewed him extensively on video. The Musée de la Mer paid for him to come to Rimouski to be there when Cousteau and his crew dived the wreck. When Cousteau finally arrived in Rimouski, he arranged to meet Beaudry at the Marine Institute. There Cousteau admitted that he had taken the information Beaudry gave him about the wreck and had already unsuccessfully attempted to dive it. The famous diving crew, uninitiated in deep-wreck exploration in the northern latitudes' frigid waters, found the wreck too big, too deep, and too dark. They would need Beaudry's help.

The next morning the *Calypso* left Rimouski with Philippe Beaudry aboard. Thinking he wasn't in their league, Beaudry found himself reluctant to dive with the famed *Calypso* team. But while dressing for the dive, he noticed he had the same gear as they did. In the water he felt he was "not any worse or better" than the world-famous underwater explorers. With this boost to his confidence, Beaudry led the French divers down to the *Empress*.

The plan called for Beaudry to take the *Calypso* divers to an area of the ship where they could retrieve some personal effects of the crew or passengers, artifacts that they would donate to the Institute the next day at a ceremony choreographed for the cameras. It was a docudrama format that Cousteau had used successfully in the past. Cousteau himself, however, would remain in Rimouski.

Beaudry suggested that the *Calypso* divers go to the captain's quarters, an area Beaudry knew all too well. It was there, two years before in 1978, that a cracked manifold (a connecting valve that joined twin tanks) had sent him on a free ascent to the surface with no air—from the ear-splitting depth of 135 feet. The memory of that dive was still fresh in his mind. On another dive he made with Alain Roy, the pair had swum past the bridge and into the captain's quarters. After several minutes inside,

André Ménard, an *Empress* bell, and *Empress* wireless operator Ronald Ferguson.
Courtesy of V. Gilligan Collection.

Beaudry emerged to find himself snarled in an errant anchor line. The ensuing struggle to free himself cost him all of his air. When his buddy came to his aid, Beaudry was unable to use Roy's octopus regulator because it was jammed under the other man's back pack. Beaudry had no choice but to bolt for the surface. From that depth he needed tremendous momentum to get off the bottom. With no air supply, he kicked frantically upward. Beaudry kept the regulator in his mouth so he wouldn't swallow any seawater when the reflex to breathe kicked in. When he reached the seventy-foot level he knew he could make it, and he had the presence of mind to slow down so he wouldn't embolize at the critical shallow depths, where air embolisms are most likely. Breaching the surface, he burst into tears, knowing he had once again just barely escaped death. Had Beaudry been down just a few minutes longer, he certainly would have been seriously "bent" by decompression sickness.

With the agreement of the *Calypso* group, Philippe Beaudry returned to the dreaded place with the three divers. In the captain's quarters, he managed to find a clock face, a razor, and an inkwell, precious finds for the cameras. The *Calypso* divers dutifully followed the unknown French Canadian around the wreck like tourists without finding any artifacts themselves.

Back on the port-side rail, Beaudry began to take the divers aft to another section of the ship, but Bernard Delamonte grabbed him. Another *Calypso* diver grabbed his other arm and began to head for the surface. They had seen enough. Their total elapsed bottom time was only fifteen minutes. Beaudry realized that the famous French divers weren't accustomed to such cold waters and were perhaps a little frightened by the dark, hulking wreck. The surprised Beaudry was used to spending at least thirty minutes on the wreck during a dive.

The Ronald Ferguson interview aboard the *Calypso* was inserted into the resulting film, *St. Lawrence: Stairway to the Sea*, with the dramatic effect intact. The *Empress* segment ran eleven minutes, including the underwater footage of the wreck with Phil Beaudry. Cousteau ended up with just what he wanted. So did Beaudry. His goal of bringing the ship and its history to Cousteau's wide, adoring public was a success. Cousteau, of course, further burnished his reputation as an intrepid underwater explorer, thanks to Beaudry's skills and tenacious nature. It was Beaudry, after all, who had badgered Cousteau to visit the wreck.

Philippe Beaudry later earned even more public recognition for the *Empress*. Beaudry and dive buddy Mark Reynolds were the expert *Empress* divers aboard when the American Robert Ballard, discoverer of the sunken *Titanic*, would visit the wreck with his film team almost twenty years later to film his documentary *Lost Liners*. But a good deal would happen during those twenty years: more intrigue, piracy, diving politics, and deaths.

The *Empress* in the Eighties: The Diving Death of Hector Moissan

Serge Lavoie would become a pivotal figure in the politics of diving the *Empress of Ireland*, though not by choice. Lavoie's immersion in controversy started innocently enough. He was a diver who loved the *Empress*; he was also affiliated with the Marine Institute and a friend of Donal Tremblay's.

Serge Lavoie, commercial diver and *Empress* explorer. *Courtesy of Serge Lavoie Collection.*

Lavoie was not typical of the divers who visited the *Empress of Ireland*. Born and raised in Schefferville, the northeastern outback of Quebec, he came to the sport of wreck diving through the back door.

Lavoie was a graduate of the University of Quebec, where he earned his degree as a mechanical engineer in 1979. He had the ambition of pursuing a career in Canada's merchant marine and had had some instruction in scuba. By 1979 he, like the rest of his countrymen, was faced with a recession in the economy: no one was hiring mechanical engineers.

Desperate for work, Lavoie took courses at the Canadian Underwater Training Center, a commercial diving school in Toronto, to expand his employment opportunities. He finally found work on the North Shore in

Quebec, across the river from Rimouski. At the time, it had an active economy compared with the rest of the country. Canada was utilizing the vast, undeveloped resources bordering the shores of the St. Lawrence, constructing a federal prison, an aluminum plant, iron ore works, and smelters. There was work for commercial divers, since ports and piers had to be built.

Lavoie quickly learned that it was dangerous business. For his first underwater commercial job in the St. Lawrence, he was given the task of recovering a ship's lost anchor. While he was dropping down to 150 feet, hauling cable secured to his weight belt, a ripping current knocked off his mask. The current also tautened his life-support line and the cable he was hauling down. His dive handlers aboard the support boat felt the tension in the lines and gave him more scope, which only made his problem worse by placing more weight on him as he descended. He tried to compensate by inflating his drysuit, but to no avail. He crashed to the bottom and found himself pinned there by the weight of the cable, while the compensating air he shot into his suit to increase his buoyancy escaped through his neck seal.

Lavoie had no choice but to release his weight belt, which still held the cable he was supposed to secure to the anchor. Because he had tried to increase his buoyancy by overinflating his drysuit, he shot toward the surface, only to crash into his support diver at the eighty-foot depth. Not only did the collision with his safety diver jar his mask loose again, but it also knocked the regulator out of his mouth.

Meanwhile, his handlers decided they had better haul up his lifeline. When they did, all they found at the other end was Lavoie's weight belt. They thought they had lost him, but he had surfaced upstream of the boat. Lavoie was not sure which surprised them more—finding only the weight belt at the end of the line or seeing him clamber aboard unannounced. This was not the desk job as a mechanical engineer he'd once envisioned for himself.

Serge Lavoie eventually wound up teaching commercial diving at the Marine Institute in Rimouski under Tremblay in 1979, and he became familiar with the *Empress of Ireland*. Tremblay had gotten in the habit of

Serge Lavoie (left) and Langis Dubé, a pioneering diver of the *Empress*. *Courtesy of Serge Lavoie Collection.*

taking Lavoie and other diving students out to the wreck for practical experience.

There were other reasons why the sunken ship so interested Lavoie. His grandparents, and later his parents, had a summer home in the quaint, slow-paced village of Sainte-Luce, ten miles downriver from Rimouski. Naturally his father had heard stories about the tragic sinking on that night back in 1914, which he would later relate to his son. Lavoie's grandfather had heard an explosion on the *Empress*, a myth that was perpetuated by locals, right after the collision of the two ships.

At first Lavoie simply wanted to explore the wreck, but after joining the world of commercial diving he too began to be driven by the obsession of other divers in Rimouski: lifting artifacts. He sometimes dived with one of the students at the Marine Institute who made dives on the wreck—Hector Moissan, a twenty-nine-year-old welder and a certified commercial diver. Moissan had two years of experience diving in the waters around Rimouski, and according to Lavoie he was a competent diver and a good athlete, was extremely cautious, and had excellent endurance for deep-wreck diving. Hector Moissan would also have the sad distinction of becoming the first diving fatality on the *Empress* since Edward Cossaboom perished during the salvage operation in 1914.

On a trip out to the wreck sponsored by Tremblay, in June 1981, Moissan was part of a team led by Louis Morin, another instructor at the Marine Institute. They were there to anchor a floating pontoon to be used as a diving base to reach the wreck. In 1981 there were no seasonal moorings on the wreck, and to find the ship local divers had to use their boat depth sounders and line up known landmarks ashore, since few had Loran-C and the global positioning system (GPS) was still over twenty years away. Once they determined its approximate position, they dragged a grappling hook until it snagged the wreck. A diver would then shackle the hook to the wreck, and diving operations could begin. It was a tedious process, frequently unsuccessful owing to poor surface conditions and fog. Often divers returned to shore without ever getting wet.

The pontoon was built by Serge Lavoie. It had a light that would be visible from land and a radar reflector so boat captains could quickly locate the wreck. The pontoon also had mooring bitts so dive boats could tie in, tethering themselves to the wreck and making dive operations easier. The placing of the pontoon promoted recreational diving on the wreck. Lavoie wasn't present on this trip; he was working as an engineer officer on an ocean research ship operated by the Marine Institute. On this excursion the divers were also hoping to recover some champagne bottles from the wreck, to be used in a raffle benefiting the museum at Pointe-au-Père. They would wear only single tanks with no pony bottles for emergency air, since the dives were to be short and not particularly deep on the wreck. Decompression would not be necessary.

The dive vessel *Rigolet*, towing the pontoon from Rimouski, arrived at the wreck site at 6:40 A.M. on June 24, 1981. Minutes later Moissan splashed in with Louis Morin to shackle the pontoon chain to the wreck. The two divers successfully secured a steel cable to a port-side winch on the forward deck of the *Empress*, just aft of the bow, and made their return ascent.

A short while later, Morin said he didn't feel up to a second dive; the seas had picked up, and he was experiencing a bit of *mal de mer*. Since he had made several previous dives on the wreck, Moissan would lead the next dive and would begin his ascent to the surface vessel once he was down to a thousand pounds of air, or one-third of his air supply. Joining him were two divers, Carol Voyer and Clément Sirois: both men were *Empress* virgins and fellow students at the Marine Institute.

The dive plan called for laying a line from a port-side winch near the new shackle point, tying in to the wreck, then moving aft to the first-class wine cellar. Moissan was wearing a wetsuit, since drysuits were still a rare luxury, and a Mae West inflatable CO_2 vest. There was only one underwater light among the three divers, since they believed the ambient light on the wreck would be enough for them to accomplish their tasks.

Once on the wreck, Moissan secured a penetration line from his reel to the winch and began to swim forward—in the wrong direction. Unwinding the line as the trio swam, Carol Voyer began to experience some squeeze in his new drysuit. He realized they were dropping down deeper on the wreck. Voyer checked his pressure gauge, and noticed he was down to five hundred pounds of air pressure, less than a fifth of his starting pressure at the surface. With such a dangerously low amount of air left, Voyer should have left the water immediately. He wasn't sure why his air consumption was so extreme. Hoping Moissan's single tank would have enough air for both of them, Voyer hurriedly checked Moissan's supply and was alarmed to see that his dive buddy had the same low amount. But Moissan seemed oblivious to the problem and Voyer, bowing to Moissan's experience, dutifully followed his leader into the darkness with their one light.

Moments later Moissan must have realized he was swimming in the wrong direction when he came to the narrowing portion of the forward deck at the bow. Moissan did a half turn and began to reel in the penetration line he had played out. His two dive buddies followed him. They later reported that Moissan's movements became "accelerated." They believed he was hurrying to complete his mission before he had to surface. His line then became snagged on the deck, but Clément Sirois was able to free it. The three continued moving aft.

Without warning, Moissan dropped his penetration reel and began to act strangely. His two dive buddies huddled around him. Sirois tried to get his attention by tapping him on the shoulder. Moissan, who was balancing himself on the port rail, reached out without warning and pulled Voyer's only regulator from his mouth and stuck it in his own. Voyer, shocked and helpless, swallowed some water and frantically tried to get his regulator back from Moissan, who was sucking hard, obviously in a panic. Sirois quickly offered Voyer his air supply and began to buddy breathe with him. In their pool sessions when they trained for scuba diving, the men had practiced sharing one air supply, one regulator. The safety procedure was a required skill, but there is a big difference between mastering the technique in a safe pool and using it in a panic situation in deep, dark water. The threesome began to struggle toward the surface.

Voyer and Sirois later said in an inquest on the incident that on the ascent Moissan appeared to be calm, even though he must have been out of air, since Voyer's supply was as low as Moissan's own. Sirois led the way to the surface while Voyer gripped Moissan's elbow with one hand. Moissan rose slower than his two buddies; he hadn't dropped his weight belt as the other two men had done.

Aboard the boat, Morin looked at his watch and realized the divers were overdue. Although he was worried, there was little he could do. Just minutes later Sirois breached the surface first. Voyer, just below him, had run out of air and was in the first stages of drowning, just feet from air and sunlight. In his panic, Voyer released Moissan and bolted for the surface, yanking his regulator from Moissan's mouth. Gasping for air and swallowing mouthfuls of water, struggling to stay afloat, he began to flail his arms, unaware that Hector Moissan was slowly sinking back to the bottom with no regulator in his mouth. Voyer yanked the cord that fired the CO_2 cartridge to inflate his horse-collar vest.

Onboard, Morin could see that Voyer and Sirois were in trouble and that Hector Moissan was nowhere in sight. He saw air bubbles percolating to the surface just feet away from where Voyer and Sirois floated. Morin was not suited up to dive and was too seasick to be of any help, and there was no other safety diver on the *Rigolet* to send in to look for Moissan. Morin could only hope that Moissan was doing his decompression stops, but that was not the case.

Finally aboard the boat, Voyer and Sirois told Morin that Moissan was in trouble underwater. There was no time to waste. Either Voyer or Sirois would have to go back down if Moissan was to be saved.

Voyer had exhausted his air supply and was in no state to attempt another dive. Sirois had only six hundred pounds of air, good for just a few minutes underwater. Morin had no choice but to send Sirois down again in a desperate attempt to locate Moissan, even though he had little air left for such a search.

Sirois descended about fifty feet down the line and couldn't find Moissan. Morin knew the situation was desperate, and at 9:00 A.M. he notified the Quebec Provincial Police in Rimouski by radio of Moissan's disappearance. Although he knew there was little hope for Moissan, and though he felt nauseated and weak, Louis Morin suited up and splashed in twenty minutes later to resume the search with a refreshed Sirois. They hunted along the bottom beneath the place where Moissan had last been seen. Fifteen minutes later they surfaced empty-handed. The somber group of divers on the *Rigolet* arrived back in Rimouski at 10:55 A.M. without Hector Moissan.

At 9:00 A.M. the next day, June 25, Louis Morin and a team of divers entered the water over the *Empress* and resumed their search for the body of Hector Moissan. Minutes later they found him. Moissan was on the forward deck of the ship in eighty-five feet of water. The fatality report issued by Transport Canadian after an inquest described the find: "The drowned man was in a seated position, with a mooring bitt (bollard) between his legs; his goggles [sic] were full of water, his regulator was floating freely near him, his inflatable vest and his weighted belt were still in place, and his submersible pressure gauge indicated zero."

The coroner in Rimouski ruled that Hector Moissan had died of an air embolism: gas escaping from his ruptured lungs had occluded blood flow to his heart. His wife and his friends at the Institute could only console themselves with the thought that Moissan had died quickly.

One telling fact did emerge once his diving gear was inspected by the DCIEM (Defence and Civil Institute of Environmental Medicine, now called Defence R&D Canada–Toronto) in Downsview, Ontario. The reserve valve on Moissan's tank was damaged and couldn't function properly. The reserve valve allows for the last three hundred pounds of reserved air to flow to the regulator once the tank is down to that final amount, possibly enough air to have carried Moissan to the surface alive.

The fatality report was critical of the Marine Institute in Rimouski. It faulted the Institute on a number of points: no one aboard the boat was aware that the divers had overstayed their time on the bottom until it was too late, and there was no safety diver ready to go in for a rescue once it was apparent the divers were in trouble. Not only was Moissan's reserve valve damaged, but the report noted that the Institute encouraged student divers to dive with their valves wide open, not allowing for a reserve of air in the tanks, a practice that compromised the safety factor inherent in the reserve valve. When properly used, the reserve air provided by the release of the safety valve could be enough to get a struggling diver out of the water.

According to the report, there were other problems with the Institute's diving practices and equipment maintenance. Over half of its scuba tanks were overdue for hydrostatic tests, which are supposed to be done every five years to test the strength and integrity of the pressurized steel cylinders. Serge Lavoie stated at the inquest that the tanks were up to snuff and were inspected regularly by none other than Hector Moissan. Moissan, a certified diving tank inspector from the Fédération Québécoise des Activités Subaquatiques, had approved the tanks for use just months before the accident. Further, none of the divers' breathing regulators were rigged with the innovative octopus rig, which might have eased the burden of sharing air for Voyer and Moissan, and later for Voyer and Sirois.

Whether a functioning reserve valve or an octopus regulator would have saved Hector Moissan will never be known. The Transport Ministry and the coast guard called for more stringent standards and regulations in recreational diving and recommended the proper use of reserve valves, employment of octopus rigs, and rigorous hydrostatic testing of scuba tanks in Quebec. But these were just recommendations. As the report noted, "There are no regulations governing recreational diving in Canada; it should be noted, however, that the Canadian Armed Forces have safety standards."

Beaudry later told me he had been diving with Hector Moissan out on the wreck the year before he died. Moissan had ignored two underwater warnings from Beaudry that Moissan was low on air. Eventually, Moissan did run out of air and in a panic grabbed for Beaudry's octopus rig; Beaudry believed in carrying one for emergencies. He and Moissan had to make their ascents and decompression stops together, breathing from Beaudry's dwindling supply of air.

Phil Beaudry claimed he had told Director Tremblay and Professor Morin that Moissan was neither qualified nor experienced enough to dive the wreck, but that both men had disregarded his warnings. Serge Lavoie said that if in fact they had disregarded Beaudry, it was because Moissan was a certified commercial diver with experience and had never had problems underwater before.

According to Beaudry, both Tremblay and Morin were responsible for organizing the dive with the goal of retrieving a bottle of champagne for a prize drawing held by the museum. Beaudry, then still affiliated with the museum, said he was against the project, since he believed the divers involved, including Moissan, weren't up to the job. He felt that the dive would compromise the museum if there was an accident. Beaudry later believed that since he was living in Montreal at the time, he was conveniently ignored.

Everybody, claimed Beaudry, knew you had to keep the sloping deck of the *Empress* to your right if you were going to the bow, and to the left if you going to the stern, which was Moissan's intended destination. Beaudry believed then, as he does now, that because of Moissan's inexperience, and Tremblay and Morin's dive plan, Moissan headed the wrong way, beginning the problems that led to his death. Beaudry told me he had pointed all this out to the Quebec Provincial Police; he believed that the police wanted to prosecute the two men, Morin and Tremblay, but because the Institute's reputation was at stake, no criminal investigation took place. Beaudry also claimed that by the time the Ministry of Transport's report on the accident came out in November 1981, both Tremblay and Morin had left the Institute. He insinuated that they had been forced out. "Nonsense," claimed Serge Lavoie, the current commercial diving instructor at the Marine Institute. Both Morin and Tremblay, he said, left years after the accident for better positions elsewhere: Morin in 1984 to start his own commercial diving company, and Tremblay in 1983 to become director of the Institute Maurice Lamontagne, a highly respected oceanic research center in Mont Joli, Quebec.

CHAPTER THREE

Extreme Diving

Courage is resistance to fear, mastery of fear—not absence of fear.

—Mark Twain

D avid Bright grew up in Niagara Falls, New York, just a mile from the Canadian border. He was an eager competitive swimmer who was a regular at the local YMCA, which also offered a scuba diving course. Bright was a history buff who lived in an area between two of the historic Great Lakes—Lake Ontario and Lake Erie—and the Niagara River. From the books he pored over at school he knew those bodies of water still held many of the ships that had gone down during the region's various conflicts: the French and Indian War, the American Revolution, and the War of 1812. Most of the wrecks, he knew, were unexplored, so at the precocious age of thirteen he earned his scuba certification, intent on rediscovering his country's history.

By doing some preliminary research at the local library, he located areas where battles had taken place and ships had sunk. In the early 1970s very little scuba diving was done there, but all through his high school years David Bright could be found diving the waters that surrounded his home. He found cannonballs and musket balls, bottles, and other artifacts waiting to be picked up. After earning a degree in biology at Pennsylvania State University, in 1981 he landed a job at Johnson and Johnson in the heart of the pharmaceutical industry in New Jersey. The New York/New Jersey corridor was also a hot spot for wreck diving in the United States. Making his home in New Jersey, he continued to pursue his first love, scuba diving. Bright honed his skills on some of the most challenging wrecks in the world.

In 1984 Bright read Clive Cussler's *Night Probe!* He was fascinated to learn that the plot vehicle for Cussler's work of fiction, the *Empress of Ireland*, actually existed. By 1985 Bright had made several forays down to the *Andrea Doria*, which divers called the Mount Everest of scuba diving, off Massachusetts' Nantucket Island. Craving to dive wrecks that were more challenging and more significant historically, Bright began to research the prospect of diving the *Empress*. He was delighted to learn of the existence of the *Empress of Ireland* Historical Society, headed by the French Canadian Philippe Beaudry.

In the fall of 1986, after the *Andrea Doria* diving season was over, Bright called Beaudry at his home in Montreal and learned that he had made hundreds of dives on the *Empress*. The now thirty-year-old physiologist, history buff, and diver asked if he could visit the wreck with Beaudry. Beaudry planned to be in the New York area for the *Titanic* Historical Society's commemoration of the seventy-fifth anniversary of the *Titanic's* sinking in April, so they could meet then.

Beaudry came to Bright's New Jersey home, and the two men talked about the *Empress of Ireland*. While there, Beaudry invited Bright to Rimouski to dive the

David Bright and first-class dish from the *Empress*. *Courtesy of David Bright.*

Empress with him. In late August 1987, the next *Empress* dive season, Bright journeyed north to spend two weeks in Quebec.

Beaudry wanted Bright to bring a particular piece of diving equipment not readily available in Canada. He told Bright he had found a large ash chute, a porthole designed for dumping ash out into the water, but he had no large lift bag to pull the chute up from the wreck. According to David Bright, helping Beaudry retrieve the ash chute was the primary reason for being invited.

With Beaudry were four divers from Ontario: Steve Brooks, Mark Reynolds, John Krahn, and Ray Stewart. The four Anglophones were all members of Beaudry's *Empress of Ireland* Historical Society. From the pier at Sainte-Luce the six men launched their two inflatable Zodiacs for the four-mile ride out to the dive site.

Beaudry told Bright the secret to finding the wreck: you had to line up some mountains on the southern shore of the Gulf that were bisected by some roads from a certain angle until they formed a perfect half-moon, and then you were in the area of the wreck. But if there was no buoy anchored to the *Empress*, Bright would later tell me, "You were pretty well screwed." He explained that they had no grappling hooks or shot lines and depended on a mooring buoy to get down to the wreck. More often than not there was one, usually placed there by Langis Dubé, a local who was regularly diving the wreck in the 1980s.

On Bright's first dive he felt like "a kid in a candy store." There were so many artifacts on the ship that it was still virtually a virgin wreck. Before that first dive on August 29, 1987, Bright had not been able to familiarize himself with the ship plans as he usually did before diving a new wreck, since none were around for him to study. But, the Canadians had deck plans and would eventually share them with him. He reached the tie-in point at the top of the wreck, and down at eighty-five feet he had to ori-

Divers launching a Zodiac. *Courtesy of David Bright.*

ent himself. What he found most notable was that after seventy-three years the *Empress* still looked like a ship—it was fairly intact. From his diving experiences and his knowledge of ship construction, he knew after swimming for a few minutes where he was on the sunken ocean liner. Bright explored the now-famous "explosion hole" made by divers in 1914 to retrieve the purser's safe, the port rail, and the forward deck. On his second dive he ventured into the third-class dining room, the bridge, the captain's quarters, and the first-class dining room.

Subsequent dives over the two-week period gave Bright a quiet confidence in his ability to find his way around the wreck. He also learned something else about the *Empress* that profoundly affected him.

Inside the explosion hole, on the top end, he swam into the first-class dining room. Bright had figured out that if he ducked down under that slanted deck, he would be able to enter the ship's mail room. He then went deeper into the wreck. He happened into a compartment where there were beds and piles of bones. Bones were everywhere, Bright would later tell me, so he called the room "the morgue." To Bright it was a sobering sight. The skeletal remains appeared not to have been disturbed, giving him the feeling that he was the first person to see them. Bright, in a personal epiphany, realized that the *Empress* was truly a grave site and deserving of respect. Diving the wreck and collecting artifacts for a museum display seemed to be the right thing to do to preserve its memory.

On an early dive that first week, the Canadians and Bright dived together to retrieve the ash chute. Bright attached the lines and the lift bag to the artifact near the third-class dining room, pulled his regulator from his mouth, and pressed his purge valve, sending a blast of air bubbles into the bag that lifted it up. It was obvious to Bright that the ash chute had snagged on something, and the Canadian divers were trying to figure out what to do. Acting instinctively, Bright immediately dropped down into the hole and found that the artifact had indeed caught on something and just needed a little jiggling to free it. Apparently the three divers were concerned that the ash chute, if disturbed, would fly upward and strike them. They were relieved that Bright had gone back in, freed it, and moved out of the way.

Bright assumed that the *Empress* was a protected wreck, based on the existence of Beaudry's official-sounding *Empress of Ireland* Historical Society. All the best or novel artifacts recovered by the divers would be given to Beaudry's organization, housed as an itinerant collection in Beaudry's home, and displayed there. Bright thought that this was "pretty cool" and that they were doing the right thing.

On one dive, Beaudry took Bright to the second-class dining room. Bright went deep inside to the pantry where cables and fallen kitchen equipment made the area very dangerous. At a depth of 130 feet, Bright dug around in the mud collected at the bottom of a large compartment that ran the width of the ship and found nineteen plates. When they returned to the surface Beaudry complimented Bright on such a deep penetration. Bright was flattered but told Beaudry that this was "fairly routine for New England wreck diving." The plates Bright found were extremely rare. They were indeed second-class plates, but they had gold leaf around the edges. They were for the few first-class passengers who wanted to sail incognito in second class.

Group photo of 1987 expedition with recovered artifacts. Left to right: Philippe Beaudry, Mark Reynolds, David Bright, Steven Brooks, John Krahn. *Courtesy of David Bright.*

On Bright's seventh dive on September 3, he decided he wanted to drop over the side of the ship, down to the muddy bottom of the Gulf. Before Bright arrived in Quebec, Beaudry had told him that the depth there was around 180 feet, a fairly deep dive by Northeast wreck diving standards. Steve Brooks had never been down that deep and asked Bright to accompany him. "No problem" was Bright's answer, happy to dive with Brooks and share his deepwater diving experience.

Alighting on the muddy bottom just off the wreck, Bright was shocked to see that his depth gauge read only 150 feet. Showing the gauge to Brooks, Bright stared at him for a moment. As Bright related later, he could read Brooks's thoughts: "Beaudry lied to us."

Bright told me that during that 1987 expedition he didn't want to create any problems. His only intention was to help collect artifacts for the historical society to exhibit. If the Ontario divers had issues with Phil Beaudry, that was OK with Bright, but he didn't want to be involved. By the time of the 1988 expedition, Bright noticed that the Ontario divers had stopped distributing the historical society's business cards.

In 1988 Beaudry had Bright pick up an underwater video camera that Beaudry had ordered from a New York City photography store so he could shoot a documentary on diving the *Empress*. Beaudry asked Bright to accompany him while filming the dive and to be in several shots. According to Bright, Beaudry had shot "crap." The Ontario divers then took over the filming. Bright related that first-time filmmakers Steve Brooks, Mark Reynolds, Russ Murray, Nick Drakich, and Ray Stewart did an excellent job and got some of the best shots ever taken of the *Empress* at the time. As they had the year before, Bright and the Canadian divers gave all the best artifacts to Beaudry's historical society.

In 1989, just days before the late August expedition, Beaudry said he couldn't make it, leaving Bright and the Ontario divers to fend for themselves—and shoulder all the costs as well. It was during that expedition that the practice of donating the unique artifacts to the historical society ended. According to David Bright, Beaudry confessed to him that he had wanted to bring "one of these hot-shot *Andrea Doria* divers up to the *Empress* and have it scare the crap out of him." But Beaudry said, according

to Bright, that it was his biggest mistake, because Bright was not intimi-
dated and wound up showing Beaudry a thing or two about deep, cold-
water wreck diving. Bright told me Beaudry never understood that he
wasn't in competition with him. He was happy to donate unique artifacts
to the society and keep the rest for his collection saying, "It was the right
thing to do."

GARY GENTILE was well known to the international wreck diving community. His diving exploits on the *Andrea Doria*, *Lusitania*, and USS *Monitor*
were well documented in newspaper and magazine articles and in books he
had written. In 1989 he sued the U.S. National Oceanic and Atmospheric
Administration (NOAA) to open up the Civil War ironclad the *Monitor*
to sport divers. His victory in the protracted lawsuit made Gentile a well-
known character in the world of sport diving, and he seemed to thrive on
the controversy he created. His high-profile presence on the *Empress*
would be no different. Besides making deep and dangerous penetrations
into the ship that had never before been attempted, he also found himself
at loggerheads with Philippe Beaudry.

After recovering from wounds suffered in the Vietnam War, Gentile
emerged from a Veterans Administration hospital intent on a life of adventure. Deep-wreck diving, mountaineering, and wilderness exploration
seemed to fit the bill. Gentile quickly made a name for himself in the insu-
lar world of Northeast wreck diving. Brash, handsome, and fearless, he led
a new wave of deep divers, pioneering dives that many said couldn't be
done. Criticism from those who were envious of his accomplishments
and suspicious of his egocentric nature didn't seem to bother him; it stim-
ulated him to push himself even further.

In the early 1970s, Gary Gentile first read about the *Empress of Ireland*
in the 1939 book *Men Under the Sea*, written by the legendary U.S. Navy
diver Edward Ellsberg. One chapter in the book was devoted to the *Empress*, and Gentile was particularly impressed with a photo of the initial
1914 salvage operation, showing the raising of the purser's safe from inside
the wreck. That divers were recovering artifacts from the shipwreck was
all Gentile needed to know. He was already a fervent shipwreck researcher

and knew the *Empress* was still rarely visited in the 1970s. It had to be laden with precious period artifacts.

Like the *Andrea Doria*, the *Empress* was a grand ocean liner surrounded by legend: extreme loss of life, heroic rescue efforts, and controversy about the accident. The *Doria* sinking may have been more famous and more recent (1956), and the ship rested in deeper water (235 feet), but the *Empress* was older and more mysterious. Like most wreck divers, besides enjoying the excitement of the sport, Gentile was also a history buff. The Philadelphia native and his good friend New Jersey diver Bill Nagle decided they had to dive the sunken Canadian ship.

Gentile and Nagle started to make inquiries through Canadian divers, including Philippe Beaudry. They didn't learn much. Gentile claimed later that a lot of the information they received was incorrect, likely a scare tactic. He too had been told that the depth of the wreck was over 180 feet, not the 140 feet where it actually rested. That extra forty feet added another atmosphere of pressure—another 14.7 pounds per square inch— on a diver, increasing the risk of decompression sickness. That deeper depth also meant colder, darker waters to deal with. Phil Beaudry in particular was singled out by the effusive Gentile as an "obstructionist" when it came to planning his dives on the *Empress*.

Gentile wrote to dive shops in Quebec and to local tourist bureaus to line up a charter boat to dive the wreck. They all gave him the runaround. One dive shop even told him that diving the *Empress* was not permitted, but Bill Nagle was not easily dissuaded. As Gentile later related, Nagle "took the bull by the horns" and in 1982 drove up to Rimouski with his wife and his dive gear. Once there he hoped to make some initial exploratory dives.

Nagle checked in with an area dive shop and was told they ran trips out to the wreck, but that they took only local people and were booked solid. Nagle was persistent and finally found out there might be some spots opening later in that week. Nagle showed up at the shop every day for five days, dive gear in hand, and each time he was told to come back later. Nagle had the feeling he was being strung along. Gentile later claimed that the shop never had any intention of taking Nagle but didn't want to say no and create a controversy about not letting Americans dive the wreck. Finally a frustrated Nagle drove back to New Jersey without ever getting wet. Gentile said the failed affair had Phil Beaudry's fingerprints all over it, since from his research he knew of Beaudry's difficult reputation in Rimouski.

Phil Beaudry later told me that he never interfered with any diver's plans to visit the wreck. If a diver had trouble booking a boat out to the wreck, he said, it was automatically assumed that Beaudry was responsible. Beaudry assured me that he involved himself only when artifacts were removed and not reported to the receiver of wreck. As for Gentile's claims, Beaudry shrugged them off as "Gentile's paranoia."

In 1990 an occasional dive buddy of Gentile's, David Bright, told him about his 1987, 1988, and 1989 expeditions to the *Empress* and about the contacts he had made there. Bright said he was organizing his own expedition to the Canadian Pacific Railway ship in 1990 and invited Gentile to come.

Gentile learned that the Ontario divers and Bright had trailered their own inflatable Zodiac boats up to Sainte-Luce, then launched them from beaches. Tidal drops in the Gulf were precipitous, frequently exposing huge stretches of mud. Pushing the heavily laden boats across deep, thick mud for several hundred yards while dressed in drysuits was brutal and exhausting. The diving was easy in comparison.

By 1991 David Bright had tired of the "yearly dramatics" of diving with Phil Beaudry and decided to run the trip himself. He hired a local, Claude Grenier, and his boat, which he kept in Rimouski Marina. Gentile eagerly jumped at the opportunity to come along. Bright also invited friends and dive buddies John Moyer and Bart Malone. By this time, Bill Nagle had purchased the dive boat *Seeker* in New Jersey and was too busy running charters out to wrecks such as the *Andrea Doria* to join them.

Gentile had done his homework on the *Empress*. After a considerable effort writing to the shipbuilders in Scotland and to possible sources in Canada, he'd finally obtained a set of deck plans. But it was Ed Suarez, another American diver who was planning a dive of his own to the *Empress*, who'd gotten his hands on a complete set of plans; he was kind enough to make copies for Gentile. Gentile pored over the plans and pinpointed areas of the ship where he thought the best artifacts would be found.

Sport diving's bag of tricks was bursting at the seams in the early 1990s. Top-performance regulators, high-volume tanks, drysuits that were less cumbersome and more affordable, and streamlined gear configurations inspired by cave divers in Florida had divers going deeper and staying longer. Breathing-gas technology responded with the development of low- or non-nitrogen mixes such as heliox (a helium and oxygen mix) and trimix (nitrogen, helium, and oxygen) that reduced the risk of decompression sickness and nitrogen narcosis, the plagues of deep diving.

Thanks to these advances, Gary Gentile had accomplished a number of firsts in deep-wreck diving. In 1989 he made the 250-foot dive to the USS *Monitor* and in 1990 the historic heliox dive to 380 feet on the World War I German warship *Ostfriesland*. Gentile was ready for the cold-water challenge of the *Empress of Ireland*.

The best time for diving the *Empress* was mid-July through mid-September. Divers did visit the wreck both earlier and later in the season, but optimum conditions—warmer water, better visibility, and calmer currents—fell within that two-month period.

On what was to become an annual August pilgrimage to Rimouski over the next four years, Gentile finally got to dive the *Empress*. Gentile and dive buddy John Moyer's first dive plan called for making a general survey of the outside of the wreck to orient themselves to its layout. Ideal visibility of twenty to thirty feet with a "touch of ambient light" on the wreck greeted the two men. Gentile shivered in the thirty-six-degree water as he surveyed his surroundings. He was used to the cold water of the northeastern United States, but the water in the St. Lawrence was at least ten degrees colder. With heat escaping from his body twenty-five times faster than in air, Gentile could feel his body heat being sucked out of him. Even with the faint glow of sunlight from above, it seemed as if he were on a night dive. The black abyss beckoned him, and he kicked forward along the starboard-lying steel hull.

Swimming over the port-side rail, Gentile slowly dropped deeper. He hit muddy bottom before he saw it. Clouds of mud engulfed him.

Bart Malone (left) and John Moyer with an *Empress* bell. *Courtesy of David Bright.*

Illuminating his depth gauge, he was surprised to find that it read only 140 feet, not the 180 feet he had been told. Gentile was used to seeing ships covered with anemones and barnacles, so he was amazed at the lack of encrustation and the nearly pristine state of preservation of the seventy-five-year-old wreck. The influx of fresh water from the river apparently diluted the salt water just enough to forestall rapid encrustation and deterioration of the wreck. Gentile could still see the lush grain of the wood on the teak decks and railings.

The pitched angle of the ship, Gentile knew, would present some problems. After all that time underwater, inner decks and bulkheads would have collapsed, creating a labyrinth ready to entrap the unwary diver. Pushing off the wreck, he headed for the anchor line that snaked its way to the surface, a faint green glow of sunlight far above him. Gentile could feel the water warming by a few precious degrees as he ascended.

Gary Gentile had seen enough on this first dive. From his years of dive experience he knew he would have to be extremely careful on this wreck. The bitter cold and dark environment and the treacherous interior of the ship would present new challenges.

From his research on the wreck's history, Gentile knew of the explosion hole in the port-side hull. With a few orientation dives under his belt, Gentile, along with Malone and Moyer, started to go inside.

The explosion hole covered two decks, including the shelter deck that had housed the first-class dining room and the first- and second-class galley. Not far into the explosion hole, Gentile discovered what appeared to be a kitchen warming table or buffet about fifteen feet long, made of stainless steel and with shelves for storing dinner plates and bowls. All that was left now were some plates that had fused together. All "the easy stuff" had already been lifted. Gentile knew from his research that few if any American divers, other than David Bright, with wreck penetration skills had visited the wreck. Gentile and his friends believed that if they wanted to return home with artifacts, they would have to go deeper into the wreck.

The Americans then found their way into the wine cellar connected to the first-class dining room, which was two decks down and farther aft of the explosion hole. There were only a handful of local divers experienced enough to penetrate this area of the ship. Gentile, Bright, Moyer, and Malone would be the first Americans. That meant there could be a plethora of artifacts to retrieve.

The room had an open hatch on the hull, through which the divers could enter. After ducking under a bulkhead and following a corridor down, they came to the wine cellar and saw intact beer and wine bottles strewn about. They would not return empty-handed from their expedition to the famous shipwreck. The elated Americans collected first-class, second-class, and third-class flatware and silverware, serving trays, kitchen utensils, and a few personal artifacts such as a passenger's pocket watch—plenty to show for their efforts. To Gentile and his dive buddies the *Empress* was every bit as alluring as a Spanish galleon loaded with treasure. What they didn't keep for themselves, they would sell to collectors for

Pocket watch from the *Empress* collection of Gary Gentile.
Notice that the time is frozen at the moment of sinking.

top dollar. Gentile and his friends were unaware of the receiver of wreck laws, but they would learn about them soon enough.

Philippe Beaudry by this time had left Rimouski and was living near Montreal. He couldn't keep tabs on what was happening out on the wreck day to day; consequently he was unaware, at least initially, of what Gentile and his dive buddies were up to. But Phil Beaudry was still the self-appointed protector of the *Empress*, a fact Gary Gentile would have to deal with eventually.

IN AUGUST the following year, David Bright's group returned to Rimouski more determined than ever. Feeling comfortable with their knowledge of the ship's layout, they decided to explore the even more remote and less accessible areas of the wreck, deeper penetrations than anyone had made. It was exciting stuff for the Americans. Top-notch divers were doing deep penetrations on the *Andrea Doria* and a handful of other deep-residing wrecks in the northeastern United States, but nowhere else in the world. It was cutting-edge sport diving—some might say "extreme diving"—and the kind of challenge that adrenaline junkies like Gentile, Bright, Moyer, and Malone thrived on.

After the lower promenade level, containing first-class passenger state-rooms, they went all the way forward to the front bulkhead and down one deck to where the first-class and second-class galleys lay.

Gentile knew, since the ship was lying at a precipitous angle with its highest point the port rail, that anything not bolted down would have slid down to the mud-embedded starboard side. "The sad thing about the *Empress*," according to Gentile, "was that there was at least twenty feet of mud there, burying most of the artifacts and making them irretrievable."

They tried digging, but the silting up of the water again made Gentile realize he was in one of the most dangerous and frightening wrecks he had ever worked. Clouds of silt engulfed the working divers, reducing visibility to zero and disorienting them. Even determining which way was up became nearly impossible. The divers had the presence of mind to wait for the silt to settle before finding their way out. That meant minutes of sitting still in blackness, an eternity underwater, where the limited air supply dwindled with each breath. The cold embrace of the water added to Gentile's anxiety. Fighting down the urge to flee tested his fortitude.

Because the ocean liner lay at an angle, there were no clear vertical or horizontal guideposts inside the wreck, compounding divers' disorientation. Consequently, Gentile's team members were tentative in their digging probes and found nothing of note in this portion of the ship. It was an area best left alone. Then and now, no tools or techniques were available to make the job easier for sport divers.

While exploring the upper deck, Gentile made a serendipitous discovery. He had swum inside all the way to the aft section of the ship near the bulk stores and cargo compartments when he and John Moyer were about to retrace their way back to the only known exit, the explosion hole. But on the return he had dropped deeper down toward the accumulated mud at the bottom of the shelter deck. Just a kick of a fin sent up billowing clouds of silt that swallowed up the divers. To make matters worse, since the ship lay on an angle, Gentile's and Moyer's exhaust bubbles would rise and then slide along the slanted ceilings above them, dislodging loose rust that rained down on them. Visibility was quickly reduced to nothing. But through the blinding clouds of silt, Gentile could make out the edges of artifacts peeking from beneath the mud. Thrusting his arm all the way down into the muck, Gentile could feel the edges of a stack of something—for all he knew, it might have been human bones. But it was a stack of dishes. Slipping his other arm down on the other side of the plates, he pulled the whole stack clear of the mud. In his grip were twelve rare first-class dishes.

The team members also found their way into the second-class dining room. It would prove more dangerous than anything they had yet attempted. The divers had to drop down through a cargo hatch in the deck, swim down a corridor, then drop deeper into the wreck to an area that widened into a big room. Gentile later said that he had to be careful to remember the route so he could find his way back out. In the late 1980s and early 1990s, wreck divers had not yet begun to routinely use running penetration lines. Had they laid out a penetration line to follow back out of the wreck's black interior, they would have had something to rely on besides their wits.

Gentile found that a smokestack extending through the decks in this area had shielded the slanted bottom of the ship from the accumulation of mud. A few feet of space under the smokestack was free of mud and wide enough to squeeze through. Gentile pulled himself through this narrow passage. It was then that he saw some brass poking out of the mud. What he found was a bizarre contraption, three feet tall, that proved to be an egg cooker. The device had chains with counterweights, receptacles where several eggs could be placed, and a reservoir for boiling water. Once a cook set the device in motion, the eggs would slowly pass through the boiling water, and after three minutes diners would have perfectly cooked eggs. It was a unique and valuable find.

Although the inside of the wreck, with its collapsing decks and bulkheads, hanging cables, and wires, was extremely confusing to navigate in, Gentile found exploring the exterior hull fairly easy. The *Empress* rested on its keel at a forty-five-degree angle in the muddy bottom. If a disoriented diver simply went to the high point of the wreck, which looked much like the peak of a roof, and saw the slanted slide of the teak deck to his right, then he would know he was kicking toward the bow. If the deck was to his left, he would be swimming toward the stern.

The American divers found that after reaching the dive site, getting down to the wreck was no less difficult. Several of their dives were washed out by three-knot running tides. The outgoing tides, working with the river flow, were impossible to swim against. Strong incoming tides, bucking against the outflow of fresh water, were equally difficult to swim in. At times the mooring buoys were almost underwater and leaving wakes because of the fast water movement. Fighting the tides proved futile, as Gentile would learn; better to reschedule the dive for another time.

In what he called his guerrilla years of diving, Gentile and his dive pals had a saying: "If you can hook it, we can dive it." He and dive buddy John Moyer tried to prove the adage true against one such ripping three-knot tide over the *Empress.* Splashing in over the stern of their dive boat, Gentile and Moyer grabbed on to a trail line that ran along the surface of the water to the anchoring line running down to the wreck. The two divers inched along the surface line in the running tide and the three-foot waves that slammed them. Because of the strain of fighting the tide and the freezing water, Gentile quickly lost all feeling in his neoprene-encased fingers. Just minutes after latching on to the line, he didn't think he could hold on any longer. Gasping for breath, he felt the muscles in his forearms burning from the effort. Not even halfway along the line, Gentile gave up and turned back toward the boat. He knew it was hopeless: not only was reaching the mooring buoy nearly impossible, but if he got there, he would still face swimming down another 150 feet of line to reach the wreck.

Gentile, followed by Moyer, slid along the length of the dive boat to the stern, where the ladder was. Because of the running tide, the trail line made a big loop behind where it was tied off on the stern. Gentile hauled himself up to the dive boat's ladder. Moyer waited along the trail line, assuming Gentile would leave the water. But Gentile found he couldn't hold the ladder with his numb hands and had to hook the rungs with his elbows. Though gasping for breath, he was afraid that if he spit out his mouthpiece he wouldn't have the strength to reinsert it if he fell back into the water. He called up to the boat as loud as he could through the regulator that he couldn't make it up without help. Ontario diver John Reekie reached down to disconnect Gentile's dive light, goody bag, and tank harness so he could help pull him from the water without all the gear.

Moyer, watching from behind, now thought Gentile was getting help reconfiguring his gear before returning to the anchor line. Moyer would later admit he was close to panicking at the thought of having to go through with the dive in these strength-sapping conditions. Once he saw Reekie haul Gentile's exhausted body onto the boat by his tanks, he breathed a huge sigh of relief. The dive was aborted, wisely.

Back aboard the dive boat, Gentile and Moyer let friends help them strip off their gear before both collapsed on the deck. It took fifteen minutes to recover their wind and strength. Gentile then announced with a feeble laugh that he now had a new saying: "If you can hook it, we can get into the water."

On the trip back, a sudden storm kicked up, throwing six-foot swells at the forty-eight-foot boat and nearly swamping her.

On Gentile's second trip to the *Empress* in 1991, he experienced the most harrowing dive of his career. As on dozens of dives before, he and John Moyer had entered the explosion hole and dropped down past the now-familiar landmark, the steel buffet table. Gentile, from the ship's plans, knew there was a pantry for the first-class dining room just aft of the table on the starboard side of the ship, the side that rested several feet in the mud. He followed the wall that separated the dining room from the pantry downward until he reached the accumulated mud and debris at the bottom of the wall. His temperature gauge read thirty-six degrees at the 120-foot depth. Beyond the reach of sunlight, it was pitch black inside, and his powerful dive light illuminated just three feet in front of him.

Enveloped by darkness, he shone his light aft and saw a narrow space between the mud and the wall that curved and ran aft. He believed that if he could squeeze through, he would reach the pantry. Before entering the silted-up passage, Gentile and Moyer explored the bottom of the area just outside the entrance to the pantry. They immediately discovered silver serving trays and china poking out from the muck. But the pieces were all junk, corroded away and leaving only the perimeters, where the silver was thickest. They knew there had to be more kitchen and dining-room artifacts nearby.

According to their plan, Moyer would stay behind and shine his light into the entrance of the tunnel, serving as a reference point for Gentile. In the passage, the silt was so deep that Gentile had only about three feet of space to squirm through. He knew that each kick of his fins would stir up blinding clouds. Gentile could also see wooden slats, boards, and cables dangling from what was left of the pantry wall. Swallowing hard at going deeper into the wreck than he'd ever gone, Gentile entered the tunnel.

After kicking along carefully, Gentile had to part a coil of cables in his path. He knew that if he got entangled in them there would be little Moyer could do for him in the confined space this far below. He was in a narrow tunnel deep inside the wreck where his only option was to press ahead and hope for a space where he could turn around to exit. After he made a slow, torturous passage of about twenty-five feet, his light illuminated an open area, the pantry. Gentile executed a half-turn and could see Moyer's beacon through the debris he had stirred up.

Gentile began to reach with gloved hands into the muck, where he could feel the edges of plates. He slowly lifted, and an entire stack emerged. He had retrieved twenty first-class plates; all turned out to be in perfect condition. Completely blinded now by a cloud of silt—what wreck divers call a "silt-out"—and 130 feet underwater deep inside the sunken ship, Gentile felt for the opening of his goody bag, lowered the plates into it, and said to himself, "I'm outta here!"

The bag, now full of loot, dragged in the mud beneath him, sending up even more silt. He couldn't see the cables that he felt brushing against his mask, dragging across his tanks, and catching on his laden bag. Looking toward where Moyer's light should be, Gentile saw that the silt had obscured everything. But he knew Moyer had to be there, so he slowly pressed on.

Gary Gentile with silver *Empress* bowls.
Courtesy of David Bright.

On his way out, Gentile was constantly getting hung up and had to brush his hands over his hooded head, knock the cables loose, and back up to free himself. Just five feet from the entrance he saw Moyer's light, which had been shining on him the entire time. Gentile later confessed that he had been shaking, and not just from the cold. The pantry foray that had taken minutes had felt to Gentile like hours.

A big cloud of silt followed him out of the tunnel like the muzzle blast of a gun, engulfing both divers. Ascending to the explosion hole, Gentile had to inflate his drysuit to compensate for the added weight of the plates he was carrying. As a result he was more buoyant than Moyer. In the ambient light near the explosion hole, Gentile's goody bag passed before Moyer's eyes, which, Gentile later remembered, grew to "the size of silver dollars." Until that moment, because of the silt-outs and little light, Moyer had assumed that Gentile's penetration into the pantry had been a bust.

As fruitful as that dive had been, Gentile would never return to the first-class pantry. As he said later: "Once was enough. It was a frightening experience, and I wouldn't go back there for all the plates in China."

ON THEIR 1992 TRIP to the *Empress*, Gary Gentile and fellow Americans John Moyer and Bart Malone ran afoul of Canadian law. The team had pulled "a ton of stuff off the wreck," according to Gentile, mostly china from the ship's dining rooms. They were met at the Rimouski dock by an officer from the Canadian Coast Guard. Someone had reported that the Americans were illegally removing items from the *Empress of Ireland*. As far as Gentile knew, he was not violating any Canadian law when he removed artifacts from sunken ships in their waters. But Gentile was wrong. Technically he was in violation of that obscure and practically obsolete receiver of wreck law.

Once, after diving the *Kolkhosnik* off Halifax, Nova Scotia, and removing the ship's helm, Gentile received an irate call from Beaudry at his Philadelphia home. Beaudry didn't like Gentile's coming to Canada and taking artifacts back with him to the United States. He also told him that he was not welcome in Rimouski. "It was OK for him to take stuff," Gentile said, "but not me."

Beaudry was proud that he was the self-appointed protector of the *Empress of Ireland*. "No one else would do it," he later told me, claiming that he had phoned Gentile and berated him because Gentile was "a public man having influence on divers and was encouraging looting in a country where salvage was banned."

At the dock in Rimouski, the Canadian Coast Guard officer confessed to the Americans that he wasn't sure whether removing the items was illegal, but that he had to respond to the complaint. He told them he would have to study the law and come back to talk with them the next day, and he instructed the dive team not to leave town. Gentile and company considered bolting, but, unwilling to risk a problem at the border, they decided to stay. On his return, the officer had photocopies of the receiver of wreck laws.

Since there was no receiver of wreck in Rimouski (the official was now stationed in distant Quebec City), the coast guard officer assumed his duties and struck a deal with the Americans. He would log all the items recovered and photograph them. If after one year no surviving family members, shipping officials, or insurance companies had come forward to claim the artifacts, the American divers would then have clear and legal ownership.

David Bright was not surprised about Gentile's receiver of wreck difficulty. In 1989, the year Beaudry failed to show up, Bright and Ontario residents Steve Brooks, Mark Reynolds, Ray Stewart, John Jevkilar, and Rhonda Jaeger got an unannounced visit at their Rimouski hotel from a man claiming to be the local agent for the receiver of wreck in Ottawa. The official, who had brought along his wife, asked to see the artifacts the divers had brought up from the *Empress*. The mysterious official said that if his wife could be made happy, he would be happy. The implication was clear. Bright and the Ontarians politely offered the lady the pick of the collection. The delighted woman chose a couple of mint-condition first- and second-class plates, and she and her husband thanked the men and quietly left.

By 1992 Bright had tired of the petty politics of diving the *Empress*. Every year, he said, there was some "intrigue or drama." It was either trouble getting a boat, or divers' egos, or misunderstandings, or the local Canadian authorities. But David Bright would have one last memorable dive on the wreck.

While diving on the stern of the *Empress* in 1993 Bright came upon an upright wrought-iron deck chair used by third-class passengers. Visibility that day was excellent, and the deck was awash in sunlight that had filtered down through a hundred feet of green water. Wearing all his gear, Bright sat down in the chair for a few minutes, serenely looked out over the wreck, and marveled at the view and how it affected him. It was better, he thought, then pulling a bagful of dishes off the wreck. Bright felt for a moment as if he were a passenger aboard the Canadian Pacific Railway ship. After eighty-six dives on the *Empress*, he had now experienced firsthand the history of the lost ship, and it had humbled him.

DURING GENTILE'S last year of diving the *Empress* in 1993, Ontario diver John Reekie was handling all expeditions in Rimouski. Reekie had hired a charter dive boat in Ontario, brought it downriver to Rimouski, and kept it there for the entire season (mid-July to mid-September) for diving the wreck. Reekie, an outsider in Quebec, was an Anglophone from Ontario, but since he was Canadian, he thought he would have no problems in the neighboring province. This was his fourth year diving the wreck. Gentile and his crew were scheduled to dive with him for a week in mid-August. After they all assembled in Rimouski, Reekie told them they couldn't dive the wreck, since the charter boat he'd hired had been placed under detention by the Coast Guard.

Two weeks later, back in Philadelphia, a frustrated Gentile received a call from Reekie saying that he had received a ruling from the Canadian Coast Guard stating that they could operate out of Rimouski. Reekie also said he had gotten the boat released and would be diving the next day. Gentile dropped everything, loaded up his car, and made the fourteen-hour drive to Rimouski.

Releasing the boat had cost $14,000 and precious time. The local lawyers argued that the boat had passed federal inspection standards and that federal standards superseded those of the Province of Quebec.

Gentile, Malone, and Moyer spent the rest of that week and all of the next diving the *Empress*, Gentile's last venture on the lost ship. After forty dives, Gentile believed he'd seen enough. Other divers had more dives on her, but few had found more artifacts. He didn't want to dive the wreck if he couldn't bring home more, and with locals like Phil Beaudry policing the *Empress*, that was the current reality. For Gentile, other diving adventures beckoned.

JOHN REEKIE was living in Port Perry, just northeast of Toronto, when he began diving in 1980. Reekie had always been fascinated by the underwater world and made the natural progression from fishing to snorkeling and then to scuba. That first summer, Reekie logged eighty solo dives in the freshwater lakes and rivers of Ontario, which harbored lots of wrecks.

Reekie, a bear of a man with a bushy head of hair, owned a busy roofing company in Toronto and had the luxury of making time for diving trips to California, Florida, and the Caribbean. In 1984 he read about cave diving in a dive magazine. He was entranced. After loading up his gear, he headed south to Ginnie Springs, Florida, a popular spot for cave divers. Reekie wound up spending over $10,000 on cave-diving instruction that first year.

What Reekie learned was technical discipline. Air management, equipment configuration, gear redundancy, hand signals, zero-visibility navigation, and the use of penetration lines and reels were all pioneered by cave divers and could be applied to wreck diving. Air management, if done properly, could ensure enough air for safely emerging from most wrecks. The lean, streamlined gear used in caving meant less dangling gear to snag or be damaged by the corroded, sharp-edged ship bulkheads. Uniform hand signals made communication among divers infinitely easier. Zero-visibility navigation made silt-outs less dangerous for divers probing inside old wrecks. But the use of penetration lines was the biggest innovation borrowed from the cavers: having a well-marked escape route from inside a dark wreck would save many lives.

Reekie quickly realized that what he had learned in Florida could be applied to diving the wrecks in the frigid waters not far from his doorstep. One of those wrecks was the *Empress of Ireland.*

In 1987, after three years of intensive cave diving, Reekie started a company that distributes cutting-edge technical dive gear manufactured in the United States throughout Canada. He began to build a reputation in the Canadian sport diving community as a knowledgeable technical diver. In 1989 he received a call from Montreal from someone who had heard of his diving ability. The caller claimed he was a filmmaker doing a documentary on the *Empress of Ireland.* At this point Reekie, like most Canadians, still had never heard of the ship, but he was eager to learn more. The Montreal filmmaker needed divers to help with the underwater lighting; the filmmaker would provide everything else: the boat, the local captain, air tank refills, accommodations, and meals.

Reekie and a dive buddy drove up to Rimouski to check it out and met the boat captain, Claude Grenier. Grenier, who'd been hired by the filmmaker, took the pair out to the *Empress* two days before the filmmaker showed up.

John Reekie didn't know what to expect when he splashed into the St. Lawrence over the grave of the *Empress.* As he dropped down to the wreck, his curiosity was instantly transformed into awe. Reekie was hooked.

The Montreal filmmaker finally showed up with a land camera he'd rented, a wetsuit, and a single eighty-cubic-foot scuba tank. That the camera was not made for underwater use was a bad sign, but the inadequate diving gear for a deep, cold dive had Reekie shaking his head.

Reekie later told me that the man could barely dive and just managed to touch the wreck on the couple of descents they made. Reekie collected a bag of artifacts from the wreck for the filmmaker to shoot on video. That was the extent of the film documentary. The man from Montreal was apparently no better a filmmaker than a diver. After a few more attempts at diving and filming, he called it quits. The man didn't even have a car or a driver's license, so Reekie had to give him a ride back to Montreal.

John Reekie with an *Empress* bowl. *Courtesy of John Reekie.*

Even though the film was a bust, Reekie was grateful that the man from Montreal had introduced him to the *Empress*. It became a love affair that would last five years.

In 1990 and 1991, Reekie and some fellow divers from Ontario hired Grenier's boat and dived the wreck. This ended in 1992 when the boat was seized by the coast guard for being unsafe. Reekie told me later that the boat was a "leaking scow," and it was only a matter of time before the authorities caught on to its lack of seaworthiness. But at the time, she was all he had. Reekie then persuaded diving acquaintances George Wheeler and Susan Yankoo to bring their dive boat, *M R Duks*, up from Lake Ontario to accommodate all his diving buddies from Ontario and the States willing to share the costs of the *Empress* expeditions for the rest of the 1992 season.

Because of the extreme danger and unpredictability of deep-wreck diving, Reekie required that all his team divers be trained in underwater caving before attempting the dive. That meant that all of them were cave-certified or were experienced wreck divers from Canada or the northeastern United States.

In 1991 John Reekie had taken part in an *Andrea Doria* expedition off Nantucket Island aboard the charter boat RV *Wahoo*, best known for being the pioneering boat that ran divers out to the Italian ocean liner. The expedition had been organized by fellow Florida caver Bernie Chowdhury. The old-time *Doria* hands had been amazed at the artifacts Reekie could recover using his caving techniques. He had slipped into areas of the sunken ship that it had taken experienced *Doria* divers five years to find using their progressive penetration techniques.

These older progressive penetration techniques were promoted by people like Steve Bielenda, owner and operator of the RV *Wahoo*. This type of penetration was done without laying out any line to act as a trail out of the wreck. Instead, it encouraged divers to make progressively deeper probes while noting their surroundings. Once thoroughly familiar with each area of the ship, divers could make deeper probes more safely.

Progressive penetration was one of John Reekie's pet peeves. He believed the technique relied too much on brainpower and memory. When you threw a wrinkle into the mix—a stressful emergency situation such as a silt-out or low air supply—time was crucial. You didn't want to trust your memory to bring you back out of the maze, not when you might also be narc'd and fuzzy headed. Reekie repeatedly harped on the fact that with a penetration line, all you had to do was turn around and follow your line out. It was your highway in and your freeway back.

But Reekie also incorporated into his gear configuration some useful pieces of equipment used by wreck divers from the northeastern United States. One such piece was a Jersey reel. The Jersey reel was a personal ascent line, developed by wreck divers in New Jersey, that was spooled on a large reel with dowels. With the reel attached to a lift bag, a diver could send the line to the surface with a burst of air from his regulator. The diver would then have an ascent line, where he could also do his decompression "hangs" without drifting away from the dive boat.

"I wanted to dive the wreck," Reekie explained to me, "and I needed other people to help pay for the boat, but I wanted competent divers. For the most part, the divers in Canada weren't competent at that time. They were a joke up here. Most of them were single-tank divers doing no deco [decompression diving]. I didn't want to babysit them, and I didn't want people dying on me. That's why I got my dive pals from the States to come up."

According to Reekie, he never made any money running the expeditions in the early 1990s. For all the work he did during the year to line up the Ontario boat for six weeks and fill it with divers, a spot for himself was his only reward. Still, despite doing all the grunt work, such as rigging the moorings, Reekie managed a few firsts. He introduced cave-diving techniques on the *Empress*, visited areas of the ship that no diver had seen before, and almost got killed in the process.

In 1992 on a cool, sunny day out on the Gulf, Reekie splashed in alone, intent on making a deep penetration into the *Empress*. Diving solo was a controversial practice in the diving community. Neophyte divers in all the training programs learned that no one should ever dive alone, but wreck divers found buddy diving impractical. With redundant systems and extensive experience, some wreck divers saw a buddy as unnecessary, even a handicap. Buddies also slowed ambitious divers, and if they got into trouble, chances were good that they'd get their buddy into trouble too.

Alone, Reekie pulled his way down the anchor line, noting the dropping temperature as he went deeper. Within two minutes he was at the tie-in point on the wreck. It was unusually bright, thanks to the sun high overhead—optimum conditions, he thought, for some serious exploration. Wasting no time, he followed the port rail aft, never stopping to peer into the explosion hole or the numerous portholes on the port-side hull. Arriving amidships, he quickly penetrated the wreck through a shaft opening. Reekie didn't bother to check his air supply, since he knew his typical consumption rate. He figured he had plenty of time to do what he had set out to do.

Once inside, he kicked farther back into the blackness until he reached a narrow shaft that angled deeper into the ship. He carefully squeezed his large body through the opening. His tanks scraped hard against the steel, and he had to suck in his stomach and hold his breath to avoid getting stuck.

Dropping down three decks, he sensed he was in a large room. He swept his powerful dive light in a gentle arc, illuminating mechanisms found only in an engine room. Scanning to his left, he could see the top of one of the giant engines; to his right he spied the still shiny brass of what had to be the ship's telegraph—ready, it seemed, for its next order. Reekie brushed the silt away and could read the last instruction spelled innocently across the white-faced indicator: "full ahead."

The advanced state of decay had produced ubiquitous yellow, brown, and black icicles of rust that seemed to ooze from the ship's pores. Two- to three-foot strands hovered in the water like tentacles in search of invaders. Loose electrical cables covered in the ever-present silt formed menacing spiderwebs that, when disturbed, rained gobs of debris on him. The murky, dark waters further clouded his brazen attempt at discovery. His exhaust bubbles loosened the eighty years of accumulation from the ceilings and walls, his fins stirred up the muck and exposed a grisly view of human skulls, pelvises, and femurs. John Reekie had never felt more alive. The realization of where he was, and that he was the first living person to be in this room since that night in 1914 made him shiver with excitement. For a man who loved history and adventure, it didn't get any better than this, or any more dramatic. Reekie left the room the way he had come in, empty-handed. He would need no artifact to remind him of this penetration.

In his long dive career John Reekie had only three close calls. Two of them happened on the *Empress*.

Manifold valve bars connecting a set of double tanks were just beginning to replace the independent twin-tank system. When joined by the manifold, the two tanks became one air supply, and a diver would not have to switch regulators to access the second tank as was necessary in an independent twin-tank system. With the newer configuration, the second regulator became a backup if the primary regulator failed. Reekie always dived with the centerpost, or isolator, valve open on his manifold, which allowed for drawing air from both tanks simultaneously. He'd been having a slight problem with one of his regulators leaking, and someone aboard the boat who was unfamiliar with the use of the isolator valve must have noticed it and shut it down to prevent the loss of the air supply. Chris Rouse, one of his American dive buddies, had also noticed the continuing leak and had shut down the valve connected to that tank, ignoring the isolator valve on the manifold. Rouse told Reekie what he'd done, and Reekie reseated the problem regulator and reopened that tank valve but never checked to see whether the center isolator valve was still open.

On a subsequent dive, Reekie splashed in and swam down and into the forward cargo hatch, a favorite spot of his. Dishes and kitchenware in the galleys and dining areas of the ship never really interested him. The personal belongings of passengers in the luggage stored in the forward cargo hold were what fascinated him. To Reekie, the artifacts found there spoke more of the human tragedy.

He tied the end of his penetration line to a piece of machinery on the deck, then played out the line from the reel as he dropped deeper into the hole. Within seconds he settled into the muddy bottom, knees first, and began to dig with his gloved hands. Visibility quickly dropped to zero. Reekie dug in the cargo hold for about thirty minutes before he noticed that his air felt restrictive. He stuck his pressure gauge in front of his silty mask and was shocked to see that he was almost out of air. He couldn't think of any reason why his air supply was almost exhausted. If he had lost that much air through the leak, he surely would have heard the bubbling of the gas escaping behind him.

He stopped digging and backed up out of the silt cloud. Dozens of skeletal remains surrounded him. He later remembers saying to the assembled bones, "Well, guys, I guess I'll be joining you."

Reekie felt queasy and began to feel dizzy. Taking in the last bit of air, he felt his head start to sink into the silt. About to pass out for lack of air, he had a sudden thought: "Maybe someone messed with my valves." With no air left in his lungs, he reached over his shoulder and found the isolator valve shut down. He hurriedly twisted the valve open; the rush of air from the shut-down tank flooded into the empty one, giving him another two thousand pounds of air, or nearly half of his full supply.

Reekie took a few moments to hyperventilate, flooding his lungs with the precious oxygen his body was hungry to metabolize. He wondered what had happened, but as he told me later, "I never panic, and that's why I'm still alive." He added, "There's no point in freaking out. I couldn't do a ballistic ascent [or bolt for the surface] because I was too deep inside the ship. I just thought I had fucked up and that was it. I never monitored my air when diving because I had done the dive so many times before that I knew how much time I had. Had I not checked that valve on my last breath, I would still be down there."

Reekie, knowing he was out of trouble, went back to digging for booty. When he finished bagging artifacts, he said good-bye to the silent witnesses of his incident, did his decompression hangs, and made it safely to the surface.

Just a year later Reekie was once again in trouble on the *Empress*. The dive boat was moored to the stern, where all the divers wanted to explore. Reekie's mooring lines and chains, which had been tied in at the *Empress*'s bow the day before, had inadvertently become separated from the buoy and sunk to the bottom. They had to be retrieved. As always, big John Reekie did the grunt work alone.

Once down on the wreck, he motored up to the bow on a new innovation in wreck diving, an underwater scooter. Scooters had long been used in cave diving, and Reekie, a caver on the cutting edge of the diving equipment business, had one of the early models, a Mark III Faralon. Scooters took a lot of the hard work out of swimming against currents at depth, and less work meant less air consumption and fatigue. Fatigue was a known culprit in decompression sickness. In the early 1990s, a scooter cost about $1,800, which made it a pricey extravagance to most wreck divers.

Reekie and his scooter ran afoul of a discarded polypropylene line that he'd failed to notice. He cut himself free and thought no more of it. Reaching the bow, he left his scooter on the deck and dropped to the muddy bottom at 140 feet beneath the surface to collect his long lengths of thick nylon rope and steel aircraft cable, which were still tethered to the wreck. He dragged them up the *Empress*'s deck on the bow to the port rail and looped some line around the rail to control the lift. He then swam over to the slanted port hull, where he knelt and went to work. Reekie tied some line from his Jersey reel to the recovered cable and line, attached lift bags, and inflated them, as he'd later tell me, "to let 'em rip." But something unforeseen happened.

Reekie had tied a two-inch piece of shoelace in a loop through the hole at the end of the fixed shaft of his Jersey reel. To this loop he'd attached a clip that could be secured to some rope so he could pull the Jersey reel off his back when needed. When he deployed the reel with all his lift bags on it, the shaft started to spin furiously in his hands. The unhooked piece of shoelace, looped around a finger on his right hand, cinched tight and pulled his right arm up around the up line, up the hull, and back through the space between the port rail and hull.

Now with his arm extended over and behind his head because his snagged finger was being pulled toward the surface, he found himself pinned to the hull. He thought the lift of the bags would yank his finger off. The pain was incredible. Stuck there, he remembers thinking, "Fuck, how am I going to get out of this?"

As Reekie fought the pain, he ran through his options. He could stay put for maybe two hours and hope he would be found by other divers. But most likely he would drown, since all the other divers were several hundred feet away on the stern and would never happen his way. Or, he wondered, could he pull his finger off his hand? If he did, he would probably bleed to death or die of hypothermia while doing his decompression stops. He then thought about the jackknife clipped to his harness, which he might be able to reach despite being pinned; if he could just get his free hand on the knife, he could cut the line and free himself. But how was he going to open the knife? He figured he had one shot at it, since he would have to spit out his regulator and then open the knife with his teeth on one breath. If he dropped the knife or couldn't open it, he'd never get the regulator back in; he was dead. The knife was rusty, and Reekie could hear the sound of his teeth cracking and scraping in an effort to free the stubborn blade. He finally worked it open, cut the line, and put his regulator back in his mouth. He was free, but not for long.

All the line, steel cable, and chain carried by the lift bags filled with air shot upward toward the surface once Reekie had freed his hand. Reekie tried to back away, but some of the aircraft cable came sweeping up against the slanted deck, wrapped around his leg, and began to drag him upside down toward the surface. Once again Reekie thought it was over for him.

"If I'm going to the surface at a hundred miles an hour," he later told me, "I'm not going to survive. But the last coil of the cable catches this little screw head on the rail that just barely stuck out. Everything comes to a screeching halt, and there I am, hanging upside down with my leg still stuck in the coil."

In that awkward position, with the air in his drysuit rushing to his legs and seriously compromising his buoyancy, he struggled to free his leg. In a burst of strength he pulled his leg free, righted himself, then backed off and punched the stuck coil free of the screw head. He watched the last of the cable streak toward the surface. Near exhaustion and sucking hard on his air supply, he swam over to his scooter and tried to fire it up. It wouldn't start. Reekie glanced at his pressure gauge. He was almost out of air from the two struggles. A long swim awaited him if he couldn't start his scooter, but then he noticed that part of the polypropylene line he'd cut from its propeller was still caught there. After freeing the propeller, he was able to motor back to the stern moorings where he'd stashed extra tanks for decompression. He also had some oxygen waiting for him at twenty feet on his decompression hang. Reekie had to do two hours of decompression hangs in the frigid water with a dislocated finger.

John Reekie had managed to cheat death twice on one dive. He was in for one more surprise when he finally rose to the surface, freezing and physically spent. The line, cable, and chain he'd worked so hard to retrieve hadn't been picked up by crew on the dive boat. They'd all seen the gear floating on the surface, but no one had jumped in to haul it over to the boat. Eventually, as Reekie hung underwater working through his decompression, the gear slowly sank back down to the bottom as the air in the lift bags escaped. Reekie was livid. As he would later tell me, "Here I had supposedly the best divers in the world on my boat, and none of them lifted a finger to retrieve the gear. The assholes just watched."

Reekie would have to repeat the whole process the next day. That time it went off without a hitch.

Not all of John Reekie's adventures on the *Empress* were so harrowing.

In 1992 Reekie had his team of U.S. divers with him once again. He was diving in his favorite spot, the forward cargo hold. Digging through the silt, he came across a big rack of moose antlers covered in barnacles. When he climbed back aboard the boat he told Gary Gentile, John Moyer, and Bart Malone about the find. They told him he was crazy or narc'd, ribbing him unmercifully and saying the moose must have been swimming across the river, drowned, and sank into the cargo hold. Among the small clique of wreck divers, as with many extreme or dangerous sports, "breaking balls" was almost a ritual. It was usually good-natured but could have an edge of malice owing to the divers' competitive natures. On their *Empress* dives Reekie, Gentile, Malone, and Moyer were constantly trying to one-up each other with deeper, longer dives and bigger and better artifacts. Reekie ignored the grinning trio of Americans and quietly went about readying himself for his second dive.

Once back in the water, he swam deep into the forward cargo hold. When he finally clambered back aboard the boat, to the stunned amusement of his fellow divers he dropped the moose antlers on the deck, saying, "Here you go, assholes."

Reekie later donated the antlers to the Musée de la Mer at Pointe-au-Père, where they went on display. Just months later the museum curator contacted him. He'd received a letter from Norway, from the grandchild of a passenger who had been aboard the *Empress* when it sank. The letter said that the writer's grandfather had been on a trophy hunt in North America before returning to Europe. The curator believed that the moose antlers, which the writer in Norway knew nothing about, had been bagged by the Norwegian big-game hunter and had resurfaced some eighty years after the hunt. The antlers remained on display at the museum.

In 1993 Reekie finally soured on his underwater sojourns in Quebec. He had received a call from a Toronto lawyer, Mark Reynolds, who was a dive buddy of Phil Beaudry's. Reynolds wanted Reekie's boat for himself and his buddies for a week of diving early in August. To accommodate Reynolds, Reekie arranged for the Ontario dive boat *M R Duks* to arrive in Rimouski a week earlier than planned and had to rearrange all the other scheduled dive trips.

Reekie then had to smooth things over with Michel Tadros, a tough boat captain and salvor who came from the Gaspé Peninsula. He and his rough bunch of salvage divers from Halifax were aboard Tadros's boat, the *Gesmere*, moored over the *Empress*. They were surreptitiously stripping the wreck of its teak.

Beaudry had been making Tadros's life difficult with his ongoing efforts to protect the wreck. Tadros, claiming squatter's rights, had ignored Beaudry and had begun his stripping operation. Beaudry had been tipped off by a local diver as to what was going on out on the *Empress* and quickly made calls to Michel Demers, the receiver of wreck in Quebec City. Demers sent Tadros a subpoena to appear in court and defend his action.

Tadros was generally feared in Rimouski and given a wide berth. Reekie, being an outsider, had no intention of crossing Tadros, who had the legal right of 500 meters clearance since his salvage was a commercial operation, and asked him for permission to dive the wreck. Tadros agreed to allow Reekie and his divers on the wreck with one condition: no Phil Beaudry.

On the dock at Rimouski, on the first day of diving, there stood Philippe Beaudry with his dive gear. Reekie thought he had made it clear to Mark Reynolds that he couldn't allow his dive buddy Phil Beaudry aboard. Since Reynolds hadn't done so, Reekie had the unpleasant task of informing Beaudry that he wasn't welcome.

Beaudry seemed to take it in stride, not really surprised. Tadros clearly wasn't happy with all the noise Beaudry was making in Rimouski about preserving the wreck, and for Beaudry, being banned from the *Empress* by Tadros meant the salvor was feeling the heat. That apparently pleased Beaudry. Reekie hadn't yet had any run-ins with Beaudry and didn't want to make any enemies in Quebec, but if he wanted to dive the wreck, he had to make sure Beaudry wasn't aboard.

After Reekie saw the dive boat with Reynolds and his group of divers depart for the wreck—minus Beaudry—he drove back to Ontario to plan for the next five weeks. On his return to Rimouski, Reekie learned that someone had managed to get a judge to put the Ontario boat, *M R Duks*, out of business.

The detainment of *M R Duks* went into effect on the Friday that concluded Reynolds's charter. Reekie thought Reynolds and Beaudry were behind the spurious seizing. He believed it was Beaudry's vindictiveness after being refused a place on his boat that spurred the legal action by his dive buddy and attorney Mark Reynolds. (Author's note: During the final production of this book, Mark Reynolds provided me with documentation from the Coast Guard confirming that neither he nor Philippe Beaudry had any involvement whatsoever in the events surrounding *M R Duks'* disposition while in Rimouski.)

Reekie, Susan Yankoo, and George Wheeler had to hire a lawyer and spend days in court. They finally got a ruling from a coast guard official in Ottawa that the boat could operate, but the Quebec provincial court balked. Reekie argued that coast guard regulations and rulings were federal and added that "Quebec [is] still part of Canada."

After three weeks the boat was released, but by that time Reekie had lost three charter groups, who had each come to Rimouski and wound up "watching the water from their hotel rooms." Reekie said he had no money to refund them from his funds, since it had all been spent getting *M R Duks* to Rimouski, maintaining the boat, and defending his share of her in court.

The entire experience permanently turned Reekie off from diving the *Empress*. As he later said of running the *Empress* trips, "I lost a pile of money, and I couldn't afford it. We were in a recession then, and here I was losing my shirt so I could provide space on a dive boat for guys with bucks. That year was it for me. Quebec, as far as I was concerned, was now enemy territory."

The *Empress of Ireland* lost a worthy and intrepid explorer. All John Reekie really wanted to do was to explore the wreck and introduce other divers from around the world to her wonders. He had been proud that she was a Canadian wreck, but no longer.

John Reekie's difficulty as a Canadian Anglophone in the French-speaking Province of Quebec was nothing new. While the rest of the country made long-overdue cultural concessions, such as bilingualism and Quebec home rule, to Quebec, the province, in a backlash, became stridently unaccommodating to its English-speaking countrymen. Bilingualism in Quebec, as a practice, had been officially eliminated by the late 1970s. Official government documents, business signs, traffic signs, and even restaurant menus were written only in French. Compulsory French language instruction in schools further embittered Anglophones.

Because of the language division and the cultural enmity that resulted, there was less exchange not only between Quebec and the broader Canadian culture but within the relatively small Canadian diving community as well. The Anglophones and Francophones (as well as the Americans) were simply unaware of what each other was doing, robbing everyone of invaluable knowledge and experience that could safeguard the *Empress* and her historical value—and save lives.

BEAUDRY LATER told me how the *Empress* finally received its government-protected status. The conflict had Phil Beaudry and salvage operators at loggerheads again about the future of the *Empress of Ireland* and her artifacts.

In 1998, five years after the aborted attempt to strip the wreck of its teak, Michel Tadros returned to Rimouski with another group of partners and a team of underwater demolition experts from Halifax in the suspiciously early month of March. This time they brought dynamite. After word was leaked to Beaudry by local divers, he called the Quebec Provincial Police.

Tadros told the police that they had come early in the season, despite ice in the Gulf, to take advantage of the better visibility, devoid of summer particulate matter, so that they could shoot a documentary. But questioning by the police apparently made the salvors wary. Five days later they disappeared.

In the meantime, Beaudry had been involved in a letter-writing campaign imploring government officials to preserve the wreck. Quebec was the only Canadian province that didn't have laws on the books that protected underwater shipwrecks as historical sites. The Salvation Army in Toronto joined the struggle. Their combined efforts to protect the wreck as a grave site eventually earned the attention of the media. Finally the

Quebec minister of culture and communication declared a moratorium on commercial salvage work on the *Empress* for one year on April 24, 1998.

The president of Pétroles Chaleur Inc., the salvage company partner to the Tadros operation, stated in a radio interview in early June 1998 that they had no intention of honoring the moratorium and were planning to blast the wreck to recover the thousand tons of nickel entombed in her holds. Up to that point, Beaudry and his concerned friends had thought the salvors were only after the teak decking. Beaudry knew what the nickel retrieval meant. To get at the valuable metal, the salvors would have to blow up several decks of the ship. The public statement on the radio and revelation of their intent caused an uproar in Rimouski, at the museum, and in the dive community. Michel Tadros and Pétroles Chaleur quietly dropped all salvage plans. When the one-year moratorium ended, in April 1999, the government of Quebec declared the wreck of the *Empress of Ireland* a protected historical site.

Pierre Derosiers, an archaeologist with Quebec's Ministry of Culture and Communication in Quebec City, told me: "The wreck was not over one hundred years old, and the *Empress* was not officially historical. We had to evolve in our thinking as to what needs to be protected. Over the years, as divers removed objects from the wreck, people and the government began to be conscious of the value of the wreck, and that realization led ultimately to the granting of protected status by the provincial government."

CHAPTER FOUR

More Fatalities

If success is a certainty, where is the challenge?

— Mark Jenkins, *Outside* magazine

The streamlined equipment, gear configurations, and mixed breathing gases pioneered by Florida cave divers and refined by wreck divers in the northeastern United States hadn't yet taken hold in Quebec in the early 1990s. The eastern half of the province spoke only French, and the diving innovations were coming from the United States— in English. New technical training agencies down in the States, such as the International Association of Nitrox and Technical Divers, Technical Diving International, and American Nitrox Divers International, hadn't made their presence known north of the border. Even when the traditional training agencies, such as the National Association of Underwater Instructors (NAUI) and the Professional Association of Diving Instructors, had come around to the new trends in tech diving and instituted programs in the States, no classes were taught in Quebec. It wasn't until 1997 when the Canadian diver Gary Kulisek taught the first NAUI tech diving course in French that tech diving officially arrived in Quebec.

Divers from Ontario and the United States, such as David Bright, Steve Brooks, John Reekie, Kim Martin, Terry German, and Gary Gentile, had a huge influence on diving in Quebec. Local divers tended to advance by copying *les Anglais*. There were two local divers, however, who had struck out on their own: Langis Dubé and Jean-Pierre Bouillon.

Jean-Pierre Bouillon was one of the few people diving the *Empress of Ireland* in the early 1990s who was a native of the shores off the dive site. Coming from a Luceville farm family, Bouillon went to work for one of

Quebec's largest employers, the shipbuilder Canadian Vickers, where he learned a trade that would help make him famous once he began his underwater sojourns on the *Empress*. He became a ship welder.

For fourteen years he worked in ship construction, laboring on both military and commercial craft. By 1984 the ruggedly handsome Bouillon was an expert in recognizing the layout of vessels that sailed the waters of the world. Fascinated by what lay below the wind-whipped seas near his home, the thirty-year-old French Canadian, following a long history of tradesmen who learned to dive, became a commercial diver.

Because a commercial diver is essentially a mechanic who works underwater, he must have superior skills as a welder, cutter, and rigger (a worker who rigs cables to lift heavy items) as well as superior diving and athletic prowess. Bouillon had all of this plus insider knowledge and good instincts about ship construction.

When Bouillon went home to Sainte-Luce on a vacation in 1984, a local diving friend took him out to the *Empress*. The two men motored out to the wreck site in a Zodiac. On their first dive, Bouillon's buddy deserted him on the bottom, a practice that didn't square with Bouillon's training in sport diving and made even less sense since this was his first dive on the wreck. With just ten feet of visibility, Bouillon quickly became entangled in some loose cables. He spent the rest of his dive trying to free himself. With little air left, Bouillon finally surfaced. After he had piled into the boat, exhausted by his effort, he and his "buddy" were unable to start the engine. Then the river turned on them as six-foot seas began to slam the small inflatable. With no radio to make an SOS call, they were reduced to waving a flag tied to an oar until a passing fisherman finally rescued them several hours later. It was an inauspicious start to what would become an illustrious *Empress* diving career.

Jean-Pierre Bouillon began to make regular trips out to the *Empress* on visits home from the North Shore of the Gulf, diving with legendary Quebec commercial diver Langis Dubé. At thirty-seven, Dubé was several years older than Bouillon. Together the two men did unheard-of explorations in the interior of the wreck. Without running a penetration line, Bouillon would enter a hole in the stern and work his way forward until he

could find his way to the explosion hole. More often than
not, he was so deep in the
wreck that had he not found
the hole, he wouldn't have had
enough air to retrace his route.
But Bouillon had an ace up his
sleeve.

To most people, the inside
of a shipwreck is a tangled,
rusted-out mass of debris. But
because of his years working in
ship construction, Bouillon
was at home with a ship's innards. His ability to navigate

Jean-Pierre Bouillon outside the recompression
chamber that would later save his life.
Courtesy of J.-P. Bouillon.

inside ships, even ships unlike any he'd ever worked on, was uncanny.

From 1989 to 1991 Langis Dubé and Jean-Pierre Bouillon were wildly
successful at finding ship artifacts on their deep penetrations of the wreck,
especially the ocean liner's solid brass portholes. Bouillon became so adept
at removing them that he often surfaced with two of the seventy-pound
portholes on each dive. They were prized artifacts to wealthy collectors
in Montreal, western Canada, and the United States, then worth about
$1,200 apiece. For most divers, removing the enormous hunks of brass was
an impossibly back-breaking ordeal, but to the strong and savvy Bouillon
it was like "apples falling off a tree."

After retrieving the portholes that had fallen inside the ship, Bouillon
and Dubé scouted out the ones that had to be "banged out." For these, the
men would run a line from one porthole to another along the inside length
of the ship. Once the brass rings were secured to this main line, the two
divers would go outside the hull. Positioned over a porthole, Bouillon
would then take a five-pound sledgehammer and hit rapidly around the
circumference of the porthole. After some eighty years underwater, the
bolts that secured the portholes to the hull were completely rusted out.
The banging would make the porthole vibrate, loosen itself from the hull,

and drop down inside the ship, caught by the fixed line. The divers would then remove the line, holding several portholes, and tie it to truck inner tubes, which were then inflated underwater by air tanks to lift the load to the surface. The inner tubes worked fine, so Bouillon and Dubé saw no need to buy the expensive lift bags the Americans used. Their farming background had taught them practical, cost-effective ways of getting jobs done.

Jean-Pierre Bouillon claimed he would sell the prized portholes only to people who recognized their "holiness," as he called it. They had to show him their respect for what the artifacts represented. A porthole in the possession of the unappreciative would be blasphemy to the hardworking diver, not to mention, he thought, to the memory of the dead.

Bouillon had other motives for knocking out the portholes. Once the portholes were removed, the inside of the ship was better lit by natural sunlight that found its way down through the choppy seas. This made exploring the interior of the wreck, and finding other artifacts, a bit easier. He was particularly eager to find vintage wine and champagne from the innermost reaches of the Canadian Pacific ship.

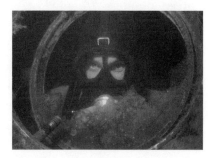

Diver behind a porthole on the wreck of the *Empress. Courtesy of Serge Lavoie.*

The bottles had been racked so that when the ship capsized and sank, some of them spilled out of the wine cellar into the passageways. Digging into the muck, which had protected the labels from disintegration, he found dozens of bottles of 1904 and 1907 champagnes and even older clarets. On one dive in 1985 Bouillon and Dubé burned a hole in a bulkhead with an underwater acetylene torch to gain access to the wine cellar where most of the bottles still rested. Most were still intact (and chilled) after seventy years under the crushing waters of the St. Lawrence.

With a penchant for the fruit of the vine, Bouillon later told me, "If there were no creatures inside them, and if they had some snap to them, we drank them." The powerfully built French Canadian with the long Gallic nose thought the champagne was delicious, and the two kept the empty bottles as mementos.

Bouillon was never happier than when he was 120 feet down inside the wreck of the *Empress of Ireland*. There he was *chez lui*—at home, in his element. He chose not to run penetration lines into the wreck. The thrill for him was swimming inside nearly to the point of no return, leaving him only one option: swimming farther into the wreck in search of an exit. If anything went wrong, he would be dead. It was progressive penetration taken to seemingly insane limits. Yet Bouillon didn't think of himself as a suicidal maniac, he was just pushing himself a bit further. He simply had confidence, drawn from his vast knowledge of ships, that he would emerge safely. It made the dives dangerous but also, to Bouillon, more meaningful.

On one such dive, Bouillon became disoriented inside the ship for seventeen minutes—"totally lost," he would later emphatically tell me. It was the longest seventeen minutes of his life; he thought he was "cooked" when he blundered into a hold of the ship and could not find a way out. He couldn't go back the way he came because it would take too much time and air. There had to be another hatch that led up and out of the ship. With the beam of his light he studied the structure of the hold to try to determine where he was and where the likely hatch opening would be. As his precious air supply dwindled, he maintained his composure and searched for an exit. With just enough air left for decompression, he located a hole and slipped through. Bouillon had found his way out by being patient and not panicking. He was also, he knew, a little lucky, but he wouldn't always be. *Chez lui* would eventually turn on him.

In 1991 Jean-Pierre Bouillon was working the wreck of the *Empress* for salvor Michel Tadros. Tadros paid good money and took on the tedious task of selling recovered artifacts. Jean-Pierre somehow managed two hardworking dives per day, sending to the surface of the St. Lawrence the prized brass portholes—trophies that brought good money for Tadros in the richer quarters of Quebec. The farm boy who had graduated to the lucrative career of treasure hunter was making a decent living doing something he loved.

But the work took its toll. Day after day he would retreat to his bed at home, dead tired after a day of diving in the frigid waters, only to get up and do it all again. It was one thing to dive this deep recreationally in freezing temperatures a few times a year, but it was quite another to work at it as hard and constantly as he did.

On October 16, 1991, Bouillon was doing his decompression hang at twenty feet when he experienced a sharp, burning pain in his back. It couldn't be a decompression hit, he told himself. He'd been doing the standard U.S. Navy stops on all of his dives. He finished his stop at twenty feet and proceeded to his ten-foot hang. But the pain intensified, and he started to lose feeling in his legs. Bouillon struggled to swim to the ladder off the stern of the dive boat for help.

The divers, during this salvage, had employed a unique system of boarding the boat. Once at the ladder, the diver would invert himself in the water so a crew member could remove his fins and he could more easily climb the ladder. But when he tried to flip over in the pitching seas, Bouillon realized he had lost control of his legs. Righting himself, he grabbed the ladder and yelled for help. But before a crewman could suit up in a drysuit and jump in, Bouillon lost his grip. The tossing seas had wrenched free his feeble grasp, and he was cast adrift. Two crewmen, finally suited up, jumped into the water and were able to flip Bouillon into a tethered inflatable. Realizing their friend was suffering from decompression sickness (DCS), they sped for Sainte-Luce, where the dive team had a recompression chamber ready for just such an incident. They hoped the recompression chamber, required by law since the salvage was a commercial operation, would reduce the nitrogen bubbles that had blocked oxygen flow to Bouillon's spinal cord, causing the paralysis and the excruciating pain in his joints and skin.

The stricken diver had to be raced four miles in the small craft across tossing seas at full speed. With every bounce over a wave, the ensuing crash down into the trough caused Bouillon agonizing pain.

After the first treatment in the recompression chamber, which was designed to simulate only to sixty feet, the attending technician knew Bouillon's condition was still serious and rushed him to the hospital in nearby

Rimouski. The chamber in Rimouski was inadequate for the severity of Bouillon's condition, so he was evacuated by air to a state-of-the-art recompression chamber in Montreal.

Once again in the chamber, Bouillon, strapped in a gurney, felt as if he had no skin and all his nerve endings were exposed. The pain was unbearable. The chamber environment was 100 percent oxygen, pressurized to reduce and eliminate the nitrogen bubbles in Bouillon's bloodstream and soft tissues. He then would be brought slowly back to sea-level pressure, minus the debilitating nitrogen bubbles.

After two hyperbaric treatments, the hospital staff in Montreal felt he had stabilized, and they stopped treatments. Bouillon was no longer in pain, but the paralysis in his legs hadn't improved significantly. Being a certified hyperbaric treatment specialist himself, Bouillon believed he needed more time in "the box," at least twenty treatments. That many, he hoped, would completely eliminate the debilitating nitrogen bubbles that had accumulated in his blood from inadequate decompression on his dives.

Bouillon now knew that his decompression stops had not been enough to prevent the residual nitrogen buildup in his system over the dozens of dives he had made. He had also been working hard and not getting enough sleep, and the water had been extremely cold. Even though he had followed the U.S. Navy dive tables, he hadn't allowed enough time for decompression to compensate for the variables involved in diving the *Empress*. He needed more time in the chamber not only to cure his paralysis but also to reduce the risk of an air embolism, which could block the blood flow to his heart or brain, causing a stroke, heart attack, or even death.

The hospital nevertheless removed Bouillon from the recompression chamber; evidently the doctors decided they'd spent enough precious and expensive time on this lone diver suffering from the ever-mysterious bends. Other patients suffering from burns, cancer, and respiratory illnesses were waiting to use "the box," where their ailments would be alleviated by the pressurized, oxygen-rich environment.

Had the recompression treatment continued, Bouillon later claimed, more of his DCS-damaged tissues could have been saved. Instead, he had lost the use of his legs. He endured painful months at a rehabilitative center in Rimouski. There a neurologist told him he would never walk again. The center promised only that he would be functional, meaning he would be able to bathe and take care of himself. Undeterred by the grim prognosis, Jean-Pierre Bouillon worked and willed his DCS-ravaged body to the point where he needed only a walker and braces to get around. Over the course of two years he progressed to two canes for walking and then to just one.

Bouillon's days of diving were over in 1991, at the age of thirty-eight, his professional prime. But he wasn't ready to let go of the *Empress* entirely. In 1993, with a small lawsuit settlement and his savings, he bought a home in Sainte-Luce with Eve, his wife, who had been his physical therapist. His new home sat next to the little village's church, on whose rectory door *Empress* survivor Gordon Davidson had knocked in search of help in 1914. On a clear day, Bouillon can see the buoy that marks the spot where the *Empress* went down and where his life changed forever.

Within a year of buying his home, Bouillon purchased a boat and named it after his mother, the *Marie A.B.* Since no one else was running dive charters out to the wreck for tourist divers, he decided he could keep his relationship with the *Empress* going. Chartering was the next best thing to diving. To Bouillon, life was all about passion, and his remained true to the *Empress*.

It was a passion I would come to understand. What brought divers like Beaudry, Bright, Gentile, and Bouillon back time after time to the sunken ocean liner was something more than just artifacts and adventure. It was a way to keep alive the story and the memory of the great ship and her passengers, and that was a noble pursuit.

A Double Fatality

On September 28, 1996, Jean-Pierre Bouillon was out over the wreck on his charter boat with a load of client divers. They were not alone, which was not uncommon during the dive season. Bouillon saw a group of *Empress* regulars on the wreck: Lise Parent; her husband, Marc Hardenne; and their close friend, Xavier Roblain.

All three were experienced *Empress* divers. Xavier Roblain, twenty-five

Marc Hardenne and Lise Parent in happier times. This photo was taken shortly before the tragic accident that took her life.
Courtesy of Marc Hardenne.

years old, was a native of Belgium and a naturalized Canadian. Blond and with movie-star good looks, Roblain had made over fifty dives on the wreck. Lise Parent, petite, pixyish, and forty-one years old, was from nearby Luceville but now lived with her husband in Montreal, where she had a successful general medical practice. Parent had almost ninety dives on various wrecks to her credit and was a certified dive master. Marc Hardenne, forty-eight years old, who had introduced his wife and Roblain to diving and to the *Empress*, had more than a hundred dives on the Canadian Pacific Railway ship. On this day they had motored out to the site not in a Zodiac (the boat preferred by locals since it could be launched from a number of places ashore) but in a twenty-one-foot hard-bottomed boat.

Out at the wreck, Bouillon, as planned, had tied up his *Marie A.B.* to the *Empress*'s amidships mooring. Hardenne and his group first checked on a submerged buoy they had previously tethered to the wreck near its bow, hoping to secure a trail line to it and dive from there. Then they tied up to one of the many seasonal moorings bobbing over the *Empress*'s bow, placed there by local divers.

The autumn day out on the Gulf was unusually sunny, warm, and calm. Hardenne helped Roblain and Parent suit up in their bulky drysuits, never an easy task since there were tight latex seals on the neck and wrists and a long zipper that had to be shut tight. He then helped them into their harnesses and tanks. Once those two were in the water, the more experienced Hardenne would have to struggle into his gear alone.

Back aboard the *Marie A.B.*, Jean-Pierre Bouillon decided that the current, moving at about two knots, was still far too strong; his group had been waiting two hours for it to slacken. Hardenne would later remember it differently. When his group arrived he thought there was little or no current, but as the day progressed it picked up until he'd "never seen it so strong." But the trio was already out over the wreck. They had come to dive, and dive they would.

At the bow mooring, Lise Parent splashed in first, carrying the loose end of the line to tie in to the submerged buoy. Minutes later, Xavier Roblain followed Parent into the water. Roblain, on a previous dive, had located a porthole. According to Hardenne, Roblain was intent on retrieving it on this dive and had no intention of helping Parent tie in to the buoy. Once Roblain disappeared under the water, Hardenne began to gear up for his entry. He planned to rendezvous with his wife and proceed to the wheelhouse, where together they'd try to wrestle a large viewing window off the wreck.

Once he was fully geared up, Hardenne realized he had a leaking O-ring on his tank valve; his air supply would escape from the tank unless he replaced it. Exasperated and eager to join his wife waiting underwater, Hardenne was forced to strip down and repair the problem. It took him about twenty minutes to replace the O-ring and suit up again. He was just about to enter the water when he saw Roblain pop up on the surface, face down and his arms and legs extended.

At first he thought Roblain was joking, since he'd often pulled similar stunts to tweak the more serious Hardenne's composure. Hardenne played along for a few seconds, but when Roblain didn't respond to his shouts, he became alarmed.

Meanwhile, Jean-Pierre Bouillon's attention was focused on his own clients. But out of the corner of his eye, he saw a diver's body floating on the surface near Hardenne's boat, spread-eagled and dangerously inflated. An overly inflated diver meant only one thing: he had rocketed to the surface without purging his drysuit of the expanding air and might have suffered a potentially fatal gas embolism. The current quickly swept Roblain away from the boats and moorings. Bouillon shouted to his divers to unclip the *Marie A.B.* from its mooring. He raced after the stricken diver.

Bouillon's client divers were all big, strong men who were able to scoop Roblain out of the water and onto the deck of the *Marie A.B.* They cut him out of his drysuit and began mouth-to-mouth and cardiopulmonary resuscitation on the unconscious diver. Overseeing the effort was a Quebec firefighter who had recently been recertified in lifesaving techniques. Hardenne called over on the radio and asked if the situation was serious. Bouillon replied that yes, it was "very serious," keeping to himself that despite the lifesaving efforts, Xavier Roblain more than likely was beyond hope.

Bouillon, with the unresponsive Roblain aboard, motored over to put one of his divers, Réal Pichette, aboard Hardenne's boat to help him find Parent. Hardenne hoped that by this time she'd tied in the line and was doing her decompression stops. Bouillon then gunned his engines and headed for Rimouski, making sure his divers were monitoring Roblain for any vital signs. But even over the roar of the engine, he distinctly heard Roblain give what sounded like his last gasping breath. At the dock an ambulance crew with a defibrillator made every effort to revive Roblain, but he never responded.

Back at the wreck site, Marc Hardenne's boat had slipped its mooring. They were adrift. Pichette didn't know how to operate the boat, so Hardenne once again was forced to strip off his gear. Losing precious time, he had to move his boat over to a different mooring ball. Hardenne tied into it, but the line came undone and they began to drift again. Hardenne decided to try to tie in on one of the other moorings attached to the bow of the *Empress*, several hundred feet from where they now were drifting. After finally securing his boat to the new mooring with Pichette's help, Hardenne geared up again and splashed in. By this time the current had picked up to about three knots, a strength he'd never experienced. Holding on to the trail line that led to the anchor line, he was pinned against the bottom of his boat by the rushing water.

Marc Hardenne knew it would take a superhuman effort to fight the current to the bottom, but he was convinced his wife desperately needed him. Struggling to resist the fast-moving current, Hardenne cried tears of frustration.

He fought as hard as he could for several minutes, but he wasn't getting anywhere against the ferocious current. He knew he'd never make it to the anchor line. He let go of the trail line and grabbed the ladder on the back of his boat. Already exhausted and out of breath from the effort, Hardenne clung to the ladder and quickly ran through his dwindling options.

He had to take a breather. Hardenne climbed back aboard the boat and with what little strength he had left, stripped off his gear with Pichette's help. After a few minutes Hardenne wanted to go

Xavier Roblain was all smiles here. He later died in the same accident that killed Lise Parent. *Courtesy of Marc Hardenne.*

back in the water and search for Parent, but Pichette convinced him that he was in no shape to attempt a search and rescue and would, at this point, risk killing himself. Close to panic, Hardenne geared up anyway, intent on finding his wife.

The two men managed to secure the boat closer to the anchor line. Hardenne splashed in and, full of adrenaline, descended the down line in the fast-running tide to the wreck of the *Empress of Ireland*. Almost an hour had passed since Lise Parent had entered the water. Hardenne was distraught when he didn't find Parent doing her decompression stops. Nor was she near the wheelhouse where she was supposed to have gone. He decided to swim forward toward the bow. Visibility was about fifteen to twenty feet. Hardenne remembers that the only thought going through his head was, "Oh, God, she's got to be here; please may she be safe."

As Hardenne neared the forward hatch, he detected a slight glow in the gloom ahead. With a final burst of hope and adrenaline he kicked hard for the beam of light. The dive light was attached by a lanyard to Parent's wrist. She was lying with her head toward the hatch and her feet toward the wheelhouse. Her regulator had fallen from her mouth, and her lifeless eyes were open. All Hardenne can remember about those horrible first moments was that he screamed into his mouthpiece and that tears were flooding his mask and stinging his eyes.

He released her weight belt and clutched her body close to his as he began to ascend to the surface; but Hardenne, in his confused and panicked state, didn't manage Parent's buoyancy well. He neglected to purge the expanding air in her drysuit. He struggled to hang onto her body, but the huge volume of expanding air ripped her from his grasp. His wife's body rocketed toward the surface.

Hardenne dropped back down and hit bottom in the mud at 155 feet, planning to follow the wreck back to the up line. But the strong current had carried him away, and the wreck was now nowhere in sight. He didn't think he'd been underwater long enough to accumulate dangerous nitrogen bubbles in his bloodstream that would require decompression stops at ascending depths. The dive computer on his wrist confirmed this.

Hardenne later said that a million things were going through his mind. He decided to ascend at a normal rate and take his chances, since he was not sure if the stress and hard work of swimming against a stiff current had dangerously increased his absorption of nitrogen gas.

Back aboard Hardenne's boat, Pichette watched in horror as Parent, finned feet first, popped to the surface. Her body was immediately carried away by the current. He picked up the radio and called Bouillon, en route to Rimouski, for advice. Should he go after the lifeless Parent or stay to assist Hardenne, who was still underwater? Bouillon told him to throw everything that would float over the side, which would create a trail leading to where her body was headed. Bouillon knew, but didn't tell the frightened Pichette, that there was little they could do for Parent, considering the almost two hours underwater and the way she had breached the surface.

After throwing the buoys, life jackets, water bottles, and seat cushions into the water, Pichette saw Hardenne surface between the boat and Parent's bobbing body. Pichette again screamed to Bouillon over the radio, asking what he should do. Bouillon told him to start the engine, but Pichette didn't know how, so Bouillon had to walk him through the steps. Finally firing up the engine, the frantic Pichette didn't bother to unhook the lines. He cut the mooring line with his dive knife and sped after Hardenne.

Approaching Hardenne, Pichette slammed the engine into neutral and pulled the exhausted diver aboard the boat by his tanks. Without waiting for Hardenne to catch his breath or stripping him of his gear, Pichette pointed the boat's bow toward the flotsam and opened the throttle. Pulling alongside Parent, the two men went about the incredibly sad task of recovering her body from the water.

By this time Hardenne was in a state of near-shock. Being back in the boat was like an out-of-body experience for him, it was so unreal. All his motions felt mechanical; his mind couldn't comprehend what had happened or what was happening now. His memories of recovering the body would remain hazy. He and Pichette managed to haul the small woman from the water with all her gear on. After removing her tanks, they cut her dry suit from her lifeless body.

Two divers in a Zodiac who had just arrived at the wreck sped over to Hardenne's boat shortly after he and Pichette had pulled Parent's body from the Gulf. One of the divers climbed aboard and helped Pichette try to resuscitate her. All three men took turns administering CPR and piloting the boat back to Sainte-Luce.

Nearing the shallow Sainte-Luce harbor, the distraught divers ran the boat aground in the low tide and broke the propeller. Still, Hardenne was able to steer the boat to the dock, where Parent's body was transferred to a waiting ambulance; but any real hope for her survival was long gone. Hardenne now faced two dead divers—his close friend Xavier Roblain and his wife.

Years later Marc Hardenne, usually strong and steady, would still struggle trying to talk about what had happened down on the wreck that day. He knew that Roblain had been intent on removing a porthole from inside the forward hatch area and was planning to tie a yellow polypropylene line to the prized artifact. Roblain likely became tangled up in the floating line inside the wreck. Since Roblain was diving with independent twin tanks, as he struggled to free himself from the line the tank he was breathing from must have run out of air. Either he couldn't reach his second regulator, attached to the second full tank, or he couldn't get the regulator into his mouth because he was tangled. Hardenne believed that since Parent's body was found near the hatch opening, she must have encountered the panicking Roblain there.

Hardenne knew that Parent had removed her knife from its sheath, since he'd found it lying next to her body on the ship's deck. In all her years of diving, Parent, to his knowledge, had never taken her knife out to use it—until that day on the *Empress*. Hardenne thought that Parent had probably tried to cut Roblain free, at which point he—being out of air—could have reflexively grabbed for her regulator. Instead of inhaling air, she would have then inhaled a lungful of seawater. She likely lost consciousness and drowned while Roblain rocketed to the surface, suffering an arterial gas embolism in the too-rapid ascent.

To Marc Hardenne, his belief about what happened on September 28, 1996, was plausible and logical. He also derived some comfort from believing that his wife had tried to save the life of a friend, a man in desperate need, though her attempt had cost the vibrant physician her own life.

At the dock in Rimouski, once Xavier Roblain's body was taken away, Jean-Pierre Bouillon shut down Roblain's tank valves to preserve evidence of the accident and so gas could be analyzed for poisons and the air amount could be preserved and noted. When the coroner, Jean-François Dorval, presented his report at a press conference months later, he stated that Roblain had died because his tank valves had been shut down and he'd been incapable of opening them once he was in the water. Consequently, the coroner concluded, Xavier Roblain had suffered an embolism in his attempt to reach the surface.

Jean-Pierre Bouillon approached the coroner after the conference and told him that the valves on Roblain's tanks had been open when he was removed from the water and that he'd shut them down himself to preserve evidence. He also said he'd reported his shut-down procedure to the authorities on the day of the accident. Bouillon later told me that the coroner had shrugged and told the flabbergasted Bouillon that "it didn't matter; the guy was dead."

By this time Bouillon was thoroughly exasperated by the provincial government of Quebec and with the Régie de la Sécurité dans les Sports du Québec (RSSQ), or the Board for the Security in Sports (now the Ministry for Youth, Recreation, and Sports) in particular. The government had spent thousands of dollars preparing rules and regulations for diving within Quebec's borders but then stood by and did nothing when a recompression chamber, much needed to treat injured divers in Rimouski, was shut down owing to a shortage of funding. To Bouillon it showed that the RSSQ failed to understand about diving safety and was blasé about correcting an obviously deficient situation. He told me with a resigned smile, "The RSSQ writes regulations for the dead and closes the chamber to kill the living."

Hardenne was diving on the wreck again a week after losing his wife and his friend. It was their passion—diving the *Empress*. He knew they'd understand his continuing to dive the sunken ship. That passion is a common thread among those who risk the plunge down to the venerable wreck.

Years later, during the summer, Marc Hardenne could still be seen in the depths of the St. Lawrence. He would think of his wife and friend whenever he visited the wreck, and in part that's why he still dived the *Empress*. He would bring flowers to lay on the plaques dedicated to Parent and Roblain that are fastened to the forward deck, small homage to the explorers who can no longer share that passion. As long as he was able to dive, he vowed, he would continue to visit the *Empress*.

The deaths of Xavier Roblain and Lise Parent seemed to buttress one argument made by wreck divers: diving solo was sometimes safer. Almost certainly one of the divers had caused the other one's death. For Hardenne that must have been a heavy burden. Would his wife be alive today if not for the underwater blunders by his best friend Roblain? It is a question he'll never be able to answer.

King of the *Empress*: Dany St-Cyr

When Dany St-Cyr started diving the *Empress* in 1990, he had never heard of technical diving or mixed-gas technology. All the fear that went hand in hand with "tech diving" didn't exist for him. Many divers, according to Jean-Pierre Bouillon, came to the *Empress* feeling a lot of pressure, since *une plongée* to the Canadian Pacific Railway ship was an "extreme" dive: a stressful and dangerous dive. But the five-foot-six, cherubic-looking French Canadian from Victoriaville, Quebec, felt none of that when he started making diving trips to Rimouski.

Although he is uncomfortable with the title King of the *Empress*, he knows there is no active diver who deserves it more. Still, he recognizes that his supremacy exists solely within his own little world, and his world is the *Empress of Ireland*. On another wreck he would be just another tourist diver.

During the winter St-Cyr drives a truck for a living, but during the summer and early fall he dives the *Empress*, exclusively. He's been diving the wreck continually since he first arrived in the area from Victoriaville. He was lured to the *Empress of Ireland* by one of his students in Victoriaville, where he was a scuba instructor. The prospect of diving a wreck farther downriver appealed to him. St-Cyr knew Langis Dubé, Jean-Pierre Bouillon's mentor and a diver of legendary status in Quebec. He had heard the stories of Dubé and Bouillon's diving exploits on the sunken ship, stories that were hugely inspirational to an up-and-comer like Dany St-Cyr, who was only twenty-five.

In 1990, eight years before seasonal moorings were placed, out-of-town independent divers were obliged to locate the wreck from local reliable sources. Dubé and Bouillon were as reliable as they came. Without the navigational aids of loran or GPS, St-Cyr and his dive buddies lined up various landmarks as instructed, dropped their lead-weighted shot lines, and made their dives. It was hit-or-miss at best, since lining up landmarks depended on good visibility, something that could not be taken for granted on the volatile Gulf of St. Lawrence. The weather could also turn on the divers and their small boats with little warning. Getting in and out of their Zodiacs in heavy seas was to be avoided if possible. Even optimum surface conditions didn't guarantee good conditions underwater. They could always count on its being cold and dark.

On that first dive, conditions were good on the wreck: they had twenty feet of visibility and little current. St-Cyr dropped all the way to the bottom of the Gulf. Near the lifeboats, he entered the wreck and found him-

self in the first-class dining room. All his life he had felt the need to dis-
cover, and he knew right then that his quest had finally begun to take
shape here, deep inside the seventy-six-year-old shipwreck.

By 1999 St-Cyr was an experience-hardened diver of the *Empress*, and
now he was searching for a way into the steering compartment, where the
ship could be manually steered if the hydraulic steering was lost from the
bridge. The compartment sat over the rudder below the waterline, all
the way aft in the ship, five levels below the lower promenade deck. It was
the most remote and difficult part of the ship to dive, an area that the tight
cadre of extreme divers who visited the wreck said could never be explored.
With the forty-five-degree slant of the wreck and the collapsing decks,
they reasoned, the ship's innards had to have been reduced to a razor-sharp
steel labyrinth, booby-trapped with silt and with hanging cables and
machinery. It was simply too dangerous to attempt. But Dany St-Cyr was
determined to find a way to penetrate the compartment; he wanted to go
to a part of the ship that no one had seen in over eighty years. He knew
he would have to do it alone. He couldn't ask anyone to accompany him on
such a dangerous dive, nor did he want anyone slowing him down.

St-Cyr knew he couldn't swim into the compartment from the engine
room; wreckage, sediment, and sealed hatches blocked the way. Through
a small hatch on the stern deck two levels down, however, he found a ventilation shaft that might take him there.

The shaft was narrow, three feet wide at best, and he had only about
three inches of clearance for his shoulders and two air tanks. Already deep
in 120 feet of water, he added to his ballast by expelling air from his lungs
and purging air from his drysuit and buoyancy device. Not really knowing what to expect, he dropped down the black shaft fins first, in a slow,
controlled descent. That way, he figured, he could escape in case there was
no place to turn around below. In the frigid black water he descended
further, easing another thirty feet down through the narrow tube. He
knew he'd reached an open compartment when his feet were no longer restricted in the shaft's enclosure. Satisfied that he'd found a way into the remote compartment but now low on air, he returned to the surface to figure out how to survive a deeper penetration.

On his second descent the next day with a fresh set of double tanks, St-Cyr dropped to the bottom of the shaft and into the compartment. The tight quarters he found himself in were the most claustrophobic he'd ever experienced. Every turn he made, every small move, made his tanks bump against corroding steel. His head banged against steel too, and he could barely flutter his fins. His constant brushing up against the interior bulkheads disturbed sediment that had coated the wreck, raising clouds of silt. Even his exhaust bubbles dislodged what time and corrosion had left behind. He felt as if he were in a coffin. St-Cyr could feel his heart pounding in his chest, and the fear of death constricted his throat, making breathing an effort. Because of the obstacles he knew he would encounter, St-Cyr had chosen a small dive light that would present fewer problems in the narrow passages. The meager beam and what it revealed constituted his only grip on sanity. Dany St-Cyr had never been so scared in his life, yet he swam on. He had come this far and wasn't about to turn back.

St-Cyr felt his way around the narrow confines and studied what his light revealed. He was in a small compartment that had to have an outlet forward. He swam down a narrow passage until he reached a roomier compartment. He made a slow 360-degree turn, watching his light beam illuminate this never-before-seen recess within the sunken ship. The light picked up the unmistakable casement for the propeller shaft. He was in the shaft alley of the *Empress*, the very bottom of the ship. He decided to swim forward toward the engine room. St-Cyr hadn't brought a penetration reel on the dive as he usually did; he figured that these deep tunnels would be too narrow for him to use it and that any extra piece of equipment would just get in the way or snag debris.

As he neared the engine room his fear was approaching a level that he felt could affect his judgment and performance. Visibility could be measured only in inches. Rust and sediment obscured what little his light could illuminate. His tanks were snagging on the alleyway's walls, and the constriction was getting tighter. Finally, after swimming several minutes, he reached a space where he could turn around, and he was able to swim back to the ventilation shaft.

Leaving the ventilation shaft on his way in, he thought he had come through a door frame, but on his return he couldn't find it. Dany St-Cyr swallowed hard when he realized there was no doorway where he thought one should be. The shaft must have rotted out where he left it, or maybe there had once been a grate there that had long since disappeared. Either way, there was no hatchway to be found. He knew it would be next to impossible to see the hole in this cloud of claustrophobic sediment, but if he was near it in the confined space, he might find it by touch. But what if he had swum too far? With a depleted air supply, he might not have enough time to find it.

St-Cyr stopped and tried to think his way out of the predicament. He knew his life depended on clear thinking, even though the chance of death hovered over him. He had a feeling he might have swum past the area where the ventilation shaft opened up. Swimming back in zero visibility, he began to feel around with his neoprene-gloved hands for an opening in the overhead decking. After a few minutes of panic, he felt something above him. It was the ventilation shaft. He was going to make it out alive. He swam back up the thirty feet of shaft and then to the surface.

What was an experience most divers would never want to repeat, Dany St-Cyr did again on his very next dive: he descended through the ventilation shaft once again. Instead of swimming forward this time once he was down through the shaft, he went aft. He swam just a few feet before he came to a wall. He was sure he wasn't at the stern, so it had to be a bulkhead. Searching with his light, he saw ship paraphernalia that hadn't been seen by human eyes since 1914. A fire hose, still intact with all its fittings and neatly rolled up, "speaking tubes" that ran up to the bridge and engine room, tools still hanging on the walls, and pulleys and chains suddenly rose out of the gloom that his dive light brought to life. To Dany St-Cyr, it was the most amazing place he had ever been on the *Empress*.

Speaking tube inside the steering compartment.
Courtesy of Dany St-Cyr.

Because the room was so narrow, he couldn't turn around. He had no choice but to swim deeper into the compartment, knowing that backing up blind wasn't possible since it was so constricted. He reached another wall. St-Cyr could go no farther and realized he was over the fantail, at the stern of the ship. The area was wide enough for him to maneuver in, perhaps three feet. Then he saw it: the steering gear for the ship's rudder. Carefully retracing his path, he swam back to the ventilation shaft. This time there would be no mistaking his escape route; the opening above him was where he figured it would be. As he left the wreck, he knew what he had to do next.

St-Cyr returned to the fantail one more time with a video camera. Since it was doubtful that any other diver would chance a penetration to this part of the ship, he wanted to document the find so that others could experience his discovery.

St-Cyr took nothing from the *Empress* but the images he captured on video. He felt that the place he'd explored so boldly housed the very soul of the ship. He had been in a holy place, a place known to underwater explorers around the world as a "pinnacle" dive, and he felt honored to have seen it. Taking an affixed artifact would have cheapened that experience. Leaving everything intact was a way to ensure its sanctity.

Years later, Dany St-Cyr would only shrug when asked if the dive was as dangerous and frightening as it had felt. He had survived it, he told me, so it couldn't have been that dangerous. Scared? Sure he was. But tasting real fear sharpens the senses, he told me, and surviving it made him feel all the more alive.

I don't think it was hubris or machismo that St-Cyr exhibited. He was offhand about the dangerous dive. He seemed to think that as an *Empress* diver myself I would understand. Dany St-Cyr was typical of the men and women you would find diving the wreck of the *Empress of Ireland*. Certainly he was the most daring and skilled, but the passion for exploring and understanding the *Empress* bound them all together. Pushing a personal diving limit was just a fringe benefit.

Pierre Lepage

Pierre Lepage, forty-six years old, learned how to dive in 1990 from his good friend Dany St-Cyr. The *Empress* was Lepage's school, and it was there, diving with St-Cyr, that he witnessed one of the more remarkable finds on the old liner.

In 1996 St-Cyr had located a cache of beer and wine bottles buried in the mud in a debris field outside the ship near the stern. On dive after dive, he returned to look for more. One day while sifting through the mud down at 145 feet, St-Cyr found a discolored and encrusted circular piece of brass. At first he thought it was a gasket with some brass on it, perhaps an engine part. "No good," he thought, as he cast it aside.

Digging deeper, he came across another piece of brass, shaped like a *P*. He waved it in front of Lepage's face mask. Dany St-Cyr realized what he'd found. The pieces of brass were the letters, fallen from the ship's stern, that spelled out *Empress of Ireland, Liverpool*. It would take two years of diving to recover them all from the muddy bottom, an effort that became their joint project. It would make St-Cyr and Lepage inseparable friends.

On June 24, 2001, St. Jean-Baptiste Day, the provincial holiday of Quebec, the two friends weren't diving together, though Lepage and his wife, Lucy Durette, had driven down to Rimouski from his home in Matane, farther east on the Gaspé Peninsula. As was his routine when diving the

Pierre Lepage and the *Empress* stern letters that he and Dany St-Cyr recovered.
Courtesy of Dany St-Cyr.

Dany St-Cyr with all the *Empress* stern letters mounted on a display board, 1999.
Courtesy of Dany St-Cyr.

Empress, he had parked his camper in Dany St-Cyr's backyard in nearby Sainte-Flavie.

Two client divers from Montreal had hired Dany St-Cyr to take them out to the *Empress*. St-Cyr's June-through-September business of motoring divers out to the wreck and escorting them around its remains was by now in full swing. He didn't have time for the dives he normally would make with his friend Lepage.

Lepage boarded his own Zodiac with his wife, also a diver, and the two of them sped out to the wreck site. Since St-Cyr, on his boat with the two clients, planned dives in the middle area of the wreck, Lepage tied his boat to the bow mooring buoy. Tied at the stern there was a third inflatable, which belonged to another dive buddy of St-Cyr's, Jacques Tardis. On a warm, clear summer day, it wasn't uncommon for several boats with divers to be out on the wreck, since by the mid-1990s its popularity had soared.

Lepage, at the bow, splashed in by himself, planning a solo dive. St-Cyr's own dive was, as he later recalled, "a piece of shit." One of his clients was a scuba instructor but was obviously in over his head on the *Empress*. Just ten minutes into the dive, he frantically signaled that he wanted to go up right away. St-Cyr saw the panic in his eyes but signaled that a free ascent was out of the question; they would have to return to the ascent line to ensure that they would be able to pull themselves back to the boat. Cur-

rents had been known to sweep divers downstream; the boat would then
have to cut its lines so the crew could go pull the diver from the water,
endangering those left below.

St-Cyr methodically returned the diver to the line and up to the boat.
Aboard the inflatable, stripping himself of his gear, he could see that Lepage's boat had cast off from its mooring and seemed to be motoring
around in search of something. St-Cyr knew immediately that there was
a problem.

Durette then pulled up in their boat and told St-Cyr in a frightened
voice that Lepage had surfaced away from the mooring line and called
for help, saying that he had a "big problem." Durette had immediately
freed the boat from the mooring, fired up the engine, and sped over to
Lepage, no more than a hundred yards away. She had almost reached him
when he suddenly disappeared beneath the surface.

Fifteen minutes had passed since Lepage went under. St-Cyr knew he
had to go in and look for his friend. They motored back to the site where
Durette had last seen him. Still saturated with nitrogen gas from his first
dive, and with little time spent on the surface to off-gas the nitrogen, St-
Cyr splashed in. He made a free descent down from the spot where Lepage had last been seen. St-Cyr hit the Gulf bottom at 140 feet. Glancing
at his compass, he decided to take a heading of due north. "I don't know
why," he later told me. "I just decided to go that way."

St-Cyr constantly looked to his left, toward the west, as he swam north.
After five minutes on that heading, his sweeping light caught something in
its beam. It was the lifeless body of Pierre Lepage. No bubbles were emanating from the exhaust ports of his regulator. Lepage was dead. Dany
St-Cyr grabbed his best friend by his harness and shook him, screaming
through his regulator, "Why did you do this? Why did you do this to me?"

St-Cyr struggled to the surface with Pierre Lepage's body in his embrace. It was a difficult task. He had to compensate for his expanding
buoyancy as well as purge excess air in his friend's drysuit with no down
line to hold onto. He reached the surface much faster than the accepted
and safe rate of one foot per second. St-Cyr made it to the boat in a fraction of that. Now it was his life that was in danger.

Stripping Lepage's body of his tanks, St-Cyr, Durette, and St-Cyr's client divers labored to pull his body aboard. St-Cyr made sure that CPR was started on Lepage, although he knew it was hopeless. He also had Durette, who was in a state of shock, alert the coast guard from Lepage's boat. St-Cyr knew that giving her tasks would give her focus and calm her growing panic. He then dropped a lead-weighted shot line to the bottom so he could go back down and do his decompression stops, grabbed an oxygen bottle, and descended to twenty feet for forty-five minutes of decompression. He could only hope that would be enough.

While Dany St-Cyr did his long, lonely decompression hang in the Gulf of St. Lawrence, he cursed himself for not being able to help Pierre Lepage. Had he not been with an incompetent client diver, he would have been with his buddy, and things might have turned out differently. Surely, he told himself in torturous repetitions as he hung on the line, he would have been there for Lepage to turn to when his trouble began. As it was, his best friend had been able to utter one feeble cry for help only to someone who had no chance of being of assistance. He had died alone on the muddy bottom.

Divers Jacques Tardis and his brother Serge sped over in their boat. Serge Tardis climbed into St-Cyr's boat and, with Lepage's body and St-Cyr's two clients aboard, opened the throttle for Sainte-Luce. Lucy Durette, fighting back tears, followed in her husband's boat. Jacques Tardis stayed on site in his boat and waited for St-Cyr to finish his decompression hangs on the shot line.

Once back at his boat launch site in Pointe-au-Père, St-Cyr called his friend Jean-Pierre Bouillon and learned that Jean-Pierre had thought that since St-Cyr and Lepage usually dived together, St-Cyr must also have been involved in the accident. Bouillon had earlier called St-Cyr's home and told his twelve-year-old daughter, Cathy, that Lepage was dead but that he had no information on her father. St-Cyr immediately called home and told his daughter he was fine. After giving a report to the police, he drove down to the hospital in Rimouski where Lepage had been taken.

In the hospital Lucy Durette, still deeply distressed, kept asking over and over for reassurance from St-Cyr that Lepage "would be OK." St-Cyr didn't have the heart to tell her he was dead and urged her to see what the doctors said. He thought the doctors were better equipped to tell her the bad news. It was hard enough for St-Cyr to accept it. Pierre Lepage never revived. He became the fifth diving fatality on the *Empress of Ireland*.

Lucy Durette deeply loved the man she had been married to for almost sixteen years. The couple were inseparable and did most things together as a team. "Real lovebirds," Dany St-Cyr would say about the two. Now Lepage was gone. Along with coming to terms with her own loss, Durette now had to drive back to Matane and tell Lepage's mother that her son was dead. But as a diver herself, who had visited the *Empress* dozens of times, Durette knew the risks she and Lepage had taken. She could find some solace in knowing that her husband had died doing what he loved. Most people aren't so lucky.

That night St-Cyr, Bouillon, and Jacques and Serge Tardis sat down at a local restaurant for dinner. St-Cyr remembers that the conversation never drifted far from the subject of death.

What happened to Pierre Lepage on the *Empress of Ireland* on June 24, 2001, still haunts Dany St-Cyr, and it is still hard for him to discuss. Lepage had made many careful dives on the *Empress* with St-Cyr, and he had made many alone as well. He was not a lackadaisical diver. He thought things through and did what he had to do like a true professional. But Lepage had been working hard on the wreck that day. His heart would have been demanding more oxygen. This may have put too much physical strain on the forty-six-year-old, and perhaps his heart had been affected by bubbles forming in his blood flow, hampering its efficiency. Lepage certainly complicated his problems when he made his too-rapid ascent to the surface. But he may have had no choice.

Lepage must have been in considerable pain on the surface, but he had at least been able to scream over to his boat that he was in trouble. St-Cyr thinks the pain would have been in his chest. His buoyancy control device was a conventional, modern vest type. His rapid ascent would have increased the air volume in the vest, squeezing him uncomfortably on the surface. Before the boat could come to his aid, Lepage might have purged some of the air to relieve the pressure, enough to drop him underwater.

He would likely have ingested water, since he'd spit out his regulator to call for help. He probably lost consciousness quickly, and then the waters of the St. Lawrence invaded his lungs.

The autopsy found no lesions on the heart indicating a fatal heart attack, but because of the holiday the coroner waited two days before performing it. Lepage may have suffered a mild heart attack, which would not have left any scarring. If the autopsy had been performed within hours instead of days, the coroner might have found some telltale enzymes in the blood showing cardiac arrest as the cause of death. As it was, the coroner listed the probable cause of death as *embolies gazeuses multiples*—multiple-gas embolisms.

R. W. Hamilton, MD, an esteemed diving physiologist, now retired, later told me that a person who dies at depth will invariably have an embolism on autopsy, but it may not be the cause of death. A pathologist would typically see bubbles throughout the bloodstream of a stricken diver autopsied at the surface. Hamilton, from years of scholarly and practical research, believes that it is not usually air bubbles in the brain that cause death, although they certainly disable a diver; rather, a "vapor lock" in the heart from the nitrogen is the ultimate cause of death.

The coroner's report also stated that Lepage's scuba equipment had been in poor repair—completely false, according to St-Cyr, who had examined the equipment, taken it apart, put it back together, and found it to be in excellent working condition. To this day, he uses the same regulators that Lepage used the day he died, without any problems. He thinks the coroner was reaching for explanations to questions he could not answer.

The death of Pierre Lepage only steeled Dany St-Cyr's resolve to continue his exploration of the *Empress of Ireland*. The death of his best friend in a place where they had spent so much time exploring together and forging such a strong bond made their experiences on the wreck that much more meaningful. The loss put St-Cyr's own existence into sharper focus. Diving the *Empress* now defined even more who he was. To St-Cyr it wasn't about winning and losing or beating the wreck; it was about feeling alive and having a reason for living.

CHAPTER FIVE

Planning the 2002 Expedition

*A shipwreck is like a crime scene. If you know how to read the clues,
you have a drama right in front of you.*

— PAUL CREVIERE JR., author of *Wild Gales and Tattered Sails*

I first saw David Creighton on screen in producer Robert Ballard's 2000 documentary *Lost Liners*. The first two steamships depicted in the film, the *Titanic* and the *Lusitania*, were certainly better known, but the story of the *Empress of Ireland* was more intriguing because so many people had never heard of her.

In August 1999, sitting on the rocky shore of the Gulf of St. Lawrence in Sainte-Luce on a gray, overcast day, Creighton read to the camera the last letter his grandfather had written to his children from aboard the *Empress*. When he read that letter, you could feel his pain at losing a grandfather he never knew.

It had become clear to me that I would begin my own quest for the *Empress*, and I knew I would have to meet this man. David Creighton would be my link to the past, a past that cannot be experienced just by visiting the historic remains. He would, I was sure, put a human face on the 1,012 men, women, and children who had died in the early morning hours of May 29, 1914.

Creighton's grandparents had been residents of Toronto, and he had written a book about his inner search for the meaning of their death, *Losing the "Empress": A Personal Journey*. When I first phoned, Creighton's voice was unmistakably the one I had heard in the Ballard documentary two years before. When I asked if we could meet, he quickly said yes and added that he never tired of talking about the *Empress*. Two weeks later I was on a plane from New York to Toronto, carrying a copy of his book with notes in the margins. There was so much I wanted to ask him.

We met at the Salvation Army's George Scott Railton Heritage Centre on Bayview Avenue, just east of downtown Toronto. It housed a museum dedicated to the *Empress* that Creighton said I "simply had to see." It was also close to historical landmarks integral to the *Empress* story. Creighton was waiting for me as I pulled into the parking lot.

David Creighton, seventy-one years old and retired from teaching high school English in Burlington, Ontario, had an easy smile and an almost unnerving way of listening carefully. He spoke clearly and succinctly, and his enthusiasm for the subject at hand was infectious, a trait he no doubt

made use of in his forty years of teaching. I liked him immediately.

After ushering me into the museum, Creighton introduced me to several members of the staff who maintained the modest exhibition. The Salvation Army has had a long presence in Toronto and since the mid-nineteenth century has been ministering to the poor and destitute of the city. The Army faithful were often mocked for their spartan, militaristic way of life and their dedication to self-denial, but the small number of Salvationists had the respect of the nation for their good works. The Heritage Centre is part of

David Creighton at the Mount Pleasant Cemetery in Toronto, 2002.

the "Sally Ann" school for followers intent on performing charitable works. We were the only people visiting the museum.

Reading letters of bereaved families who had lost loved ones on the *Empress*, studying press clippings reporting that long-ago tragedy, and seeing artifacts recovered from the chill waters just after the sinking and during later excursions to the now silent tomb made visiting the exhibition a somber experience. Creighton pointed out artifacts in hushed tones.

We came to an elaborate cloth spread across a table, beautiful handiwork of another era. The maroon material, embroidered with a floral pattern and fringed with gold, had warmed Alfred Keith, Salvation Army member and survivor of the *Empress of Ireland*. This was the tablecloth that Captain Andersen's wife had taken from their cabin on the *Storstad* to cover Keith after he was pulled freezing from the waters of the St. Lawrence. Alfred Keith had stepped off the collier in Rimouski wearing only this. In generous gratitude for his life, his descendants had donated the tablecloth to the Heritage Centre so that others might know of the Christian charity extended to their grandfather. David Creighton and I stared at the display for several quiet moments.

Walking on, we came to an array of musical instruments, military uniforms, and faded black-and-white photographs. Creighton pointed out Guido Whatmore, one of the band members in a group photograph, brought home to Toronto in a coffin on May 31, 1914.

Creighton's Aunt Edith had been sweet on young Guido: they had chatted discreetly apart from her parents on the train platform at Toronto's Union Station on the morning of May 27, 1914. Creighton had read about his aunt's infatuation with Whatmore in her tattered and yellowed letters, which he'd inherited when she died. The train would take both her parents and Guido to the *Empress*, away from the eighteen-year-old girl forever. "Sad, isn't it?" Creighton asked. "Yes," I replied, and I meant it. So often, distant events seem unreal, but seeing firsthand the everyday, humble remnants of those lost lives brings an event closer to the heart.

CANADA'S LARGEST CITY, Toronto, was the hardest hit of all the Canadian municipalities by the *Empress* sinking. One hundred and seventy Toronto residents lost their lives aboard the ship, and 148 of them were Salvation Army members. The Army's profound loss was mourned by the city.

Sixteen of the Salvationists who perished on the *Empress* were given wakes and eulogized at the Mutual Street Hockey Arena in downtown Toronto on Sunday afternoon, June 7, 1914. Over six thousand mourners filled the cavernous arena on that uncommonly hot summer day. After singing rousing hymns, the mourners watched as pallbearers moved the coffins to waiting funeral wagons draped in purple crepe, each drawn by four black horses. The Salvation Army Band played Chopin's "Funeral March" as the cortege wound through downtown Toronto and up Yonge Street, the city's major thoroughfare, to the Mount Pleasant Cemetery. Over 100,000 people lined the route, some wanting to glimpse the sur-

vivors who marched behind the dead in the largest public funeral in Toronto's history.

Mount Pleasant Cemetery had been the grand old burial ground of the Toronto elite since 1876. As Creighton and I strolled through its bucolic grounds, the towering skyscrapers of downtown Toronto were visible through the venerable oaks and maples. Mount Pleasant held massive mausoleums, stunning on hilly green expanses. Plots here had been hard to come by in

Toronto's memorial service for Salvation Army victims, the largest public funeral in the city's history. *George Scott Railton Heritage Centre.*

1914. The cemetery was as majestic a last resting place as one could ever hope for, and thus an odd place for the humble Salvation Army members who lived and worked among the poor. Apparently the city of Toronto and the surviving Salvationists thought otherwise.

Just off Yonge Street in section R, sixteen Salvationists had been laid to rest. A beautifully chiseled obelisk of Vermont red marble rose some fifteen feet above the lawn. Emanuel Hahn, a well-known sculptor at the time, had been selected to carve a memorial based on a design by Salvation Army Major Gideon Miller.

Carved into the stone was a large crucifix topped with a crown. Near its base were ocean waves with a seagull flying above a cliff. Creighton explained to me that death for Salvationists was not a cause to mourn but a reason to rejoice, since it meant the dead had been "promoted to glory." The crowned crucifix symbolized that those sixteen souls, and the unaccounted for, were now "kings in Heaven." Creighton smiled as he recounted their simple beliefs. Modernity and science, he related, made him a skeptic.

Around the base of the memorial were the names of the 148 Salvationists who died. I found Major David Creighton and Bertha Creighton listed, although they weren't among those found and laid to rest beneath the simple slab markers in the lawn. There were more than sixteen buried there. I found David Reese's stone, but I knew the body of Canada's Salvation Army commissioner had not been recovered until a month after the sinking and was interred here later.

I asked David Creighton about the grandparents he never knew. In his youth, he told me, they were just "those old people" in a photograph on the piano in his childhood home. His father, Wilfred, sixteen at their death, never talked about his parents or the ship that had taken them from him. Since Creighton didn't want to reopen painful wounds, he never asked about his grandparents. It wasn't until his stunningly beautiful Aunt Edith, who had loved Guido Whatmore and was the last of the *Empress* orphans, had passed away in 1988 that Creighton began to research his family roots. It would lead to his book and his involvement in the Ballard documentary.

"You know," he told me, "I've often

Mount Pleasant monument over the graves of the Salvation Army victims.

thought about my grandparents' last night on the *Empress*." For just one precious day, the couple was alone together. They must have felt some excitement, he thought, about being away from their five children, aboard a luxurious ocean liner bound for faraway England. Creighton told me he wondered if they'd made love that last evening. And did they die in each other's arms? David Creighton likes to think so. It's a poignant thought, inspiring and noble.

EVERY YEAR on the anniversary of the sinking, the Salvation Army holds a memorial service at Mount Pleasant. For many years after 1914, the service was well attended by survivors, until that number dwindled to just one.

Grace Hanagan was only six years old when she boarded the *Empress of Ireland* in Quebec City with her parents. Her father, Adjutant Edward Hanagan, was the Salvation Army Band's leader. But her father and mother were not among the survivors. Little Gracie was one of only four children aboard the *Empress* who had been rescued from the freezing water. Even late in life, she would confess that the sound of water running

in a bathtub could rekindle horrible memories of that night. Grace Hanagan, who had married and become Grace Martyn, died two weeks before the 1998 memorial service. The last survivor of the *Empress* was gone, marking the end of an extraordinary era.

David Creighton, a gracious host, guided me around the city later that day, pointing out the downtown building that once housed the Canadian Pacific Railway headquarters, where travelers could book passage on one of the Empresses of the Atlantic. He also took me to Toronto's Union Station, now a teeming international hub, where both the dead and the living had

Grace Hanagan and her parents before the fateful voyage, 1914.
George Scott Railton Heritage Centre.

been returned after the sinking of the
Empress. I weaved through the crowds
behind him to an old section of the
building with limestone portals leading to train tracks long gone, where
the "pitiful remnants of this ghastly
tragedy," as David Creighton said,
had been delivered home. Members
of the Salvation Army had been there
in great numbers, with Creighton's father and aunt and uncles among them,
devastated not only for the loss of
their parents but also because they
had no bodies to bury.

When one person began singing
the doxology, "Praise God, from
whom all blessings flow," the rest of
the assembled mourners joined in,
and their song filled the train station.

Last living survivor of the *Empress*
tragedy, Grace Hanagan Martyn at the
eightieth anniversary of the disaster in
1994 at the Mount Pleasant Cemetery.
George Scott Railton Heritage Centre.

David Creighton sang a few bars of the hymn for me as commuters strode
by. Eighty-eight years later, the tragedy still resonates deeply within him.

Over dinner in a downtown restaurant Creighton asked why I thought
the *Empress of Ireland*'s story was so little known compared with that of
the *Titanic*. One reason, I thought, was that the locale of the disaster, the
Gulf of St. Lawrence, was not particularly glamorous or well known. The
ship also hadn't sunk on her maiden voyage, as the *Titanic* so dramatically
had done; the *Empress* had made ninety-five uneventful Atlantic crossings. And there had been fewer international celebrities on the *Empress*.
Perhaps most critical, the *Empress* had sunk just before the outbreak of
World War I. The horrors of trench warfare quickly pushed the *Empress*
story to the back pages and then out of the newspapers altogether.

David Creighton nodded thoughtfully at my reasoning, but like a good
teacher he wondered aloud if there might be one more reason for the
tragedy's lack of notoriety. I couldn't think of any.

"It sank in just fourteen minutes," he said. "The *Titanic* took almost three hours to go down. There was no time on the *Empress* for the chivalrous deeds so widely reported aboard the *Titanic*. In any tragedy, people want to believe that there's hope, but there was none aboard the *Empress*. It was not a night to remember, but a night to forget."

I remembered the words of the stoker William Clarke, who had survived both sinkings. The time in which the *Titanic* went down seemed interminable, but the *Empress* had rolled over "like a hog in a ditch." I found myself nodding in agreement. Perhaps the public's insatiable appetite for dramatics, whether cowardice or heroics, was simply not piqued by the *Empress*'s story, and thus she was forgotten.

I told Creighton that his reading of his grandfather's letter in the Ballard documentary had seemed heartfelt. But he told me that what happened on the *Night Wind*, the boat moored above the *Empress* during the filming, had affected him even more profoundly.

David Creighton had been to Rimouski before and had visited the museum at Pointe-au-Père, but he had never been out over his grandparents' watery grave. Creighton wasn't a diver, and the grave site was far from his home. During filming, however, he hovered above the area for four days. Creighton did everything the director asked him to: laying a wreath on the water, reading the letter, and reflecting thoughtfully on camera. But it was when he was alone on the deck of the *Night Wind*, as he stared into the opaque waters of the St. Lawrence, that the realization overwhelmed him: this was where his grandparents had gone down and remained with six hundred other lost souls. He wept.

The director, with a cameraman in tow, approached him and said, "Something happened just then. How do you feel now?" David Creighton obliged and recounted his thoughts for the film crew. He was willing to open himself up on camera, he told me, and do what was necessary to bring the *Empress* story home to people's lives.

Réal Gagnon, the *Night Wind* captain, saw David Creighton withdraw after the moment was captured on film. He joined him where he'd retreated to the bow to sit alone. For a few moments, they made small talk and joked. Finally, Gagnon said the obvious in his halting English—that this was where it all had happened, the panic and the deaths. He placed a hand on Creighton's shoulder. "Anyway, enjoy the sunshine," Gagnon said, "while we're still alive." Creighton thought it was the most poignant sentence he'd ever heard.

Leaning over the rail, he stared again into the water where his grandparents had been "promoted to glory." Creighton could only imagine the place where his grandparents were entombed, but his personal connection to the *Empress of Ireland* made it seem very real. I was grateful to him for sharing his thoughts and feelings about the *Empress*, and it did help me better understand the history and the tragedy. My connection to the *Empress* was personal, too, because I was a diver. I wouldn't have to depend on my imagination. I would become part of a small group of divers fortunate enough to see the wreck, touch the ruins, and share the passion of experiencing the lost ocean liner.

Finding a Charter

Rumors about the difficulty of diving in Quebec and wild speculation concerning the future of the sport there were rampant on the Internet in 2002. Because of some recent diving fatalities on the *Empress*, most notably the death of Pierre Lepage in 2001, the provincial government of Quebec was studying ways to make the sport safer, and not in ways deep-wreck divers approved. Getting permission to dive the wreck only after proving your experience to French-speaking bureaucrats was infuriating.

To an American, it seemed that the government of Quebec also exhibited an overly paternalistic attitude toward its citizens and how they spent their free time. The Secretariat for Recreation and Sports (Secrétariat aux Loisir et au Sports, the SLS) reports to the Ministry for Youth, Recreation, and Sports. One can imagine the howl of protests that would be let loose by American skydivers, mountain climbers, or other extreme sport athletes if anyone ever proposed a position in the U.S. government that would demand certification by a government authority before they could participate in their sports.

In 2002 Quebec was considering closing the *Empress of Ireland* and other wrecks in its waters to divers and restricting diving to depths of no more than sixty feet. If I didn't sign on for an expedition and get up there soon, I might never have the opportunity to dive again on the *Empress*. That was a disturbing thought, since my first dive on the wreck in 1971 had hardly been a fulfilling experience. The impending regulations gave urgency to my quest to reconnect with the *Empress*.

I'd been making inquiries of outfitters and groups running expeditions up to the *Empress of Ireland*. North Atlantic Dive Expeditions, operating out of Beverly, Massachusetts, and run by Captains David Caldwell and Heather Knowles, was planning a dive expedition to Rimouski in late June 2002. But Caldwell's time frame for diving the wreck was too early for me. In June the weather was still too temperamental, the water bitterly cold, and the currents too swift. True, diving could be good then, but historically, early season diving on the *Empress* was a crapshoot.

Mad Dog Expeditions, run by Englishman Andrew Driver out of New York City, looked promising. The outfitter had a solid reputation and had been running trips to the *Empress*, the *Andrea Doria*, and the *Bianca C* in Grenada, West Indies, for several years. His pricing at $1,500 seemed reasonable, but his mid-July dates for the *Empress* dives seemed a bit shy of the traditional seasonal window: in the latter half of August and the first half of September, the weather is warmest and the sea conditions are calmest.

Most encouraging was that Mad Dog chartered Jean-Pierre Bouillon's boat for ferrying divers out to the wreck. Bouillon was without doubt *the* guy in Rimouski to dive with. Still, Driver, as a Brit, was an outsider. I wanted a Quebecois who knew the ins and outs of provincial politics, current laws, and local French euphemisms and colloquialisms, who could act as a buffer between the fiercely protective local diving community and an *Anglais* like me.

In late March 2002 at the Beneath the Sea Exposition in Secaucus, New Jersey, the largest dive show in the world, I put the word out that I was looking for an outfitter for an *Empress* trip. Along with the usual resort staff from warm climates, the show was well attended by Canadian outfitters. Most of them were English-speakers from Ontario who restricted their diving to the Great Lakes and Thousand Islands region of the St. Lawrence River. Then filmmaker and dive operator Dan Crowell approached me and said he thought he'd found the perfect operator for me: Gary Kulisek.

I had dived the *Andrea Doria* and a number of other wrecks off the coast of New Jersey with Crowell from his boat *Seeker*. Not only was Crowell probably the best deep diver in the northeastern United States, he also ran a highly regarded dive operation. I had great respect for him and his abilities and believed he had an innate sensor for bullshit, so I trusted his recommendation. He told me that Kulisek seemed to be a "real character," and in that respect, Kulisek didn't disappoint me.

Gary Kulisek and his company, Alp-Maritimes Sports, had plenty of diving experience. From May through October, most of his trips involved running diving expeditions in Ontario and Quebec, though he also had extensive experience in the Caribbean managing dive resorts, as well as doing commercial diving work in Canada. One of his commercial jobs had involved underwater surveys in abandoned mines that were inundated with sulfuric acid. The guy had all the right credentials, and he spoke nine languages, with a working knowledge of three more.

I didn't meet Kulisek at the show, but back home I exchanged e-mails with him in his St. Sauveur home, forty miles north of Montreal. We bandied about the possibility of my joining an already-set expedition versus an expedition that I would fill with divers of my choice. We agreed on a tentative date for my own *Empress* expedition.

In early April 2002 I caught Kulisek at home late one evening. After answering his phone in French, he smoothly switched to English once I spoke. Kulisek sounded tired. But he spoke to me in a friendly tone, though he was clearly a bit harried. Kulisek talked about an ill-conceived off-season project that involved running ski resorts in Quebec, which explained the "Alp" in his corporate name. His phone tirade was laced with profanities, and his flawless English was punctuated by the inevitable Canadian "Ey?" "The last four days I've been going nuts," he told me. "In the winter I take on management contracts with ski businesses, which I swore I'd never do again, and it's killing me. People have lied to me, something I have no time for. But fuck that. Don't worry, though. Your dates on the *Empress* are locked in. Nobody is going take them."

In his colorful way, Kulisek went on to outline his dilemmas. He hadn't come up with a price for me because he hadn't nailed down a Sainte-Luce hotel owner on a price. Kulisek told me that it was the "nicest place in town" and that he ran a first-class operation. Only the best of accommodations, food, and diving, he told me, would do for his clients. My own bullshit detector went up right away.

Kulisek also promised to line up as many relevant interviews as he could for me in Rimouski. They would include, he told me, all the "normal human beings" as well as the "bullshit divers with the hidden agendas." He told me the obvious: that as an author it was my job to "filter out the bullshit," adding, "I don't want to aid and abet the liars and fakes."

Timing and available space wouldn't allow me to join another expedition; Kulisek would have to remove another diver to make room for me, and he didn't want to do that. So the week of August 17, 2002, was mine. It became my responsibility to recruit other divers to fill out the trip. That wouldn't be an easy task. Finding qualified divers willing and able to take a week off and drive up to remote Quebec, dive in the frigid waters of the St. Lawrence, and pay a hefty sum for the privilege would keep me busy. Kulisek would be basing his fees, $2,000 U.S. each, on six divers, his ideal number.

Jean-Pierre Bouillon would be the boat captain. I was well aware of his *Empress* expertise and his accident out on the wreck. Bouillon chartered his boat to various outfitters, and now I had a Quebecois as well to grease the local wheels for me. Besides providing rooms and meals, Kulisek would also organize the dives, supply the breathing gases, and lead underwater explorations.

The Expedition Team

Finding five qualified divers to join me was even harder than I expected. Tech divers represent less than 1 percent of the recreational diving community. For the most part they live in the northeastern United States and usually plan the time-consuming logistics for their expeditions a year in advance. The kind of money Kulisek required from each diver was about the same as the price tag for diving Truk Lagoon, the exotic and ever-popular dive destination in the South Pacific. I had also started late. It was already April; August diving dates were just over the horizon. The main thing I had working for me was a committed time slot on the *Empress of Ireland*—a pinnacle dive that I hoped at least five tech divers would find irresistible.

The first to sign on was Peter Piemonte from Belchertown, Massachusetts. "I'm in," was all he said when I told him I had the dates. An aviation manager and head pilot for a large international construction company, Piemonte was forty-eight and had just returned to diving after a decade's hiatus. Somewhere along the line he'd picked up a bad case of the technical deep-diving bug. A former motocross racing champion, he told me that tech diving had fulfilled that "living on the edge feeling" that dirt bikes and the early days of flying had once given him. He still needed that edge, he told me, but with the wrinkle of control thrown in. Tech diving, with all its cutting-edge gear, configurations, precise breathing gases, and dive computers, gave him that measure of control over his life that he now wanted. It was a common thread for technical deep-wreck divers: the adrenaline high we all aspired to was tempered by the need for some measure of control. Control meant having complete confidence in our diving skills and mastering the advanced equipment so we could survive in such a dangerous environment.

Piemonte had taken part in a number of deep dives with me on forays into the black depths of Long Island Sound (diving with us had been Pete Johnson, a tech diver with a penchant for locating new wrecks, and Gary Gilligan, aboard Gilligan's always temperamental *Minnow*). I knew Piemonte was up to the task of diving a dangerous wreck like the *Empress*.

A big, affable guy with a contagious laugh, Pete Piemonte, like me, loved underwater exploration. Treasure and artifacts didn't interest him. Seeing and probing a challenging wreck with a reputation like the *Empress's* was something he just could not pass up.

Darryl Johnson became the second diver to sign on. Johnson was an Air National Guard weapons analyst near Hartford, Connecticut, and a dive buddy of Peter Piemonte's. He had accompanied us on several Long Island Sound dives and had proved himself an expert diver. Johnson, also a scuba instructor, had commercial dive experience and had made several dives on the granddaddy of all wrecks, the *Andrea Doria*. Johnson took his diving seriously and was not one to joke around on dives. It had been on one such *Doria* dive back in 1999, aboard the dive boat *Seeker*, that he'd witnessed the death of diver Charlie McGurr. Such an experience understandably can make a diver serious; it's not a sight one can forget.

But Johnson had a sense of humor too. Over a couple of beers after a Long Island Sound dive, he told me about a rather unusual commercial dive he'd done for a large gambling casino in Connecticut. He'd had to be lowered down a narrow clogged sewer line complete with toilet paper and other unspeakable nastiness and manually clear a filter grate in the brown sludge. Diving in murky, cold water on a sunken ship, I thought, shouldn't pose a problem for this guy.

Money, however, was an issue for Johnson. But when an *Andrea Doria* trip he had signed on for was canceled because of weather, he sent me his check for the *Empress* expedition.

In July I was still looking for qualified divers. Some had expressed interest or given oral commitments but bailed out with precious time running down. Then I got a call from Colin McRavey. Twenty-nine-year-old McRavey was new to the sport—only two years of diving under his belt—but his experience seemed just right for what we were attempting to do up in the St. Lawrence. A native of Scotland, McRavey had quit his job as a computer programmer at a large pharmaceutical company in Hartford and was spending his summer diving. Besides logging dozens of dives on the deep wrecks off the New Jersey shore, McRavey had made several dive trips up in Canada and had dived some of the wrecks in the Thousand Islands region of the St. Lawrence, including the deep-residing *Jodrey*. The *Jodrey* was a 640-foot ore carrier that had gone down in 1972 and had bottomed out at 242 feet, making her a pinnacle dive for technical divers. Although McRavey did not have the several hundred dives I would have liked to see logged, the ones he had made proved what he was capable of doing. The clincher was that Colin also told me he grew up just five miles from where the *Empress* was built in Glasgow, Scotland.

I told Gary Kulisek that Colin McRavey would likely be the last diver

I'd be able to enlist for the *Empress* expedition. Kulisek said he'd put the word out to his e-mail list of tech divers and offer the two open spots. This late in the game, the prospects did not look good for filling the trip. The downside was more expense for divers who did go; the upside was that the boat would be less crowded. For a tech diver, with all the accompanying gear, more space is always a bonus.

An Eerie Double Death

On August 6, 2002—just eleven days before our expedition was to start—I received some terrible news that would give me pause. Bill Schmoldt, a diver aboard Captain Joe Terzuoli's *John Jack*, had suffered a decompression sickness hit while diving the *Andrea Doria*. Apparently he had become lost on the wreck or had not carefully monitored his gas supply; he had run out of air and had to bolt for the surface without doing his decompression stops. He had been picked up by a U.S. Coast Guard helicopter at the wreck site, sixty miles south of Nantucket, and had been flown to a hospital with a recompression chamber in North Providence, Rhode Island. In the chamber he suffered multiple heart attacks and was pronounced dead while undergoing treatment. Schmoldt, fifty-four, from Brielle, New Jersey, had been a computer science teacher at a private school in New Jersey.

Considering the 235-foot depth where the *Doria* resides and its location far out at sea, the complications Schmoldt encountered in the chamber were no surprise. Time is always crucial when treating a bent diver. Once Schmoldt reached the surface in the throes of the bends and was pulled into the dive boat, he was looking at a two-hour wait and a painful helicopter ride to reach a hospital that had a chamber. The inert gas bubbles that had not been expelled by decompression stops had plenty of time to form and course through his body. Schmoldt's death was the first one on the *Doria* in two years, bringing the total number to thirteen since divers started regularly visiting the wreck in 1980.

After the initial e-mail, a flood of e-mails about the accident crowded my computer. Mad Dog Expeditions was the charterer of the *John Jack*. The dive had been billed as a "rebreather only" dive. Rebreathers were the

Bill Schmoldt, killed diving the *Andrea Doria*, 2002. *Courtesy of John McNally.*

new wave in diving technology. These breathing units recirculated unused oxygen and scrubbed carbon dioxide from the mix. Since breathing gas was recirculated, rebreather tank packs were smaller than the open-circuit double tanks and consequently considerably lighter. Schmoldt was diving on scuba and was the second captain aboard the boat; coast guard regulations require a licensed second captain aboard any charter vessel operating offshore.

Whether anyone really had enough experience and training, and the right temperament, to dive a deep, dangerous wreck like the *Andrea Do-*

ria was an ongoing controversy in the diving community. Schmoldt's death would fuel the fire.

While reading the multitude of e-mails on Schmoldt's death the day after the accident, I came across a note from Colin McRavey, the most recent addition to the *Empress* expedition. He'd sent a link to the *Montreal Gazette*, with an article headlined "Divers Can't Resist the *Empress*; One More Drowns." The story was eerily dated August 6, 2002. Serge Cournoyer, thirty-three, of Quebec, had died diving the *Empress* on the same day Bill Schmoldt perished on the *Doria*. The article gave the usual background information provided by other divers and dive operators in the area. The reporter duly noted that the wreck was deep, in cold water, and treacherous. The one new bit of information I gleaned from the article was that Cournoyer had had years of experience diving the *Empress*.

Cournoyer's death was another chilling reminder that experience and diving skills do not make a diver bulletproof. I wondered if Serge Cournoyer had accepted that. Something that wreck-diving guru Gary Gentile had told me came to mind: "Many people in extreme sports do not recognize their limitations, and when they do, they are about to die."

The two wreck-diving deaths didn't scare me off the upcoming expedition. The five fatalities out on the *Doria* during the 1998 and 1999 dive seasons had in some ways desensitized me and made me realize just how dangerous this kind of diving was. Long ago I had accepted the risk involved. I also tried to learn from these tragedies. That's why I made a call to Gary Kulisek.

Several hours of busy signals had me wondering whether they had call-waiting yet in Canada. Finally an exasperated Gary Kulisek answered the phone at his St. Sauveur home. He had been fielding calls from the press all day. Apparently Kulisek had a high profile in the diving community in Canada.

Not only were the two deaths on the *Empress* and the *Doria* raising questions, but there had also recently been a diving death out west in British Columbia and two diving-related deaths in the United Kingdom. Gary confessed that he was "tired of talking about dead guys." He knew, of course, that he would have to do it one more time when he took my call.

Kulisek told me that Dany St-Cyr had been there on Cournoyer's dive and that he'd recovered the body. Kulisek also told me he knew of Serge Cournoyer. Cournoyer was not the kind of diver Kulisek wanted aboard his charter boats. In a defiant stance against the trend in tech diving, he had told Kulisek that he dived with "independent twins" and was a proponent of progressive penetration. The problem with independent twins is that you have to switch regulators underwater when your air supply in one tank is near exhaustion. You also have to monitor your air supply in both tanks and know when to switch. With a set of tanks joined by a manifold and an isolator valve, you don't have to switch regulators. Since you're breathing from both tanks and have to rely only on one pressure gauge, monitoring your gas supply is simplified. Independent twins were yesterday's technology that few divers still adhered to.

Progressive penetration, a technique that was used throughout the 1980s and into the 1990s, was viewed by many in the wreck and cave diving community as dangerous, since it shunned the use of a penetration line. In theory, progressive penetration was sound if you had ideal conditions, but that rarely happened.

Dany St-Cyr later gave me the whole story on the Cournoyer accident. He told me there had been three boats tied up to separate moorings on the *Empress* on Tuesday, August 6, 2002: St-Cyr was on the bow, Jean-Pierre Bouillon and his clients were amidships, and Cournoyer and his buddy, Michel Abbot, were on the stern. St-Cyr said that he didn't like what he saw from the two divers who were moored over the stern. He could see that their dive configurations were all wrong for deep-wreck diving. "They even had snorkels," St-Cyr said with an incredulous look. He had a bad feeling about these guys. St-Cyr could only shrug his shoulders and allude to the old cliché about leading a horse to water. Deep-wreck diving, to him, was all about personal choice and responsibility. St-Cyr completed his dive, stashed his gear, and motored back to Pointe-au-Père.

Serge Cournoyer was diving alone. He had Michel Abbot with him but, as Kulisek described it, they weren't buddying up closely as you do in recreational diving; it was just "two guys in the same ocean."

"Diving solo" is another hotly contested topic in the dive community—but not among technical deep-wreck divers. Proponents of the recreational buddy system point out that most accidents occur when buddies get separated or when people are diving alone and that a buddy can provide help in an emergency. Tech divers counter that with redundant equipment (independent tanks, stage cylinders, and regulators), advanced training, and experience, the buddy system is outdated and an unreliable crutch. There is also the unstated but widely held belief among many tech divers that a panicking buddy in an emergency will often take you down with him.

On August 6, Michel Abbot had swum off to investigate another portion of the wreck. When Abbot completed his dive, he returned to the surface and waited in the Zodiac for Cournoyer to appear. After a half hour had passed, he called over to Jean-Pierre Bouillon's boat to find out if he was on their mooring line decompressing. He wasn't. By this time Cournoyer was well past his allotted time on the bottom. One of Jean-Pierre's clients, Clément Pouliot, went in and took a quick look around the wreck but saw no sign of him.

Jean-Pierre Bouillon suddenly noticed that small air bubbles were bursting on the surface, not the large bubbles indicating a diver outside a wreck. Small bubbles, broken up after percolating through the holes and cracks on the wreck, meant only one thing: Cournoyer was somewhere inside the massive wreck. Bouillon immediately knew Cournoyer was trapped. Then the bubbles stopped.

Bouillon later told me that at that point Serge Cournoyer was "no longer a danger to anyone," meaning that no one would have to risk his life to save him. Every diver knew that encountering a desperate diver on the bottom could have dire consequences for the rescuer. A panicked diver, pumped up with adrenaline, could easily overpower a Good Samaritan, killing them both. Such a scenario was likely the one that cost both Xavier Roblain and Lise Parent their lives on the *Empress* in 1996.

A diver aboard the *Marie A.B.* called the Quebec Provincial Police on his cell phone, knowing that journalists would be monitoring the VHF frequencies. Savvy journalists always listened in, in hopes of getting wind of a developing tragedy and an attention-grabbing story. There was only one thing left to do: search for Cournoyer's body. But Bouillon's clients, he told me, were "all gassed up internally and out of gas externally," too saturated with nitrogen to dive again. If the body was to be recovered, a local diver would have to do it. If it was left to the Quebec Provincial Police or the coast guard, the crabs would surely get him first, since neither agency had the resources for such a dangerous recovery.

Motoring into Rimouski, Bouillon met diver Richard Beaudoin on his way out. He alerted him that there was a diver missing. After arriving at the wreck site, Beaudoin splashed in and took a look around the wreck but couldn't find Cournoyer. In the meantime, back on shore, Bouillon called Dany St-Cyr's home and told his wife, Linda, that an *Empress* diver was missing.

St-Cyr, the "king of the *Empress*," knew the wreck better than anyone. If anybody could find Cournoyer, he could. When Linda told him that someone hadn't surfaced from a dive, St-Cyr immediately thought it must be one of Bouillon's clients. He drove to Pointe-au-Père, topped off his scuba tanks with gas, and motored to the wreck site some six miles out in the Gulf with his friend and sometime dive buddy Simon Pelletier.

When they arrived, St-Cyr saw that there was another dive boat moored over the wreck. It was empty. From the bubbles percolating up to the water's surface, it was obvious that some divers were searching for the body. He decided to wait and see if they could find Cournoyer, and if not, find out where they had looked. When Michel Abbot and another diver surfaced, St-Cyr couldn't get much information from the two about where they had searched. He had the feeling they didn't want him to find the body. According to St-Cyr, the divers likely wanted "the stripes," as he called it, for finding the victim. Just before St-Cyr splashed in, Pelletier was able to ascertain from Michel Abbot that Cournoyer had been planning on entering the cargo hatches on the forward deck.

St-Cyr dived down and took a circuitous route, weaving his way down through the ship's access hatch and then into the cargo hold. Cournoyer, St-Cyr thought, must have penetrated through two decks that were lying at a forty-five-degree angle, confusing since the angle and the collapsing decks inside the ship made its innards a maze. Perhaps Cournoyer had descended into the starboard side cargo hold to dig in the accumulated mud for artifacts. But St-Cyr could not find any evidence that Cournoyer had been there. The mud on the bottom had not been disturbed.

St-Cyr then thought Cournoyer might have descended through the cargo hold and swum into a passageway, then overshot the entry point when he tried to retrace his route. Perhaps he then swam past one bulkhead too many and became disoriented by the angle on which the ship lies and found himself trapped between two bulkheads? Maybe Cournoyer thought there was a hatch giving access to the cavernous cargo hold but couldn't find it? St-Cyr told me later that because Cournoyer was unfamiliar with this portion of the wreck and had not laid out a penetration line, "he was fucked."

I had a pretty good idea of the terror Serge Cournoyer must have experienced in those last minutes as he sucked on his air supply and watched the needle on his pressure gauge slowly drop into the red zone. As much as I loved exploring the deep holds of a sunken ship, I dreaded getting lost inside. On one dive early in my career, on a wreck in just sixty feet of water, I had become disoriented inside the engine room. I'd been with a buddy, but we'd gotten separated. I vividly remember sweeping the beam of my light frantically around the steel room I had blundered into, with my heart beating double-time. With my free hand I groped for the door and found only metal. I had no clue where my entry and escape route was; I had relied on my buddy's penetration route, since he was much more familiar with the wreck than I. And now I was lost and on my own.

I can still taste the panic, a burning acid that welled up in my throat as I followed the beam of my light with my terror-filled eyes. All I could see was steel. I thought, "This is it, I'm going to die in this metal box under the water and never see my wife and family again." Every few seconds I flashed my light on my pressure gauge and watched the needle drop with every exaggerated, panicking breath. I groped around like a blind man, hoping to find an exit from this underwater prison. It took only seconds, but it felt like hours, before I found the hatchway. I lived to tell about it. Serge Cournoyer did not.

DANY ST-CYR meticulously searched the underwater labyrinth around the cargo hatch he knew so well. In the cul-de-sac, his powerful underwater light illuminated a leaded weight belt lying against a slanted wall. St-Cyr followed the beam as it slowly crawled up the silty, dark interior of the ship's innards. He saw the tips of a diver's fins. Grabbing them with his free hand, St-Cyr pulled gently downward and the lifeless body of Serge Cournoyer passed before his faceplate.

Cournoyer's mask was askew and filled with water. His regulator had dropped from his mouth, and St-Cyr could see that in his desperation he had chewed through his lip.

Later Kulisek, called as an expert at the coroner's inquest, would say he believed that nitrogen narcosis contributed to Cournoyer's death. The narcosis could have explained his becoming hopelessly trapped inside the wreck. "The guy went in there," Kulisek told me, "realized he was lost, and freaked out. Probably he could handle narcosis under normal circumstances, but add to that the stress that you could die in a few minutes and the narcosis took control."

Kulisek's assessment of the fatal accident intrigued me, so I asked R. W. Hamilton, a consultant on the effects of various breathing gases under different pressures, if narcosis could have been triggered by panic. He said he would expect stress to be more than usually debilitating to someone who is also "narc'd" but added that the effects of both stress and narcosis are highly individual.

Cournoyer's body was close to being neutral in buoyancy, since by this time he had swallowed a lot of seawater. St-Cyr, knowing the wreck as he did, had no difficulty in extricating the body from the interior of the ship. There was no need for CPR; Serge Cournoyer had been underwater for over four hours.

Cournoyer's dive equipment was of particular interest to Jean-Pierre Bouillon and Dany St-Cyr. From past experience, they knew that the coroner and the police would undoubtedly rule Serge Cournoyer's accident as death by drowning, generally the expedient way for overworked bureaucrats to finish their paperwork. But the two friends now took it upon themselves to inspect the victim's dive gear and the gases used to see if equipment was the culprit. There seemed to be nothing amiss. However, they did find one chilling thing: when Bouillon tried to purge Cournoyer's regulators so they could be released from the tank valves, he heard not even the one tiny hiss you'd expect when the air pressure was relieved. Serge Cournoyer had sucked every ounce of air from the system before succumbing to the dark, frigid depths.

According to Jean-Pierre Bouillon and Dany St-Cyr, word started circulating that Serge Cournoyer had shown an interest in following a certain dive plan that local divers had been discussing. It was a plan to retrieve some of the remaining portholes from the wreck. At the time, the coveted portholes from the decomposing ship were still fetching thousands dollars from collectors. Although technically against the law, poaching artifacts from the *Empress* was still a thriving enterprise in Quebec. For Cournoyer, it was also a fatal one.

SERGE COURNOYER's body was the second Dany St-Cyr had recovered on the *Empress of Ireland*. First he had retrieved his friend and dive buddy Pierre Lepage, and now this stranger who had overstepped the boundaries of common sense and, apparently, his expertise.

St-Cyr later confessed to me that he wondered what he had done to bring such an odious burden on him. He did not like looking for "dead people," he said, in his meager English, but he felt it was his job. "It's the right thing to do," he told me. "It's the human thing to do, to render service." He was never callous or indifferent; he understood that he had a responsibility to put his diving skills to a worthwhile use. As with any title conferred or assumed, being "the king of the *Empress*" had its obligations.

Pondering both deaths on August 6—Bill Schmoldt on the *Doria* and Serge Cournoyer on the *Empress*—I could not help wondering about the eerie coincidence, the tragic results on the same day of the same year. So while I didn't consider aborting my upcoming *Empress* expedition, I did pause. Those deaths had me contemplating my own mortality. Was participating in such a dangerous activity wise? Perhaps not, but if success were guaranteed, it wouldn't be much of an adventure, and adventure and history are two passions that give meaning to my life.

CHAPTER SIX

Adventure

Life is either a daring adventure or nothing.

—HELEN KELLER

In August 2002 Darryl Johnson, Peter Piemonte, Colin McRavey, and I convoyed up to Canada in two vehicles. We had been on the road seven hours before we finally caught sight of the St. Lawrence River. Traveling northeast on Quebec Autoroute 20, we saw the river appear just as the city of Quebec rose high on a nearby promontory. We still had another two hundred miles to go. Quebec had been the departure city for the *Empress of Ireland*, and it was not hard to envision the 550-foot vessel taking on passengers years ago amid the bustle at quayside.

Autoroute 20 hugged the river's shoreline east of the city and followed the St. Lawrence as it widened dramatically to several miles across in its northeasterly flow to the Gulf of St. Lawrence. Green mountains on the North Shore framed the moving blue waters, and puffy white cumulus clouds mushroomed in the azure sky. In the brilliantly clear, warm afternoon, I imagined the *Empress* steaming downriver toward her destiny. Passengers aboard must have been merry with the excitement of transatlantic travel and, for some, the prospect of reuniting with loved ones.

Our diving group arrived in Sainte-Luce late in the afternoon on August 17, 2002. Sainte-Luce is ten miles downriver from Rimouski, although "downriver" is a confusing term on the St. Lawrence. The river flows northeast, up into the Gulf of St. Lawrence, where its mouth opens to the Atlantic Ocean. "Downriver," moving with the natural direction of river flow on the St. Lawrence, means any place along the march of water flowing outward to the Gulf. "Upriver," moving against the natural flow, actually describes a southwesterly direction, toward distant Quebec City and Montreal.

The center of Sainte-Luce has a looping seawall crowned with a promenade that follows the Gulf's edge, disappearing east into the distance. When we arrived the tide was out, exposing an expanse of rock-strewn mudflats stranding a solitary boat at the harbor breakwater.

When we pulled in that Saturday, tourists up from Montreal and Quebec City strolled the picturesque promenade in their sandals and socks, meandering along the narrow road that followed the river and dropping in to little shops and restaurants that faced on the water. With no T-shirt shops in sight, it was hard to believe I was still in North America. The scene seemed a portrait of traditional French culture.

The waterfront and church in Sainte-Luce. *Courtesy of Edie Summey.*

I'd planned to meet Gary Kulisek at the Hôtel Navigateur, run by local diver Marc Doucet, which overlooked the Gulf. The bell tower of the Church of Sainte-Luce loomed grandly, her somber graveyard a buffer between the sea and the church. I felt a chill in the overcast air, and after rummaging through my bags, I found a sweatshirt. When I called my wife, Vicki, in New York, to let her know I'd arrived safely, she told me the temperature at home was in the nineties. The Maritimes of Quebec were not quite so balmy.

Gary Kulisek and I embraced like old friends. He looked just as I had imagined, with his close-cropped hair and wisps of gray in his sideburns. Lines from mask squeeze were permanently etched on his suntanned face. Dressed in shorts and a T-shirt, he had tattoos of ship anchors and diving helmets. Scar tissue—not produced by a surgeon's scalpel and in all the

Gary Kulisek, owner-operator of Alp-Maritimes Sports, *Empress of Ireland* diver, and charterer. *Courtesy of Gary Kulisek.*

wrong places—lit up in the late afternoon sun. Crushing a cigarette underfoot, Kulisek spoke in his wonderful raspy voice. Not only did he look like Wallace Beery in the role of Long John Silver, he sounded like him too. The guy looked like a pirate, his nine languages aside, but he was *our* pirate.

After the other divers and I settled in at our accommodations, Kulisek wanted us to gather down at Jean-Pierre Bouillon's house next to the church's rectory. There he would brief us on the dives, check our gear, and analyze our breathing gases.

We had each brought a set of double tanks filled with the latest tech-dive gas. We knew the wreck bottomed out at 140 feet, so our tanks contained nitrox, the newer oxygen-enriched air blend appropriate for that depth. Normal breathing gas for recreational scuba is the "regular" air you breathe every day, only compressed. Compressed air contains roughly 21 percent oxygen and 79 percent nitrogen, the right air mixture to breathe at sea level. But for every thirty-three feet down you go underwater, the pressure increases another 14.7 pounds per square inch because of the weight of the water. The pressure forces excessive amounts of these gases to be absorbed into the blood and soft tissues, and these absorbed gases have to be released upon ascent or the buildup of bubbles will cause decompression sickness (DCS). By increasing the percentage of oxygen and reducing the nitrogen, tech divers can decrease the amount of nitrogen absorbed and lessen the chances of a decompression hit. Nitrox, with its 32 to 26 percent oxygen and 68 to 64 percent nitrogen, also lessens the effects of nitrogen narcosis, known as "rapture of the deep."

Nitrox would let us reduce our decompression stop times, so we'd spend less time in the frigid water. One thing we kept hearing about diving the *Empress* was how cold the water was in the Gulf of St. Lawrence.

A pair of Canadian divers told us they had recently taken a temperature reading of thirty degrees Fahrenheit on the wreck; a reading below freezing is possible in seawater because of the salinity and the movement of the water. Cold water not only could cause hypothermia, but it could increase the odds of taking a decompression hit. While the hypothermia factor was another underwater effect not entirely understood by the medical community, some physiologists were sure it was a factor in DCS.

All of us brought our heavy long underwear to wear under our drysuits, but the sapping cold of the Gulf would take its toll nonetheless. There were battery-operated heating pads on the market that could be worn under the drysuit, but they required cutting a hole in the suit to run the wire in, something I was loath to do. Holes compromised the watertight integrity of a drysuit. I didn't want another potential source of leaks, and the battery-operated pads hadn't increased comfort at the bottom to my satisfaction.

At Bouillon's house we also had to sign expedition waivers—nothing as complicated as those in the States, Kulisek assured us, but a sobering reality check for any diver at all unsure of taking the risk of extreme diving.

Bouillon's house was as close as you could get to the *Empress* and still be on dry land; the shipwreck that had been his obsession, that had crippled him, and that now gave him a way to make his living, lay within sight. I followed Kulisek's outstretched arm to a white dot on the horizon, four miles distant. Squinting, I could just make out the white buoy, reflecting the late afternoon sun, that had been placed over the wreck by the Quebec government in 1999 when the wreck was declared a historical landmark. To my right stood the door of the church rectory where Gordon Davidson knocked in search of help back in 1914 after swimming four miles from the disaster scene.

As I stared at that door, I could imagine Gordon Davidson standing there in his soaking pajamas, shivering in the predawn darkness. Looking out to where he had come from, I marveled at the feat. I'm a long-distance swimmer myself, yet what Davidson accomplished was mind-boggling. Jolted awake in the dead of night and dropped into the near-freezing water wearing next to nothing, Davidson had still made it to shore.

In our meeting in Bouillon's house, Kulisek quickly addressed the issue of cold. I had always worn a wetsuit hood and gloves with my drysuit. That meant that my head and hands, unlike my body, would be heated by a thin layer of water, warmed by my body heat to a relatively comfortable level. It had worked for me in the forty-degree-plus temperatures I was accustomed to in the waters around the northeastern United States.

View to the wreck site from Sainte-Luce cemetery. The wreck lies just four miles from this spot.

Kulisek didn't believe that wearing "wet" gloves would be wise in these waters. He adjusted the wrist seals of my drysuit and lent me a pair of dry gloves. The trick to the dry gloves' working was a rigid plastic tube tucked into the underside of each wrist, under the tight-fitting latex wrist seals, so pressure to the gloves could be equalized. Kulisek told me my dives and decompression hangs would be much more comfortable.

Kulisek also didn't like the way my "short hose"—the hose to my secondary breathing regulator—was configured. Telling me not to be mad at him for shifting my gear around, he tackled the first stage (the valve seated on the tank) of the regulator with a wrench and rearranged my low- and high-pressure hoses to lower ports on the first stage, making them hug my torso more closely. I mumbled that it was only the second time I was using the new regulator and that I'd been meaning to change it.

I never doubted trusting his expertise in this new and foreign environment, for I knew that even with my thirty-five years of diving I could always learn something from those with more experience. In wreck diving, egos could interfere, since it seemed the sport attracted very competitive people. Taking advice, borrowing ideas, and learning new techniques could be hard for divers already comfortable with their abilities and gear configurations. But up here in Quebec, I thought there was a lot for me to learn about tech diving while I was experiencing the *Empress*. Gary Kulisek would be a teacher in more than one way.

Besides Jean-Pierre Bouillon, who would be piloting the dive boat, Kulisek employed two divers. His seventeen-year-old son Matts, who'd been diving since he was five and was the youngest diver ever to explore the *Empress*, would be the emergency backup diver; this critical diver would remain on the boat at all times, suited up and ready to splash in if suddenly needed. Tyler Bradford, from the Toronto area, would lead two of us on our dives. Bradford was a former undercover police officer in Ontario with more than seventy-five dives on the *Empress*. Kulisek would escort the other two divers in their exploration of the wreck; but he told us that when he felt we were familiar with the layout and he no longer had to worry about us, we could dive solo.

Once we were all checked out with our equipment, we went to Bradford's room at the Hôtel Navigateur for an orientation to the wreck. Unrolling the ship's plans, he went over the layout of the ship as we all hung eagerly over his shoulder. He gave us several options for our first dives the following day. The one he suggested, and that made the most sense to the four of us, was an exploration of the forward deck area. Bradford assured us that the dive would give us a feel for the wreck and orient us to the mooring lines, our escape routes. He told us to expect a current—always. There would be a trail line from the mooring buoy to the stern of the dive boat. After splashing in, we would pull ourselves along the trail line to the anchor line at the buoy, then pull ourselves down to the wreck. The dive teams would then assemble at the tie-in point on the wreck and proceed with the dive.

Bradford called the *Empress* "the most dangerous place in the world," and as an undercover cop, he'd seen some dangerous places. He explained one of the biggest problems with the wreck: a diver could be swimming along the bottom following the hull and, because of the lack of ambient light and poor visibility, could stumble into one of the ship's exposed, angled compartments without realizing it and get fatally lost. Bradford's warning somewhat contradicted what Gary Kulisek had told me about the *Empress* in one of our many phone conversations: if you're on the outside of the ship, nothing should happen to cause you to panic and bolt for the surface, another deadly mistake. Kulisek now amended his statement by saying that only a flooded drysuit would force him to make a hasty exit from the depths. As he said, "I'm gonna choose. Either I'm gonna die from hypothermia or chance the ride up," meaning risk getting bent from DCS or triggering an embolism.

"Great," I thought. "Now I have two things to worry about: accidentally entering the ship and getting trapped, and flooding my suit from an untested seal from the dry gloves and having to bolt for the surface." For my initial dive, I resolved to restrict myself to the wreck's open decks with a clear shot to the surface and to monitor my dry gloves constantly for leaks.

Later that night, as I lay in the unfamiliar bed and stared at the ceiling, I found myself wishing I had drunk more than just a bottle of beer. The alcohol, I'm sure, would have calmed my jittery nerves and had me drifting off a bit quicker after the long drive; but alcohol causes dehydration, another contributing factor in DCS. I was about to find out whether I would fare any better on my second *Empress* excursion than I had on my first, thirty years ago.

The First Dive

Bouillon's twenty-seven-foot boat, the *Marie A.B.*, was berthed at Rimouski Marina. Surrounded by a breakwater, the marina sheltered boats belonging to the Canadian Coast Guard and the Quebec Provincial Police as well as Canada Fisheries research boats, pleasure craft, fishing boats, and the HMCS *Nipigon*. *Nippy* was a former Canadian Navy destroyer that had been rotting in mothballs in a naval shipyard in Halifax until Bouillon brought her here. He had won her in a two-year government auction that had almost bankrupted him. Bouillon had put together a nonprofit group and prepared her for sinking, and he was now waiting for the final go-ahead from the Quebec and federal governments to send her to the bottom. The *Nippy*, Bouillon proudly told me, would rest just a mile from

Rimouski Marina, where all dive operations were run from. *Courtesy of Edie Summey.*

the *Empress*, but in shallower waters to attract recreational divers, at 115 feet versus the *Empress*'s 140 feet. His goal was to make this part of Quebec, his beloved home, a mecca for all levels of divers.

Loading the *Marie A.B.* was a chore. With seven divers and all the gear needed for our technical plunges to the bottom, the vessel was packed to the gunwales. Balancing the boat so she would run trim was critical to getting out there and back safely. Because of the tight space, we all dressed in our drysuits before setting out. And we all wore our diapers.

Wearing diapers was nothing new to me. Deep-diving guru Billy Deans of Key West had been a proponent of them since the early 1990s, when I took a photo of Deans modeling his preferred Depends brand for an article in a dive publication. Kulisek passed the Depends out to us before we suited up. There was no head aboard the *Marie A.B.*, and we were look-

ing at a twenty-five-minute run out to the wreck site, another fifteen minutes to put on our dive gear, a forty-five-minute to one-hour dive, and the required two to six decompression stops of twenty to thirty minutes each, all done in bitterly cold water after drinking several cups of coffee and hydrating liquids. Wearing a diaper, though mortifying, was a no-brainer.

On our first day heading out, the sun shone brightly and the seas were

Real divers wear diapers; on a four-hour trip, the last thing any diver wants to do is short-change crucial decompression stops because he (or she) has to take a leak.

Pointe-au-Père Lighthouse today.

calm. Bradford hollered into my ear over the roar of the boat's engine that we were lucky. The weather, he told me, was not always so accommodating.

We sped past the lighthouse at Pointe-au-Père, where the *Empress* had dropped off her river pilot and letters to be mailed, David Creighton's last letter to his family among them. I thought about that as I watched the lighthouse grow smaller and the *Empress* site's white buoy on the horizon grow larger.

Kulisek interrupted my reverie by expounding on the confusing river geography. Since all river pilots had been dropped off at Pointe-au-Père back in 1914, Pointe-au-Père officially marked the start of the open sea, or the Gulf of St. Lawrence, as far as I was concerned. "Of course," Kulisek said, "it was salt water all the way down to the Pont Pierre Laporte Bridge in Quebec City, so one could make a case that the ocean started down there." But most people, I learned, still considered the waters surrounding the *Empress* to be the St. Lawrence River, when in fact at that point it wasn't a river at all but an estuary.

The wreck site had three sets of buoy markings bobbing in the swells, maintained by Bouillon and Dany St-Cyr. Dany St-Cyr placed them on the bow, amidships, and on the stern every spring for his and other divers' convenience, then removed them in the fall. The large white marking buoy placed by the Quebec government, proclaiming in English and

French that this was a protected wreck, floated a hundred yards downriver of St-Cyr's buoys tethered to the wreck. Bouillon steered the boat in a loop around the big government designation buoy; *Empress of Ireland* was emblazoned in bold black letters.

Kulisek, leading Darryl Johnson and Peter Piemonte, entered the water first, making room for Tyler Bradford, Colin McRavey, and me to gear up and splash in.

Before any deep technical dive, nervousness pervades the air. You're beginning to overheat in your suffocating drysuit, and the constriction hampers any last-minute adjustments you're trying to make in your gear. You have to temper your impatience to get into the water with diligence in making sure all the right valves are open and all your gear is properly

The tombstone of the wreck of the *Empress of Ireland*. The buoy denoting its protected status was placed there by the government of Quebec in 1999.

placed and easily accessible. I have made every mistake possible in thirty-five years of diving: I have forgotten to don my mask, fins, or weight belt; overlooked connecting my low-pressure hose to my drysuit to equalize water pressure; and neglected to turn on my air supply. What, if anything, had I forgotten this time? The environment I was now confronting was perhaps the least forgiving I had ever faced.

Sitting on the *Marie A.B.*, I started to sweat heavily inside my drysuit. Had I been wearing cotton underwear, it would have presented a problem. Cotton retains moisture and, when wet, conducts heat away from the body, increasing the likelihood of hypothermia. I was wearing polypropylene and Malden Mills fleece, which not only are warm but retain heat when wet. Still, perspiring heavily makes the underwear clammy and uncomfortable, and being uncomfortable before diving can unsettle you. Before a deep, dangerous dive, you don't want to be unsettled.

I was stressed, anxious to go, and starting to worry about what I would encounter once I entered the water. Would the visibility be decent? Would

Colin McRavey (left) and Kevin McMurray.
Courtesy of J.-P. Bouillon.

Peter Piemonte (left), Darryl Johnson, and
Gary Kulisek ready to make the plunge.
Courtesy of J.-P. Bouillon.

the freezing water keep me from thinking and performing clearly? And, of course, the real question: Why the hell was I here? I had thought I knew, but now I had my doubts.

We had agreed on a dive plan. Bradford would take us down to the wreck to the mooring point amidships, where the chains hooked through a double porthole, at eighty feet, and lead us along the promenade deck rail forward to the bow. Visibility would then dictate where we would go. Sitting on deck waiting to go, I avoided testing the water temperature, refusing to give myself that excuse for not making the plunge.

Matts offered me a looped entry line that wrapped around my wrist. As I splashed in backside first, Matts, topside, gave a forceful tug on the line, and I was quickly righted in the water. Still on the surface and now upright, I gave the fingertips-to-head sign that everything was all right and kicked forward along the trail line to the mooring buoy. The water didn't seem that cold, but being dressed in a drysuit for the past hour had me yearning for a cool dip. The Gulf of St. Lawrence was a welcome immersion.

I was surprised to see Darryl Johnson coming back along the trail line. He said something about an equipment problem and swam back to the boat. The three of us in our group met at the buoy. We nodded to each other, deflated our buoyancy-compensator vests, and began the dark descent.

Light from the midmorning sun streaked the waters beneath me. It was an abyss; nothing was in sight but the beckoning dark green depths. I gave my drysuit inflator valve a punch to equalize the squeeze of the depths and equalized my mask pressure by exhaling a vigorous burst of air through my nose. Then I dropped like a stone.

As I dropped into the darkness, I met ascending diver Peter Piemonte. He made some frantic hand signs that befuddled me. After a moment or two I realized he was asking the whereabouts of his dive buddy, Darryl Johnson. He wanted to know if Johnson had made it to the surface. I gave Piemonte the hand signal thumb to forefinger, indicating that Johnson was all right: I could see the relief on his face through his dive mask.

Seconds later, and thirty-one years after my first visit, I found myself kneeling on the hull of the *Empress of Ireland*.

It was a familiar scene even after the passing of so many years. But this time I was less nervous and wasn't shivering from the cold. I held a massive underwater light that brightened my surroundings considerably. I was pretty sure I was in the same area of the wreck where I had been back in 1971. Sure, I was a lot younger and stronger back then, but I was a helluva lot better prepared this time. As a result, I was eager to begin my exploration of the *Empress* and knew I was about to become more intimate with her.

My light picked up things I hadn't seen before. The teak decking, machinery on the forward deck, and the gaping hole of the cargo hatch emerged from the darkness. It was like seeing the scene for the first time. The excitement of the dive made me press on, hungry to see more of the grand old ship.

I did a 360-degree turn while I clutched the anchor line and took in what I could. I guessed the visibility to be about ten feet, not much on a wreck that stretched almost the length of two football fields. Imagine trying to find your way around an unfamiliar sixty-story building lying on its side at a forty-five-degree angle, in pitch blackness with only a flashlight. Throw into that equation over a hundred feet of water overhead, and you'll have some understanding of what it's like diving the *Empress*. The starboard-lying wreck stretched out before me in both directions and disappeared into the murk, while my world shrank to a lit circumference of ten feet. Bradford and McRavey were ghostly figures in the distance, following their narrow beams of light and hovering over the wreck in an eerie stillness.

The mooring chain was tethered to a set of sixteen-inch double portholes near the gangway doors for first- and second-class accommodations. Bradford had told me that the double portholes could be found nowhere else on the wreck. I noticed how the chafing of the chain against the hull had worn the metal to a sheen. The rest of the ship, as far as I could see, was covered in an endless waving field of sea potatoes, puffy marine animals related to the sea anemone, giving the illusion that I was in some nightmarish poppy patch. Exchanging the finger-to-thumb OK sign, McRavey and I fell into line and followed Bradford forward along the

The hull of the *Empress* and the ubiquitous sea potatoes. *Courtesy of J.-P. Bouillon.*

wreck. I cast a glance above me and saw the reassuring green glow of the distant sun.

Bradford, McRavey, and I followed the rail of the ship's promenade deck, swimming forward in our pressure-compressed drysuits that clung to us like leather hides. The railing was our lifeline, the key to understanding where we were on the ship. It was the "trail" forward and aft, and the highest point on the wreck. If any of us got lost, all we had to do, as Kulisek had told us, was follow the wreck up to its shallowest point and follow the lateral rail. We would eventually run into one of the three mooring lines—on the bow, amidships, or on the stern—which we could ascend, doing our decompression stops along the way. It sounded simple enough. Had I known the layout and pitch of the ship in 1971, perhaps my first dive would have been a bit more satisfying.

We followed the promenade deck rail to a cutout where a rail dropped down to the forward deck. The three of us were suddenly buffeted by a substantial current across the deck. Encountering unexpected currents is common on the wreck. Because of tidal movements and river flow and how the wreck lay, divers could never be sure what they'd meet. In this fast-moving water, we followed Bradford down into the darker depths along the sloping deck. Suddenly I found that the current dissipated to nothing. The current was running across the outside, or port-side section, of the hull. On the sloping deck dropping down to the starboard side we were in the lee of the current. We no longer had to kick and breathe so hard, saving precious air.

Just minutes into the dive, I began to see why the wreck could be so dangerous. It was not only the depths, or even the poor ambient light, but her precipitous lean to her starboard side, where the fatal blow had occurred. The awkward lie of the ship made me collect my thoughts and reorient myself to my escape route. I dropped down, trailing my left glove across the surprisingly smooth teak decks. I glanced at my dive computer: the depth read 120 feet. I was surprised to see my water temperature gauge read thirty-six degrees. I felt warm. The cold, it seemed, wouldn't plague me on this dive. Hideously ugly snow crabs scurried out of my path.

Bradford leveled off and kicked forward, stopping intermittently to point out various pieces of machinery that were bolted to the severely leaning deck. I came across what looked like the remains of the forward mast, which had held the lights that so confused the *Storstad*. I stopped breathing for a moment.

Finally, Bradford stopped and joined his hands in a V, an almost prayer-like gesture. Shining my light over his shoulder, I could see that we had reached the bow. Then I glanced to my left, and as I peered into the darkness I could just make out McRavey hovering there with his light shining. I kicked after Bradford as he dropped over the port rail to the left side of the ship where the hull disappeared into the depths. Again we swam into the current and kicked harder to move through it. Visibility was poorer on the port side of the hull, no more than five feet, because of the particulate matter picked up by the current. There was no ambient light, just total blackness.

It has often been said that diving the *Empress* is like a night dive. I couldn't agree more. The complete darkness I was experiencing was familiar indeed. Besides the cold, the blackness was the one strong memory I'd carried from 1971.

As we dropped to 125 feet, visibility improved dramatically. That's when I noticed the current had stopped again. It couldn't have happened at a better moment; we had something more interesting to focus on. On the encrusted hull, a massive hunk of metal appeared to protrude from its side. All three of our powerful lights illuminated the upper portion of the *Empress*'s five-ton anchor, at least fifteen feet across. I slowly glided deeper down, letting the beam of my light draw the anchor's features from the darkness. It was an incredible sight. I looked over at Bradford and shook my head in wonder. I thought I saw him smile behind his faceplate.

The three of us then kicked up along the hull, still engulfed in darkness. Just a few feet below the rail, Bradford stopped and rubbed his gloved hand across the silt-shrouded hull. I should have known what he was doing, but it didn't register until, under a cloud of silt, the letter *E* emerged. I ran my hand across the hull toward the right. More letters began to appear under the clouds of silt. Kicking backward a few feet, I could see the name "Empress" appear. The letters were raised, and once we brushed a couple of times, their brass came shining through, illuminated by our dive lights. Kicking to my right, I saw the word "Ireland" reveal itself. Seeing the ship's name, still there after eighty-eight years, made the reality of the dive even clearer to me. I told myself I was really here. I was touching a remnant of history that told a powerful story, bearing witness to a profound and heart-wrenching tragedy.

It was then that I found myself shaking my left hand. "Fuck!" I thought. "My damn glove is leaking." It may have been leaking for a while, but the emotion of the past several minutes had lured my

The *Empress*'s bow letters. © *Dan Crowell.*

mind elsewhere. I was making my way back to the mooring line and thinking of the warmth of the sun above. The icy grip of seawater on my hand and the slow trickle under the wrist seal into the drysuit chilled my forearm. We had been down for only thirty minutes, and because of the oxygen-rich breathing mix of nitrox, we faced only minimal decompression hangs. I figured I could tough it out. The leak wasn't that bad.

Colin McRavey had a more serious problem. On our hangs, he appeared to be in considerable discomfort. He wrapped his arms around himself and shook, miming that he was severely chilled. The screens on our dive computers cleared, indicating that we could surface—not a moment too soon for McRavey.

Once we were back on the boat, it was obvious that McRavey was suffering from hypothermia. We helped him strip off his drysuit. His underwear was soaking. His lips were blue, and he shook uncontrollably. While I'd had a minor glove leak, he'd had the more serious problem of a main seal or zipper leak. He could barely speak. We sped back to Rimouski, with McRavey bundled up in all the warm clothes we could find. Once he could finally speak, McRavey told me in his heavy Scottish accent that he didn't think he was up for a second dive that day.

Johnson's Free Ascent

As we headed toward the marina, Peter Piemonte told me about his dive with Gary Kulisek and Darryl Johnson and what had gone wrong. Their plan had been similar to ours. Once they were on top of the wreck at the mooring point, they swam forward along the rail. Kulisek led, followed by Johnson, then Piemonte.

At a depth of ninety feet, Piemonte found himself in a wake of silt kicked up by Kulisek and Johnson. He swam out past the rail, to their left and behind them, to escape the billowing cloud, then continued along the leaning hull, kicking hard against the current. About twelve minutes into the dive, Piemonte looked forward and could not see Kulisek. His dive leader had been swimming along, he said, at a "pretty good clip" and had simply disappeared into the darkness. Piemonte wasn't alarmed, since he knew where he was, and he figured that Kulisek was just beyond the limits of his visibility. He then noticed Johnson was above him and swimming upward. As Piemonte shone his light on him and watched him swim for the surface, he realized Johnson was making a free ascent, bolting to the surface without following the anchor line.

Piemonte knew that a free ascent was dangerous under these conditions: deep depths, poor visibility, and raging currents that could take a diver beyond the sight or reach of the dive boat. It was an emergency procedure usually done only when there was absolutely no alternative. Piemonte froze, unsure of what to do. Was Johnson out of air or in some other catastrophic situation? Should he risk his own safety, face getting swept away from the dive boat, and bolt up after him? As these thoughts filtered through his mind, he watched Johnson disappear above him into the dark. "In the end I decided I couldn't follow him up. I stayed on the rail and watched him go. By that time I was afraid I might not be able to find him and that I'd lose sight of the ship myself. I knew I had to find Kulisek and signal him about Johnson's dangerous ascent."

Piemonte knew that the rest of us wouldn't be expecting to see anyone surface so soon, only twelve minutes into the dive, and so far from the mooring point. For all Piemonte knew, we could already be in the water. Jean-Pierre Bouillon's physical handicap and his inability to speak English meant he would be of limited use in rescuing a diver by himself. Matts was aboard the boat as the safety diver, but apparently in his moment of confusion Piemonte thought he was following Bradford, McRavey, and me into the water. Piemonte was afraid that Johnson might be swept away from the boat and a difficult search would have to be mounted—or worse. Swimming as fast as he could along the rail, Piemonte caught up with Kulisek.

Piemonte gave the signal that they had to go and assumed that Kulisek would notice that Johnson was no longer with them. Kulisek then swam back toward the anchor line. Piemonte thought they would be returning to the surface.

But Kulisek swam past the amidships mooring line with Piemonte in tow, then up to the infamous explosion hole. Piemonte thought he was searching for Johnson, so he followed. At the explosion hole, Piemonte finally got Kulisek's attention again by pointing his thumbs up, signaling him to ascend, but Kulisek began to shine his light into the hole as if to indicate that Piemonte should drop down into it. Piemonte grabbed him by the shoulder, frantically signaled No! and then gave the sign to ascend again. They began a series of hand signals between them that apparently neither recognized. Had the two been diving together before and agreed on a system of hand signals, the confusion might have been avoided. In his frustration Piemonte finally wrote on his slate, "Darryl left." Kulisek showed no alarm, thinking Darryl Johnson had simply decided to leave and ascend up the anchor line following normal procedure. Piemonte then began banging on his own chest to add urgency to his message, and gave the "let's ascend" signal, hoping his widened eyes expressed how quickly they had to get out of there.

At that point Kulisek swam back to the anchor line. "Good," Piemonte thought, "he's finally getting it." But where the anchor chain was secured to the wreck, Kulisek seemed to be searching for Johnson. Piemonte grabbed his elbow and pulled him upward. Kulisek still seemed puzzled by his attempts at communication. Piemonte thought about scribbling something on his slate again, but since time was being wasted and he had Kulisek's attention, he figured his ascending should get the point across. Kulisek followed at last.

Their bottom time had been only seventeen minutes. Although not required by their decompression schedules and computers, Piemonte and Kulisek did a safety stop at twenty feet. Piemonte had been thinking about writing another message on his slate when I ran into him on my descent. After the initial crossed signals between us, Piemonte was clearly relieved once he knew Johnson had made it to the surface.

When Piemonte boarded the boat, he saw Johnson sitting on the bench along the gunwale "looking," as Piemonte later said, "no worse for wear." Piemonte asked what had happened. Johnson told him the story: when he got down to the deck, he noticed a "heavy draw" on his regulator, making it difficult to inhale from the mouthpiece, a problem that worsened as he moved along the rail. He felt as if he wasn't getting enough air and noticed the needle on his pressure gauge had dropped dramatically, indicating that he was running out of air. Johnson realized he had to get out of there. He signaled Piemonte that he was going up, but apparently Piemonte didn't see the signal. Johnson noticed little current moving at that time, so he believed it would be safe to make a free ascent instead of swimming back to the anchor line and ascending from there. With the reduction in pressure as he swam up, the heavy draw on his regulator disappeared, but he switched to his stage bottle, his decompression gas tank, just to be safe. His bottom time had been only twelve minutes.

Piemonte told Johnson that he thought the free ascent was "a pretty serious decision to make" and asked why he didn't turn to him for help, since he was so close by. Piemonte carried twin tanks, each containing 120 cubic feet of air, "all the air in Canada," as he said. Why didn't Johnson make a stronger effort to let him know he was in trouble and intended to make a free ascent? Johnson claimed he didn't want to disrupt their dive; still, he apologized for making a "bad decision."

Gary Kulisek, too, was concerned about what had happened and approached Piemonte after getting Johnson's explanation. Piemonte assured him that it was an unusual decision for Johnson to make and that in the eight dives the two had made together, many of them in worse conditions than they'd just experienced, he had never done anything like that. In Piemonte's view Kulisek had nothing to worry about. Piemonte later confessed to me that he was surprised by Johnson's actions but said he was not concerned.

After off-loading all the empty tanks, we drove into Rimouski to get some lunch. We had a couple of hours before the tides turned and slackened out on the wreck. Bouillon stayed behind on his boat in the marina to monitor the weather conditions and the Canadian Coast Guard reports issued out of Pointe-au-Père.

Back at the dock after lunch, I noticed the sky had turned slate gray, and the wind had the marina's flags snapping briskly in the wind. Wind, of course, was always to be expected. Unfortunately for us, though, it was blowing out of the northeast. Kulisek had been up front about the possibility that dives could be "blown out." The final decision on a "go" would always be with Bouillon, and he usually based his decision on the forecast

Resting between dives at the Rimouski Marina dock.

out of Pointe-au-Père. If the winds were out of the northeast and greater than seventeen knots, he would cancel the dive. Northeast winds came in unobstructed from the ocean and down through the Gulf of St. Lawrence, making the narrows of the Gulf an inhospitable place. You didn't want to be out over the wreck during a blow. Not only did it make getting in and out of the boat extremely difficult for divers, it also risked the safety of the vessel itself. Bouillon canceled our second dive.

The long drive up the day before, the nerves leading up to the first dive, and the dive itself had all taken their toll on me. I was a bit relieved that the dive was called off. The prospect of a relaxing dinner and turning in early was calming. I felt I would be ready for our two scheduled dives the next day. After dinner we all went to bed. No one reported trouble falling asleep.

The Braille Dive

Day two in Rimouski looked promising. Scattered clouds amid blue skies and warm sun had us all dreaming of ideal conditions underwater. Speeding out from behind the breakwater onto glassy flat seas seemed to confirm our good luck.

Our first dive of the day later became known as "the braille dive." McRavey and I wanted to retrace our dive of the day before, to get a better feel for the layout of the forward area of the bow and see what we'd missed. Arriving at the tie-in point on the wreck, we quickly realized that any ambitious plans for the dive were dashed. Visibility on the high point of the wreck, the part of the ship most washed by the sun, was extremely poor—three feet at best. But McRavey affixed a pulsating strobe light to the chain links on the mooring line, and off we went.

There was a stiff current buffeting the wreck, making conditions on the bottom all the more unpleasant. The forward deck of the ship was engulfed in darkness. Even with my high-powered light, it was almost impossible to make out any of the deck's features.

We dropped over the port rail again in search of the anchor but couldn't seem to locate it. We did find the raised nameplate letters again, but I nearly had to plant my face on the hull to decipher them. I gave Bradford a sign, pointing to my eyes and indicating with a shrug that I couldn't see anything, and hugged myself to tell him I was cold. The damned left glove was leaking again, even after I had checked for leaks, found none, and made fast the seal and plastic tube. The dive was just not worth it; I wanted out. Bradford and McRavey nodded enthusiastically to my hand signs indicating "let's get out of here," by pointing to the surface. McCravey later told me he'd been hoping someone would call the dive; he was on the verge of doing it himself.

Kulisek, Piemonte, and Johnson's dive went off without a technical hitch. They tried to drop down to see the anchor, since they had missed it the day before because of Johnson's free ascent. This time the poor visibility and lack of any ambient light stopped them. They had to stick around the forward deck area.

Once we were all back on board, we motored back to Rimouski to get some lunch and full tanks for the second dive. We also needed some surface interval time, a respite between dives where a diver can rest and allow nitrogen levels in the blood to drop.

The second dive was a go, but not until after Bouillon hemmed and hawed about the deteriorating weather. The marina flags were snapping, and some ominous clouds were building up in the east. Although Kulisek and Bouillon were obligated to get in as many dives as possible for their paying clients, they were also obligated to make sure the dives were done under safe conditions. Rough seas not only made diving extremely difficult but endangered everyone aboard a small craft like the *Marie A.B.*

Since Kulisek, Piemonte, and Johnson would be the first in, Kulisek would send up a Styrofoam cup as a signal that the visibility had improved. The pressure of deep water would compact this air-infused material; when released upward, the cup would expand in a crumpled form and rise to the surface. If we didn't see the cup, we'd know the visibility was still poor, and we could decide whether to dive. The cup came up. All of us ecstatically began to ready our gear for another plunge to the wreck.

Visibility on the bottom was better, but not by much; it went from three feet to about ten feet. We again swam along the port rail. Halfway down the rail, I felt the maddeningly familiar trickle of water entering my dry glove. Considering the poor visibility, fatigue from the early dive, the hurried fifteen minutes to gear up for the second, and now this pesky leak, I opted to abort the dive. I signaled to Bradford and McRavey with a swift motion of my hand across my throat that I was aborting and swam back to the tie-in and slowly made my way up the line. Bradford and McRavey continued exploring the forward deck area, poking into the forward cargo hatch, examining the wave shield, and peering into the crew's mess area before retracing their route. Before making their ascent, they went over for a look into the explosion hole.

I had borrowed another pair of dry gloves from Kulisek, tightened the wrist seals, and moved the plastic tube to the top of my wrist for this dive, but the left glove had still leaked. I was finished experimenting with the dry gloves; I would use my neoprene wet gloves from here on. I reasoned that my hood was wet, and I hadn't experienced any great discomfort from the cold water on my head, so my hands should be all right. Sitting up on deck, I was clear on what I would wear for my dives tomorrow. "Your decision" was all Kulisek said, with a resigned shrug, when I told him what I intended to do.

Over lobster at a restaurant in Sainte-Luce, we all agreed that it was time we explored the lifeboats on the starboard side of the wreck. When the *Storstad* knifed into the starboard side of the *Empress*, the ship had listed quickly, rendering that entire row of lifeboats useless; many of them were still tethered to the ship by their davits. It was a must-see for any diver on the *Empress*. It was also the deepest part of the wreck, and arguably the most dangerous, since the lifeboats rested on their keels in the mud of the St. Lawrence.

Trouble on Day Three

We switched team leaders for the dives on day three. Kulisek wanted to assess the skills of all the divers. Bradford would dive first with Piemonte and Johnson. McRavey and I would follow with Kulisek.

At the tie-in point, a red-and-white maple leaf, the unmistakable Canadian flag, waved in the current. Kulisek quickly pulled it off the chain. I suspected it was placed there by the "federalist" Bradford, as Kulisek called him. There was constant ribbing between Bradford and Kulisek about being a nationalist or a federalist. Half serious, Kulisek liked to refer to the Canadian flag as the symbol of the "occupation army." Though of Slavic heritage, Kulisek was still an ardent Quebecois, proud of his province and its independent French bent. Bradford, the Anglophone, clearly believed in a united Canada, which he thought Quebec damned well should remain part of. As an American, I found it interesting to gain some insight into the politics of Canada. The separatist movement in Quebec had always been just an item in the newspapers, but here I was getting a firsthand look at how the two distinct cultures interacted. It seemed to me there was unease between Anglophones and Francophones, at least in Quebec. Good-humored ribbing, I surmised, was the time-honored way to defuse hostility.

Back underwater, following the now-familiar route forward along the port rail, I followed closely behind Kulisek with McRavey behind me. Visibility here was good, at least twenty feet along the rail. At the rail cutout, we then followed the first-class bulkhead topped by a teak rail down the angled slope of the forward deck.

Using the rail as a guide, I slid into the darkness with Kulisek's white tanks as my beacon. The deeper we went, the blacker it became, as the light from the surface was swallowed up by the depths. Even though he was just a few feet in front of me, Kulisek's tanks were now just barely visible. His dive-light beam was only a faint glow in the darkness that surrounded us. Before reaching the bottom of the rail, Kulisek stopped. He faced me and shook his head; he didn't want to continue down to the bottom. No argument from me. Instead of descending farther, he led us along the sloping forward deck toward the bow.

Kulisek stopped and beamed his light onto two plaques bolted to the deck. Both had been put there by divers. One commemorated those lost in the disaster; the other marked the deaths of French Canadian divers Lise Parent and Xavier Roblain in 1996. Real weighted wildflowers adorned both plaques, much like a roadside fatality memorial.

We explored the deck around the plaques. There was plenty to see: cargo loading machinery, the number one cargo hold, the metal shield forward breakwater, the rotating shaft of the capstan for hauling chain aboard, and assorted squat bollards that once held the *Empress* taut to wharves at her ports of call. I could dive hundreds of times in this area and not see it all. I felt a deep kinship in that moment, and a greater understanding for the passion that drove Gentile, Beaudry, Reekie, Bouillon, and St-Cyr. It was a lot different from summiting a natural challenge like Mount Everest, for here I was exploring a marvel of human ingenuity and engineering that had disappeared in fourteen tragic minutes during my grandparents' time. To truly understand this time capsule, I knew I would need a more intimate knowledge of her. That meant diving the wreck, and diving it a lot.

On our ascent, McRavey seemed to be lagging behind. The Scotsman, I would find out after this dive, was a proponent of the new technical dive theory of deep stop decompression, or outgassing the inert nitrogen that causes the bends.

According to Tim O'Leary, director of technical operations for NAUI (National Association of Underwater Instructors), one of the largest internationally recognized certification agencies, the stops at the deeper depths "are a huge benefit because you're treating the bubble." Deep stop decompression, as O'Leary would explain to me, unlike the standard decompression models, looked at the "correct physics," the phase model of bubble dynamics.

The phase model tried to manage the "seeds" of bubbles, called micronuclei, where bubbles are born. This new decompression technique (Reduced Gradient Bubble Model or RGBM), first written about by Bruce Weinke in 1995, restrained the critical radius of the bubble and thus the cumulative volume of bubbles in a diver's system during ascent. Within the constraints of the phase model algorithm, the diver stops deeper, earlier in the ascent, and for shorter lengths of time, using the natural hydrostatic pressure (the weight of the water) to squeeze the inert gases out of the bubble and keep the bubbles smaller.

O'Leary told me that deep decompression is safer because it gets the diver out of the water faster, with shorter shallow hangs, and essentially prevents the problem of accumulated gas saturation before it arises. The deep decompression nips bubble formation in the bud. No bubbles, no bends.

Bradford, Piemonte, and Johnson had the same dive plan that we did. But again something went amiss.

Descending following the teak rail over the first-class bulkhead, the three men thought things were going according to plan. The bottom of the rail terminated at the starboard-side staircase. My team had not gone that far because Kulisek thought the visibility was too poor. Bradford stopped at this point to make sure everything was all right with Johnson and Piemonte. Bradford was familiar with the area and was ready to proceed, but he was going to let them decide whether they wanted to swim over to the lifeboats. Johnson and Piemonte both gave Bradford the OK signal, so he turned and kicked softly, trying not to disturb the sediment, toward the lifeboats on the pitch-black bottom along the starboard side.

Suddenly one of Johnson's fins knocked Bradford's mask from his face. Bradford quickly replaced his mask and cleared it of the invading frigid water. Then he saw Johnson's camera and attached strobe falling in front of him. As he grabbed them, he caught a brief glimpse of Johnson's fins disappearing toward the surface. Bradford took a few moments to compose himself, and with Johnson's camera still in his grasp, he swam over to Piemonte.

Before the dive, Piemonte thought he detected "a certain nervousness" in Johnson. Johnson had made it a point to tell Piemonte that he had to keep his position in the rear. Piemonte was a little miffed, since he considered himself an "accommodating guy" and thought Johnson was out of line "barking orders to me." He'd also noticed that Johnson had snapped at Matts Kulisek, who had inadvertently stepped on his mask on the deck before the dive. Still, Piemonte had thought the dive was going according to plan until they reached the starboard staircase.

Bradford had been twelve feet deeper than Piemonte. He may just as well have been a hundred feet deeper; they couldn't see each other. Piemonte had barely been able to see Johnson's light, and he'd been only four or five feet away. Piemonte had glanced at his depth gauge and noted the depth: 125 feet. At that moment Johnson had swum past him, without giving him a sign or even a look. In seconds Johnson was gone, out of sight above him.

Piemonte thought the dive had been called because of the poor visibility. Instead of following Johnson, he decided to wait for Bradford, who appeared out of the darkness clutching Johnson's camera and strobe. For a moment he wasn't sure if it was Bradford. Perhaps the diver swimming by him earlier had been Bradford and not Johnson. Piemonte shone his light on the diver's face; it was Bradford.

Bradford threw his hands up, shrugging the "what's going on?" sign and scribbling on his slate. He put in front of Piemonte's face: "Where's Darryl?" Piemonte threw up his hands in confusion and pointed to the surface, indicating that all he knew was that Darryl Johnson had left.

Tyler Bradford later confessed that he then thought Johnson had to be dead. A panicking diver ascending from that point could inadvertently enter the wreck and be trapped. Even if he was free and clear, which was unlikely from that part of the ship, he could still suffer an embolism if he ascended too fast.

Piemonte, on the other hand, wasn't particularly worried since he'd seen Johnson exit via the teak rail, which meant that in all likelihood he had made it to the port rail and then to the mooring line. Piemonte wished he could communicate that to Bradford, but he couldn't; it was too long an explanation for the slate. Both divers agreed to abort the dive and swim back to the line, with Bradford thinking they now had to mount a body recovery.

At twenty feet they ran into Kulisek, waiting for McRavey and me to make our way down. He made it clear that Johnson was all right and up on the boat. Breaking the surface, Bradford gave Piemonte a look that said, "What the fuck is going on here?" But Piemonte had his own concern: he was angry. He had assured both Bradford and Kulisek that Darryl Johnson was up to the task of diving this wreck. Piemonte had told them that he and Johnson had been diving on wrecks more challenging than this. Now Piemonte "felt like an asshole." He'd already decided against saying anything to Johnson before he clambered up the ladder onto the boat. From past experience, he knew that confronting someone when he was pissed off was not a good idea.

Bradford was not so reluctant. He wanted to know what the hell had happened. Johnson told him he'd had a "free flow," meaning that he was breathing gas in an unchecked flow rather than a controlled flow through the mouthpiece, and thought it was best to return to the boat. Bradford had turned around on the bottom to keep going after Johnson gave him the OK sign, only to get his mask knocked off by Johnson's fin and have Johnson drop his camera. He accused Johnson of making another free ascent.

Johnson argued that he hadn't made a free ascent and didn't realize he had dropped his camera, that the lanyard must have slipped from his wrist. Given any standard, Bradford said, Johnson should have shut down the isolator valve on his tank manifold, isolating the free-flow regulator, and then shut down that tank. He wanted to know why Johnson didn't do that.

Johnson's answer was only "I guess I made a bad decision." He'd tell me later, "It wasn't my proudest moment, and I didn't like the way I handled it. It was just that I wanted to get out of the situation. Unfortunately, I didn't execute emergency procedures properly."

On board the boat after the dive, Piemonte told Johnson that it was twice now that he'd turned around with Piemonte right behind him, where Johnson had so adamantly insisted he be, and then simply bolted. Both times Johnson had had a problem and didn't look to him for help or even say he had a problem. Johnson had twice left him in deep water with a lot of questions. "Why are you doing that?" Piemonte demanded. Johnson's only defense, again, was that he'd made a bad decision. That wasn't good enough for Piemonte. He told Johnson to stop the bullshit now, because things were going to get ugly. Piemonte then stripped off his gear and sat up on the bow, taking himself "out of the mix." He was angry because Johnson had worried him, but more than being angry, he was disappointed. Piemonte had vouched for Johnson. "I ran my mouth," Piemonte later said, "and I was wrong." "I think I would have noticed," Piemonte told me later, "if he had a free-flow problem. I had my light on him. I would have seen all those bubbles. In my mind, we had another panic situation. From that moment on, I decided I was going to be a solo diver."

In Johnson's defense, what he'd done underwater on those two dives was not all that wrong. A lot of divers who suddenly think they're in a dangerous situation would have done the same. Divers learn to perform the tank-valve shutdown and often practice the maneuver, but usually only in a pool or during shallow-water training. It's different when the crisis is real and you're in deep, dark water.

On both dives Darryl Johnson had spent little time on the bottom, so no decompression stops were required. Many divers would have dutifully made their way back to their ascent line as they'd been trained, spending more time on the bottom accruing decompression time while exhausting their precious air supply, a consideration if in fact an equipment malfunction was causing the loss of gas. Surfacing from a wreck in a free ascent is perceived to be bad form because it's thought to result from panic, or because "the moron couldn't find his way back to the anchor line." But all boat captains have stories of divers who wound up dead or in the hospital because they didn't want to look like a moron by making a free ascent, instead staying down longer to find their way back to the distant anchor line.

The only thing that could have proved fatal to Darryl Johnson was getting caught up in the overhanging wreckage or "embolizing" from holding his breath during the ascent. He had done neither. The case can be made that he did the right thing. He didn't drown, suffer a DCS hit, embolize, or trap himself on the wreck in his quick ascents. He may have not been so lucky if he had followed accepted procedures.

On the way back to Rimouski that afternoon, we saw some whales, which made me think of some of the passing shadows I had seen on the bottom. If anything, it removed any question about where we were diving: we were visiting a wreck in a vast ocean. This was no river.

Diving the Lifeboats

The afternoon dive on our third day, with high sun and still waters, provided some of our best visibility underwater.

Kulisek, McRavey, and I agreed on a dive plan that would take us aft of the mooring line, to the explosion hole, and back to the stern.

The port rail was well lit by the sun from the surface, and I didn't need to turn on my light. We kicked aft until we reached the huge explosion hole, blown out by salvors in 1914 to remove the purser's safe from deep within the ship. The hole was a prominent feature on the upward side of the sunken vessel and a popular entry point for divers intent on penetration and looking for artifacts. Flicking on my light, I peered into the gaping void. I followed the light beam with narrowed eyes but could see nothing but some dangling debris hanging from the collapsed decks. "Another time," I thought, and kicked aft after Gary Kulisek.

It was a leisurely swim back to the stern. We stopped often to investigate openings and portholes on the port-side hull. Only snow crabs and sculpins, sedentary fish that seem to stare mournfully at interlopers, bore witness to our intrusions.

After swimming almost half the length of the giant ship, we came to the collapsed area near the stern. This part of the ship was a tangled mess of debris. We drifted over it, probing the area with our lights. Visibility dropped precipitously here, down to about five feet, making the search for the propeller shafts and engine area too difficult for us neophyte *Em-*

press divers. With hand signals, the three of us agreed to vacate the stern and swim back amidships, where there was more to see. Back at the explosion hole, we dropped in.

Gary Kulisek and Colin McRavey entered the jagged hole where the explosion had blown out the steel on the hull side. I was hovering over the promenade deck and noticed that the decking had rotted away, providing a back door into the explosion hole. That's where I made my penetration into the wreck.

We could have run a penetration line and dropped even deeper into the ship, but we were approaching our turnaround time. The grand staircase, which was a hundred feet farther from the explosion hole, would have to wait for another dive.

ON OUR SECOND-TO-LAST day on the wreck, we all agreed that it would be a good idea, finally, to get down to the lifeboats. Bad visibility and a lack of ambient light wouldn't turn us back this time.

Topside conditions seemed perfect. Once Bouillon secured the *Marie A.B.* to the wreck's mooring line, I surveyed the placid seas around us. Through the glaring sunlight, I caught sight of Ernest, the resident seal who had made the *Empress* his fiefdom. Like all reefs, natural or artificial, the *Empress* was a magnet for sea life, making the deteriorating hulk an attractive playground. Ernest eyed us for several moments before quietly slipping beneath the surface. No doubt he was used to divers invading his underwater turf and left us alone after satisfying his curiosity.

We had had our tanks filled with a "lighter" oxygen mix, less oxygen than usual, since this would be the deepest dive on the wreck, at 140 feet. Tyler Bradford had filled the tanks with 500 pounds per square inch of oxygen, and Dany St-Cyr had then topped them off with air using his portable compressor in Jean-Pierre Bouillon's backyard.

Peter Piemonte dived solo. Bradford took Darryl Johnson along on his dive, where he planned to lay some line from the starboard staircase to the lifeboats, which we all could use as our guide. I'd be diving with Gary Kulisek and Colin McRavey again.

Conditions down below on the port rail were encouraging. Visibility was in the fifteen-foot range. We continued farther down to the now familiar first-class bulkhead.

At the bottom, we stopped at the starboard staircase. Kulisek turned to McRavey and me and pointed out the line that Bradford had set leading to the lifeboats. On the muddy bottom it looked like midnight on a moonless night.

Kulisek spun to his left after giving me the OK sign, and his white tanks gave off a faint glow as he swam aft. I took the guideline between my fingers and followed. So far the wet gloves were providing me with enough protection from the cold.

We had gone perhaps twenty feet when I bumped into Kulisek. He had stopped and was running his light up the sides of something that I couldn't quite make out. I pulled up alongside of him and probed the darkness with my light as well. Ribbings of the interior hull of a steel lifeboat appeared from out of the gloom. I thought I could make out the benches. Giving my buoyancy-compensator vest a blast of air, I lifted gently from the bottom. The curvature of the hull materialized, and I realized I was in-

Number one *Empress* lifeboat resting on the bottom next to the wreck of the *Empress*.
© *Gary Gentile.*

side the lifeboat. Now I understood what Bradford had told me the night before, when he spoke of the danger of losing sight of the wreck down near the lifeboats; it was disorienting to be inside an overturned lifeboat, hanging off the bigger wreck above it.

On a dive three years before, Bradford had taken two divers to the stern section of the ship. A half hour into the dive, one of the divers had called off the dive and Bradford had taken him back to the anchor line. Bradford and the remaining diver then decided to go into the wreck to see the grand staircase. Deep inside the ship in pitch blackness, Bradford found the bottom stair tread and rested his right hand on it.

It was too dark, and the other diver never saw it. Bradford decided it was time to get out, but a line they hadn't noticed before had wrapped around the other diver's high-pressure-gauge hose. She was stuck and Bradford could see the panic building in her eyes. The silt started to cloud the vicinity, but Bradford managed to free the diver from the line. He got her out and back to the anchor line, and since he had plenty of gas left, decided to stay behind.

Even though he was well into "deco time," past the point in the dive where decompression stops would become necessary, he descended to the lifeboats just aft of amidships. Visibility on the bottom wasn't bad, perhaps ten feet. He could clearly make out the teak on the sloping decks of the *Empress*. Once he sank to the bottom, Bradford executed a 360-degree turn. He looked around but couldn't see any wreck debris. Visibility had worsened, and the current had picked up. Bradford realized he had drifted away from the ship. He was lost.

Quickly assessing how much gas he had left and how much deco time he had accumulated, he thought about deploying a lift bag that would carry a line to the surface and serve as his escape route. The current, however, might flatten his bag on the surface, emptying the air it would need to float. He looked around for some debris to tie off to and anchor the line. There was nothing. With his options severely limited, he pulled out his dive knife and stabbed it into the sand. Bradford remembered his next thought: "How did I get myself into this mess?"

He tied off his penetration reel line on the hilt of the knife and began to do circular, incremental sweeps. In what seemed forever, but in reality was just a couple of minutes, he came across large pieces debris from the ship. He looked up and could just make out the hull of a lifeboat. Following the side of the lifeboat and then the ship up, he made it to the port-side rail. His misadventure, however, was not over. He knew that early in the season there was only one mooring line on the wreck, not the usual three—one at the bow, one amidships, one at the stern.

"As I was going up," Bradford told me later, "I thought: Do I turn left or do I turn right to find the anchor line? If I swam the wrong way, I would have to swim three hundred feet back the other way. I was down below a thousand pounds of air." He had less than a third of his air supply left, with decompression time still to be made.

Bradford guessed correctly and found his way back to the anchor line. He thought about what had happened as he decompressed. He estimated that he couldn't have been more than twenty feet from the wreck when he got lost. "It was just another example," he told me, "proving that you can't just dive this wreck casually or you'll get into trouble. You have to plan the dive and dive the plan, or else you're fucked."

GETTING INTO TROUBLE was paramount in my mind as I now searched the inside of the lifeboat with my light. Kulisek seemed to be looking for something. It came to me suddenly what that was.

It was well known among *Empress* divers that skeletal remains hung in one of the lifeboats. With deep-wreck divers, the subject of human remains always comes up. It's one of those perverse or macabre subjects, depending on your point of view, that eventually works its way into questions about what to expect on the wreck. Over six hundred souls were still entombed in the wreck, including David and Bertha Creighton.

Gary Gentile, John Reekie, Philippe Beaudry, Dany St-Cyr, Gary Kulisek, and Tyler Bradford had all told me that they routinely encountered human bones. I too had seen my share in other underwater sarcophagi. The bones on the *Empress* had long ago been cleaned of their flesh and now, like the china plates and tureens, poked haphazardly from the muck. The remains were simply a reality, a testament to the tragedy. They deserved our respect, and as far as I was concerned, they received it. To me, diving the *Empress* was like exploring the hallowed battlefields of Gettysburg, Verdun, or Normandy. Bearing witness was our way of bestowing respect.

Victim's skull inside the *Empress*. © Dany St-Cyr.

Above me, a lifeboat still hung from its davits. After the sinking of the *Titanic*, new regulations required all ocean liners to carry enough lifeboats to rescue everyone aboard. Had the *Empress* not sunk so quickly, perhaps the boat above me could have carried many of the passengers to safety. I thought that the skeletal remains somewhere here in the darkness might have belonged to some poor soul who thought this small lifeboat was the ticket to survival. Instead, it had become a tomb.

I could see Kulisek check his gauges. He looked at me and gave a shrug. Poor visibility and accumulating bottom time then had him pointing toward the surface. We followed Bradford's guideline back to the staircase. It seemed darker now than when we had first kicked aft at the start of our search for the lifeboats. I glanced down at my light and noticed how dim the beam was. I gave it a couple of raps with my left hand. Nothing. The light was crapping out on me. I reached into a pocket over my right hip for my emergency backup light. Since it was used only in emergencies, it wasn't as powerful as my primary light. On any other wreck that wouldn't have presented much of a problem. But the *Empress* was another story. Kulisek was several feet in front of me and was unaware of my situation. He swam forward along the deck leading to the bow.

Because my light wasn't quite up to the task, I swam hard to catch up to Kulisek and then stayed close to the tips of his fins, afraid of losing him. I knew where to find the port rail, our escape route back; it was up the inclined deck to my left. But I wanted to see more, and I knew there were not many dives left. If I stayed close to Kulisek, even with my meager light, I could still explore the wreck.

Along the forward deck we again passed over the dedication plaques, the purple wildflowers still waving in the current. Back on the anchor line, we did our decompression hangs.

Kulisek had forgotten to strap on his dive computer, so he went by mine. Waiting impatiently for the nitrogen bubbles to be expelled from my system, I could think of little but the cold. I couldn't feel my fingers.

Along with Kulisek, I relied on my dive computer to determine my decompression times. It had a built-in safety factor based on one of the more conservative algorithms computing air consumption and outgassing. My oxygen-enriched nitrox called for shorter stops, and I knew I was in the safe zone once I had only ten more minutes of decompression left to go.

Kulisek and McRavey had both left for the surface, leaving me alone and shivering in the thirty-four-degree water. I had had longer bottom times and gone deeper than they had. After another minute of suffering, I headed for the surface. My computer started to belt out its warning beep. I ignored it. I had "bent" my computer by not following the required decompression stop times, making it useless for the afternoon dive.

A bent computer and a blown primary light didn't bode well for the afternoon dive. The accumulated fatigue over four days of diving in the frigid water had begun to take its toll. I mulled over making the dive and finally persuaded myself to do it. It might be the last dive, I reasoned, since the weather forecast for the next day wasn't good.

Warmed by an excellent meal of fresh halibut at a Rimouski restaurant, I helped load up the boat with fresh tanks, my spirit renewed. On the brisk ride out, I decided that if the conditions were good, I'd follow Kulisek down to the explosion hole for a penetration dive. Again, Bradford would lay some line from the hole to the grand staircase for us to follow.

WITH THE DRAMATIC scenes from the movie *Titanic* on any wreck diver's mind, diving the *Empress* was not complete without a penetration dive into the ship to view the grand staircase. It had been, like the staircase on the *Titanic*, an ostentatious passageway that connected the Edwardian-appointed first-class dining room with the upper deck. There was noth-

ing much left of the wooden staircase, just the bottom riser and the anchoring post. Still, it was a must-do dive. Bradford said it would be about a hundred-foot lateral swim from the explosion hole.

Conditions had worsened on the bottom since our morning dive. Particulate matter in the water was dense, and any ambient light from

The deteriorated grand staircase today.
© Dan Crowell.

above had disappeared. I dropped to the bottom and waited for McRavey. Kulisek vanished in the direction of the bow. That didn't make much sense to me, since the explosion hole was in the other direction. McRavey made some signs asking if we should follow. I motioned that I was staying fast, thinking Kulisek would return for us and we'd swim aft to the explosion hole. McRavey indicated that he would swim after him. While I waited, instead of sitting there like an idiot on the hull, I thought I would take a peek into the explosion hole.

I almost missed it, a pretty hard thing to do considering its large, un-mistakable shape. I found Bradford's line tied off on the perimeter. I shone my light on the white line and tried to follow it down. I could see only a couple of feet before it melted into the darkness. I hesitated. I didn't feel comfortable descending the line. I was alone, about to enter a section of the ship I had never ventured into. Visibility was poor, and I was fatigued. My curiosity almost got the best of me, but I told myself there would be other opportunities to venture deep into the wreck. I swam back to the mooring line.

McRavey returned and gestured for me to follow him. I shook my head, pointed to myself and then to the surface, and gave myself a hug indicating I was cold. I was done for the day.

WE HAD ALL decided to make just one dive the following morning, our last one, and then leave for home. But before leaving, we wanted to take in the Musée de la Mer in Pointe-au-Père. Since the afternoon's dive had been cut short, the time was right to visit the museum on our second-to-last day.

On our way out to the Pointe-au-Père museum, we stopped at the Canadian Pacific Railway memorial to the *Empress of Ireland*. It was a driz-zly gray afternoon when we pulled over to pay our respects.

The monument, like the *Empress* memorial stone in Toronto's Mount Pleasant Cemetery, is a simple monolith of granite surrounded by a chain anchored by granite posts. It sits by the side of a two-lane road that leads out to the point. The narrow roadside plot is flanked by a grassy knoll and a hardy clump of pines. The wind blows constantly across this

Canadian Pacific Railway mass grave and monument to *Empress* victims at Pointe-au-Père.

weather-beaten, rocky point of land. It's an austere place, the perfect site for so somber a memorial.

Beneath the stone rest many of the dead, most of whom went unidentified. Each of us, after studying the monument, turned to stare out to sea where the *Empress* now rests.

I found myself thinking of the lives lost and hoping that those who never made it off the ship died quickly and painlessly, but I doubted many of them were so lucky. However they had perished, perhaps this simple stone memorial gave their families some solace as it did me.

The present Musée de la Mer, which opened just two years earlier in 2000, lay across the street from the lighthouse and the sea. Designed to resemble the sinking ship, it appeared to lean precipitously to its right side. On the roof stood two smokestacks. We had an hour's wait before the next showing of the English documentary on the sinking, so we strolled around the exhibit room before collecting for lunch across the street at a small café next to the lighthouse.

Next to the café stood another part of the museum complex maintained by Parks Canada. On the second floor we found what we were looking for. The whole floor, dedicated to the exploration of the wreck of the *Empress of Ireland*, held artifacts recovered by divers, underwater video, and testaments by divers of close calls. The infamous moose antlers, which John Reekie recovered from deep within the cargo hold, were in a glass-enclosed recess. As I studied the imposing barnacle-encrusted rack, I could not help smiling, remembering how Reekie had ventured back deep into the wreck to prove they were there.

We all huddled around a model of the ship resting on the bottom, complete with little divers on various levels of the wreck exploring it with lights in their hands. Above hovered a dive boat. We pointed out various spots where we'd been and other areas that beckoned. It became obvious that we all intended to return to the *Empress*. The passion for the sunken ship had been instilled in us.

The film blended poetic license and historical fact. I watched a young girl from steerage class romp through the sepia-toned images of the first-class public rooms and dining areas. Outside, the fog collected ominously. Fog horns brayed their mournful warnings. Inside, passengers readied themselves for sleep as the *Storstad*

Musée de la Mer, Pointe-au-Père, with the lighthouse in the background. *Courtesy of Edie Summey.*

sliced through the ghostly fog, impaling the heart of the *Empress*. Screams of panicking passengers, falling bodies, and splashing water reached a horrifying climax. Then silence, but for the somber narration.

Visiting the museum gave me yet another perspective on the *Empress of Ireland* story. I was impressed that this display of archival photographs, ship models, and artifacts retrieved from the wreck by divers drew over forty thousand visitors a year to this remote place, proof that the *Empress* has not been forgotten. I felt proud to be part of the dive community that helps perpetuate her memory.

La Fin du Monde

Since just one more visit to the wreck awaited, a sense of accomplishment pervaded us all. As so often happens after a successful physical adventure, a raucous party mood took shape.

Tyler Bradford told us we had to try some "outrageously good" local beer he called the End of the World. The Quebec beer is actually called la Fin du Monde. Whether Bradford was unsure of his command of French or just exhibiting Anglo-Saxon pride, I'm not sure. If it was the latter, it was another example of the cultural divisions existing in Canada. In any case, since it was our last night in Sainte-Luce, he supplied us with a couple of six-packs of the brew.

Before drinking I noticed the alcohol content on the label: 9 percent versus beer's usual 4 percent. "Ass-kicking stuff," as my friends back home would call it. And it was. Although drinking too much alcohol, which causes dehydration, is not a wise thing to do the night before diving, we did it anyway. The expedition's near end called for a little celebration.

The following morning a blustery, cold wind blew out of the northeast as I stepped from my hotel room and into the morning sun. I was pretty sure what that meant.

On board the dive boat, Bouillon was listening intently to the weather forecast over his VHF radio. He gave us the familiar noncommittal hand dance when asked if the weather gods were cooperating. It had become a daily ritual. We knew the routine.

Without wasting any time, we off-loaded the tanks and dive gear from the trucks and stashed everything in the boat's cabin. We slipped on our diapers, struggled into our drysuits, and waited for word whether it was go or no go. Kulisek, after further consultation with Bouillon, came to me shaking his head.

"No good," he said. "High winds and heavy seas. Looks like we're not going out." The weather forecast for the afternoon didn't look good either. So that was it. We were done.

It was an abrupt, anticlimactic end, and I was disappointed. All the work and time it took to get here, and the successful dives we had made, demanded a more fitting farewell. I resolved right then that I would come back.

Kulisek and Bouillon were standing on the aft deck of the *Marie A.B.* when I told them I intended to return for more dives on the *Empress*. Kulisek chuckled and translated for Bouillon. Bouillon said something in French with a wide smile. Kulisek, placing his hand on my shoulder, translated for me: "You, my friend, now have the passion."

CHAPTER SEVEN

Return to the
Empress of Ireland

Too much of a good thing can be wonderful.

—MAE WEST

J ean-Pierre Bouillon, Dany St-Cyr, and Gary Kulisek firmly believed that once the HMCS *Nipigon* was sunk, the new wreck would take some of the diving pressure off the eighty-nine-year-old *Empress of Ireland*. The shallower and more accessible wreck of the *Nipigon* would also be an excellent place for beginners to train for exploring the more challenging *Empress*. Kulisek thought diving in Quebec was on the cusp of a golden age. That was enough reason for me to travel to Rimouski in July 2003 to witness the sinking. It was also another opportunity to dive the *Empress* and to discuss with Kulisek the prospect of having one more diver join the August expedition I had planned over the winter. Peter Piemonte and I made the nine-hour drive north.

I was surprised that Piemonte wanted to dive the *Empress* with me. He had just had a close call diving the World War II German submarine the *U-853* off Block Island, Rhode Island. Piemonte had bought one of the new rebreathers and had taken only a handful of training dives with it when he decided to test it out on the deep-residing U-boat. He felt confident about the unit and his ability to use it as he descended to the hulk, resting on the bottom at 130 feet. Rebreathing systems have their quirks, however, and a lot of divers were still leery of them—me included.

The technology of the rebreather system had been around for some time but had made the jump from the military to the sport diving world only in 1997. By 2003 rebreathers were all the rage in the technical diving community. Converts to the new scuba system extolled the virtues of the expensive units—from $3,000 to $15,000 each—with a religious fervor. It was easy to understand why, since rebreathers make possible longer dives and shorter decompression times and are lighter and less cumbersome. They can be compact because the unused oxygen in each exhaled breath is recycled, with the carbon dioxide "scrubbed" from the air before it is circulated back to the diver. In the more expensive, "fully closed" units, oxygen sensors also monitor the partial pressure of oxygen as the depth changes and, based on that information, add oxygen to the breathing mix as needed. Consequently, no large reserves of gas are necessary. In addition, the air is warmed and moistened by the diver's lungs, unlike the cold, dry, compressed air of the high-volume scuba tanks, lessening the chance of hypothermia, which is known to affect decompression adversely.

Compared with the traditional heavy and cumbersome twin-tank scuba systems, rebreathers obviously appeared to be the future of the sport. But as with all new technologies, there were problems. One rare but unnerving propensity of the system was the delivery of a "caustic cocktail." Peter Piemonte's dose almost cost him his life.

Piemonte was eager to operate the unit at the stated maximum depth of 130 feet. He hooked up to the rebreather, a forty-cubic-foot stage, or decompression gas, bottle containing 100 percent oxygen, and a thirteen-cubic-foot "bail-out" bottle with air that was also used for inflating the drysuit and buoyancy compensator wings. He splashed in alone and kicked down the mooring line.

The mooring line was attached to the wreck near the aft gun mount, twenty to thirty feet from the conning tower. Piemonte swam past the conning tower and elected to penetrate the submarine through a blast hole on the forward deck. Because there was only a small hatch leading into the control room, the six-foot-two Piemonte had to remove his big oxygen stage bottle to squeeze through.

Piemonte spent five minutes in the control room and was pleased to notice that visibility was better with the rebreather, since he was not expelling exhaust bubbles that loosened rust particles inside the wreck. Going back out through the blast hole, he thought for a moment about leaving the stage bottle there on the deck and picking it up on his return. He opted to put it back on before dropping down to the sand near the submarine's port-side bow planes. That decision probably saved his life.

Swimming forward along the bottom, Piemonte began hearing what sounded like gurgling emanating from his rebreather when he exhaled. He assumed it was air bubbling out of his relief valve on the top of the unit and continued to kick forward. In fact, a plastic clip had loosened and depressed a release tab, letting seawater into the unit. The bubbling he was hearing came from his exhaled breaths being expelled into the sea instead of circulated into the scrubbing canister. Seawater flooded into the canister.

Piemonte then heard the gurgling when he inhaled. He stopped swimming. He knelt in the sand and, being the professional pilot that he is, analyzed the situation. Instead of going immediately to the bail-out bottle as he was trained to do when he heard gurgling on inhalation, he experimented with trying to clear the mouthpiece of water. He took a deep breath so he could try to expel the water with a forceful exhalation. Piemonte did not get air. He got a mouthful of foul-tasting liquid that burned his throat. The interaction of seawater and soda lime (the carbon dioxide scrubbing agent) had created a high-alkaline liquid known as a caustic cocktail. Piemonte felt as if someone had put out a cigar on his tongue.

Piemonte grabbed for his regulator, attached to his bail-out bottle. With his clumsy, neoprene-encased hands, he frantically fumbled across his chest for the lifesaving regulator. He couldn't find it, so he searched for the hose that led from the bottle to the regulator, then ran his hand along it to the regulator, which had shifted somehow during the dive. Jamming it into his mouth, he took a deep breath.

Piemonte took two calming breaths before starting to swim up and aft of the U-boat toward the anchor line. At the deck level, or roughly at 110 feet, breathing became extremely hard. He knew that at such a deep depth the low-volume bail-out bottle was almost out of air. While he swam up,

Piemonte began to deploy his oxygen bottle. At the conning tower he ran out of air.

Angling up and aft, he kicked for the anchor line, which he knew from experience was just above him in the dark. Piemonte knew that the pure oxygen in his stage bottle at this depth could be toxic, sending him into convulsions that could make him lose consciousness. If that happened he would drown.

At the eighty-foot depth Piemonte desperately needed to breathe. He had no option but to take a hit of the oxygen. He did not want to breathe gas from his buoyancy compensator wings, in case the caustic cocktail poisoned him and knocked him unconscious. Keeping the wings inflated would ensure his arrival on the surface. He was careful to exhale on his ascent to avoid embolizing.

With his dive computer clutched in front of his face mask, he was careful to take a breath of oxygen at sixty feet, exhale, and kick; then at forty feet, exhale, and kick. The rapid-ascent alarm was beeping furiously.

Finally, on reaching thirty feet he stopped. He knew it was a bit deep for breathing 100 percent oxygen, but not dangerously so. Piemonte calmed himself down, then sucked in some seawater and swished it around his mouth to get rid of the terrible-tasting caustic cocktail. He was still afraid he had been poisoned and was careful to keep himself buoyant.

Since Piemonte's bottom time had been only thirteen minutes, he was not in a decompression situation; nonetheless, he stayed at twenty feet until he was almost out of gas. He finally clambered aboard the boat, glad to be alive.

Piemonte later told me that had he stayed longer inside the narrow confines of the U-boat, as initially planned, and taken the caustic cocktail there, he never would have made it out. He would have joined the bones of the long-dead German submariners.

PETER PIEMONTE couldn't pass up another opportunity to dive in the Gulf of St. Lawrence. Although he was interested in seeing the *Nipigon* sunk and then diving her, that would be a sideshow to his real purpose, which was to revisit the *Empress*. I shared his goal, but I also needed to discuss with Kulisek in person the prospect of another diver's returning to the sunken Canadian ocean liner: Veronica Gilligan—Ronni.

Ronni Gilligan's Return

I had called Ronni Gilligan not long after I returned from the *Empress* in September 2002. A fellow diver from the 1970 *Empress* expedition, Diane Strong, had given me her phone number and urged me to call her since she had been the first woman diver on the *Empress*. I was pleased to learn that she lived in nearby Long Beach, New York. When I told her I'd like to interview her about her dives on the *Empress* more than thirty years before, she immediately warmed to the conversation. She seemed stunned that anyone would be interested in her story and agreed to talk to me. It took just an hour and a half to reach her beach house in her oceanside community on Long Island.

At sixty-two years old, Ronni Gilligan still dives, although she admitted that diving had been an afterthought during her vacations to warm latitudes. When prodded, she told me that she was proud of being the first woman to dive the *Empress* but it was something she didn't think much about when she did it. There was something she was more proud of: she was part of the team, with Fred Zeller and Pete Perrault, that first penetrated deep into the dangerous inner compartments of the Canadian Pacific Railway ship.

Gilligan had retired in 1995 from working as a peripathologist with the vision impaired. She kept busy by volunteering with a lay group of Catholics affiliated with the Maryknoll order. The volunteer work gave her the opportunity, she told me, to meet with like-minded people and talk about God and good works "without having people look at you funny." She was spending three to four months a year overseas teaching English to Buddhist monks in Thailand and

Ronni Gilligan and the *Empress* builder's plaque she recovered with Peter Perrault in 1970.

children in Nepal, Bolivia, and Albania. When not involved in charitable work, Ronni Gilligan could usually be found on the beach just down the block from her home. As she said to me, tongue-in-cheek, "Someone has to be down there to make sure the waves are coming in right and that the sand is still there."

I learned that in the summer of 2002 she had revisited the Gaspé Peninsula after a long hiatus and made a point of stopping by the Musée de la Mer in Pointe-au-Père. She was impressed with the exhibition, its location, and its goals; and it started her thinking: Did she have one more dive on the *Empress* in her?

Gilligan told me she hadn't kept up with the advances in scuba, so she quizzed me about all the "newfangled breathing gases" and the certifications needed to use them. She also asked me about drysuits as opposed to the wetsuits that she wore into the frigid waters back in the 1960s. During our conversation it was apparent that she hadn't lost the adventurer's spirit. I asked if she would consider returning to the *Empress* with me for one more dive. She gave me a big grin and said, "Nah, I'm too old and out of shape." Gilligan grew quiet for a few pensive moments, then she shrugged her shoulders and said "maybe."

Gilligan and I continued to communicate over the following months, and she showed a growing interest in the expedition to the *Empress* I was planning in August 2003. She finally asked if I thought she could dive the wreck again. I wasn't too sure, and I told her so. Her age, her lack of physical conditioning, and the fact that she hadn't done any deep cold-water diving in a long time all worked against her. I held out one hope: Gary Kulisek. Perhaps Kulisek, a tech-dive instructor and an experienced *Empress* hand, I told Gilligan, might be able to get her up to snuff.

Kulisek liked the idea of bringing Gilligan back to the *Empress*. He agreed to "run her through the ropes" in Clayton, New York, in the Thousand Islands region of the St. Lawrence River. The river waters off the upstate New York town were relatively warm and clear, the perfect training ground for an *Empress* dive. Kulisek said he wanted her up there in June 2003, when he and his assistant Will Allen could work with her.

I hadn't had a chance to talk with Kulisek after Gilligan's training session. In one brief e-mail he wrote cryptically that "we had to talk about the Gilligan thing." The "Gilligan thing" was very much on my mind as we sped along Quebec Autoroute 20 as it followed the banks of the St. Lawrence on our way to Rimouski.

On my own return to the *Empress* after a long hiatus, I had developed renewed respect for the wreck. There was no question that it was not for the casual recreational diver. It was freezing cold, dark, deep, and haz-ardous—no place for anyone but an expert diver. But the prospect of re-uniting one of the pioneering divers with the *Empress*, thirty-two years af-ter she had last dived it, was intriguing. Ronni Gilligan's experience might give me a better feel for what the siren call of the *Empress* was all about. Yet that desire was tempered by the thought that I was encouraging this wonderfully engaging woman to put herself in a dangerous situation.

Kulisek pulled me aside shortly after I arrived at the Hôtel Navigateur in Sainte-Luce: "I have to talk to you about Gilligan." Gilligan, Kulisek told me, had come up to Clayton to do her training dives, but instead of the agreed four days, she had stayed only two. She said she had felt com-fortable enough to dive the *Empress* but had "only a couple of dives left in her." She didn't want to waste them in Clayton. Kulisek told me she had the temperament, will, and skills—although rusty—to survive an *Empress* dive. He would have felt more comfortable with letting her participate in the *Empress* expedition if he had had more time to assess her skill level and teach her the ins and outs of drysuit diving. Kulisek was inclined to let her dive, but only under careful supervision. That said, he told me it was "my call," since it was my expedition. The onus was on me.

Diving the *Empress* Again

The imminent sinking of the *Nipigon* created a sensation in Rimouski and Sainte-Luce. The towns were swarming with reporters and TV news crews from around Canada there to cover the story. The 376-foot retired Canadian Navy destroyer was set to be sent to the bottom in a blaze of fireworks and explosives. It would be the first vessel sunk as part of the new artificial reef program in Quebec.

Piemonte and I were there to help, but we were also there to dive the

Empress. Gary Kulisek, Dany St-Cyr, and Jean-Pierre Bouillon were caught up in the excitement of the event and were at their wits' end trying to make sure the destroyer would be sunk on time in full view of all the network cameras. Future funding was still an issue, as was the weather. It would be touch and go until the final minute.

Despite the turmoil around us, Piemonte and I were provided with Zodiacs for dives out on the *Empress*. We would be taken out to the wreck from Pointe-au-Père by Jacques Tardis and Eric Boulanger, local divers with hundreds of plunges down to the wreck. As I suited up on shore under the shadow of the lighthouse, I wondered if diving today was such a good idea.

When we arrived in Rimouski the weather was balmy, but it had quickly changed, as it was apt to do in the Quebec Maritimes. Winds had begun to whip out of the west, and ominous clouds closed in, forming a wall of impenetrable vapor. That Wednesday morning before our first dive I gazed out into the Gulf and couldn't see past the Pointe-au-Père breakwater. I was thinking that motoring out to the wreck site would be madness, but Eric Boulanger asked if we were ready to go. A steady rain began to fall, but the wind had died down and the Gulf was as smooth as glass. We jumped aboard the inflatable and held on as Boulanger eased the boat out from behind the breakwater and opened the throttle. Engulfed in fog, Boulanger relied solely on his global positioning system. The diving, thankfully, didn't reflect the surface conditions. The next three days brought some of the most spectacular conditions on the *Empress* I'd ever seen.

Dropping down the anchor line, I was amazed to see the wreck materialize when I was a good fifty feet above it. Reaching the tie-in amidships, I could look in either direction and see vast portions of the *Empress*. We swam over to the forward deck following the familiar port rail. Piemonte gave me a nod and pointed to the first-class bulkhead that dropped down to the lifeboats. I nodded in agreement, purged some air from my buoyancy compensator, and plummeted into the waiting darkness.

On the muddy bottom there was enough ambient light to make out some of the wreckage, debris, and the number one lifeboat. Our dive lights cast an eerie glow on our surroundings. Following the beam of the light up, I was alarmed to see that we had blundered inside the wreck without realizing it. Carefully retracing my path, I was relieved, after a few kicks of the fins, to no longer have metal overhead.

Kicking forward, I slowly followed the teak deck up, past the memorial plaques, forward cargo hatch, bollards, and winches until I reached the port rail. Intent on getting reacquainted with an old friend, I dropped over the side of the hull, found the brass letters spelling out *Empress of Ireland*, then dropped down to the anchor. Reassured that it was all still there, I swam back to the anchor line.

On Thursday, after waiting out the weather, we again left Pointe-au-Père in a fog, ahead of three other inflatables waiting for their turn to launch. Because of the big *Nipigon* event, it seemed as if every diver in Quebec was gathered in the Rimouski area. Trailered inflatables could be seen all over town, and there wasn't a hotel room to be had. Consequently it was busy out over the *Empress*. There were three other dive boats there when we arrived at 10:00 A.M. We tied in to the stern mooring and splashed in within minutes of our arrival. Visibility, again, was spectacular.

On our previous expedition to the *Empress* I had never had the chance to explore the extreme stern of the ship. With forty to fifty feet of visibility, Piemonte and I didn't hesitate to follow the port rail to the transom, follow the hull down, and drop into a debris field on the bottom. It was a part of the ship I had never seen before, and again I found myself marveling at her size and majesty. The teak decking climbed up the incline to the rail, and the faint sunlight from above backlit it, creating an eerie shadow. I stroked the ship's side as if she were a living thing, and in a sense she was. It was cold at 130 feet, approximately thirty-four degrees, but the filtered sunlight brought a spiritual warmth. Had I tried to communicate my feelings at that moment, I would have failed. I was awed by what my eyes took in.

The next two days brought less than desirable conditions on the wreck. It seemed that when conditions topside were good, the underwater environment rebelled. Dives three and four from Tardis's boat were "braille dives." As poor as visibility was, I had now reached a comfort level on the wreck. I was confident I could find my way around her without difficulty. Instead of worrying how I would get back to the anchor line, I found myself studying the smallest of the ship's details with renewed interest, oblivious to the cold and darkness. I no longer feared the *Empress*. I had found communion with her, and a true sense of accomplishment pervaded me.

Nipigon

Nipigon had been towed out of the marina the day before and was now anchored above her last resting spot, a mile west of the *Empress*. On Saturday morning I got up and looked out from the promontory where the hotel sat. I could clearly see her proud gray profile four miles offshore, due north of the church spire in Sainte-Luce. Jean-Pierre Bouillon was giving a live interview on television in French with the image of *Nipigon* shimmering in the distance over his shoulder. After seven long and difficult years he was finally achieving his goal, and I was happy for him.

Kulisek assigned us all—Hal Watts, Will Allen, Pete Piemonte, and me—to various boats and told us we would be the first divers in the water once *Nipigon* sank. Our job, he said, was to make sure all the explosive charges had detonated, blowing holes in the hull below the waterline of the navy vessel. I was to leave with Kulisek on his boat, a thirty-footer he had trailered up from Thousand Islands that week.

Nipigon waits to go down.

I surveyed the scene around me at Rimouski Marina. Just about every boat was manned, and they were all pulling out from their slips. Helicopters circled overhead, people were yelling over the roar of idling engines, and others scurried about picking up last pieces of gear and provisions in a mad dash to make it out to the sinking.

Because one of Kulisek's boat engines was giving him trouble and he continually had to stop to attend to it, we caught the front end of bad weather that had moved in from the west. Six- to eight-foot seas began to pitch our little boat about. I kept watch on the following seas, alerting Kulisek when they were upon us so he could steer away from them and ride them out like a surfboard. More than once I thought we'd capsize. I zipped up my drysuit and advised the others aboard to do the same. Even with a life preserver on, an unprotected capsize victim wouldn't last long in these cold waters. The *Empress of Ireland* had proved that.

We finally arrived at a crowded scene that was enlivened by a fireworks display from the deck of the ship at 12:30 P.M. The Canadian Coast Guard and the Quebec provincial police boats patrolled a half-mile-wide safety zone around the doomed destroyer. Kulisek, who had officially been given the task of getting divers in the water to inspect the wreck, blithely penetrated that zone. There was a lot of screaming and cursing in French between Kulisek and the harried authorities. Not understanding a word, I assumed Kulisek had made his case, since we moved closer to *Nipigon*.

Minutes before it was to be sunk, at precisely 1:00 P.M., Kulisek pointed his bow toward *Nipigon* and put his engines in neutral. There were no loud explosions, just "pops" and puffs of smoke rising from the ship's hull. It immediately started to sink, evenly and slowly, upright and proud. Only a minute had passed when the bow of old warship suddenly pitched up in the air, the stern dropping beneath the waves. Within seconds it disappeared in a rush of bubbles and lingering smoke. From the detonation of the first charge to its settling on the bottom, two minutes and twenty seconds passed. It seemed quicker than that.

Because of the pandemonium at the docks, our diving gear was spread out among three boats. Kulisek had assured us that things would be straightened out once we were above *Nipigon*. But because of the

Nipigon sinks after the explosives detonate.

pitching seas and frenzied scene out at the sinking, some divers and their gear didn't get reunited. Hal Watts was one such diver. Watts is a dive celebrity from Florida who has a host of deep-diving records and owns and runs the Forty Fathom Grotto, a popular dive destination near Ocala. Kulisek asked me if I would pass up diving and lend my gear to Watts. I was coming back in a month and would have plenty of opportunities to dive *Nipigon*, so I helped Watts suit up in my tanks.

Weaving in my unfamiliar gear, Watts went in, but he made it down only nineteen feet before he realized his drysuit had flooded. In the five-foot swells, it took Stefan Kulisek (another of Gary's sons) and me ten minutes to pull Watts in his flooded suit out of the water. I almost lost my gear.

Diver Will Allen came up our anchor line equally distressed. Over in Dany St-Cyr's boat, he had strapped on Hal Watts's gear, since his rig was being used by Dany St-Cyr, whose rebreather had malfunctioned. Down on the wreck at a depth of 116 feet, one of Watt's regulators froze up in the cold water. Unfamiliar with Watts's configuration, Allen had trouble locating the secondary regulator and almost drowned before finding it. As he surfaced in the tossing sea, I could see that Allen was clearly shaken. Once he was aboard the boat, he collapsed on deck without saying a word. Watts offered to help me into my gear, but I declined. The way things were going, I thought, the day might get worse.

St-Cyr boarded Bouillon's boat, and Will Allen was now with us in Kulisek's boat. That left only Simon Pelletier on St-Cyr's boat, and he needed another body to trim the inflatable for the rough ride back to Pointe-au-Père, so I transferred to his boat. The two of us got back without incident, but I wound up stuck in Pointe-au-Père, still zipped up in my drysuit in the pouring rain, until Kulisek remembered to pick me up three hours later and take me back to Sainte-Luce.

On Sunday morning Piemonte and I made one last dive on the *Empress* before loading up his truck and heading back to the States. There was a stiff, half-knot current on the wreck and visibility was poor, no more than five feet. With little ambient light from above, we contented ourselves with exploring the familiar forward deck area, protected from the current buffeting the hull side. It was an anticlimatic dive, given all that we had done and seen over the past four days, but as Piemonte said, "Every dive on the *Empress* is precious." And it was.

August 2003 Expedition

Three other divers were joining me on the August *Empress* expedition. My friend and dive buddy Gary Gilligan was the first to sign on. A crew member on Steve Bielenda's RV *Wahoo*, Gilligan (no relation to Ronni Gilligan) had close to a hundred dives on the *Andrea Doria*. He and I regularly dived from his dive boat the *Minnow* on several wrecks that lay just offshore from his home marina in Bridgeport, Connecticut. The fifty-year-old Gilligan was one of the most experienced and skilled wreck divers in the northeastern United States.

Matt Robinson, twenty-nine years old, had come highly recommended by Rhode Island wreck diver Bill Campbell. Campbell was another old *Doria* hand, and a recommendation from him was all I needed even though Robinson, a police officer in East Providence, Rhode Island, had been diving only two years. In that short period he had racked up hundreds of dives on deep-residing wrecks off New England and Long Island.

Dan Crowell, captain of the renowned dive boat *Seeker*, had lately been establishing a name for himself as a maker of underwater documentaries. He was intrigued with the Ronni Gilligan story and thought it might make a good film. Crowell, forty-five years old, had thousands of deep dives, with over 150 on the *Andrea Doria*, more than any other diver in the world.

But Crowell had never visited the *Empress*, and he thought it was time. Gary Kulisek had a diver from Illinois, Edie Summey, who had signed on, which left one spot. Ronni Gilligan's commitment was in my e-mail box when I got home from the *Nipigon* sinking.

The expedition was to run the week before Labor Day, starting on Monday, August 25, 2003. We all arrived in Sainte-Luce the day before and met at the Hôtel Navigateur early in the evening. Kulisek set out the prerequisites for Ronni Gilligan's dive. Conditions would have to be optimum: no current, no chop, and good visibility. Will Allen, Kulisek's safety diver, would "hold her hand" for the duration of the dive.

On Monday morning at Rimouski Marina, after conferring with Jean-Pierre Bouillon, Kulisek decided that Gilligan's dive to the *Empress* would have to wait at least another day. As he explained to me, he and Bouillon were concerned about the weather. They were expecting a "blow" out on the Gulf with the winds coming in from the northeast. Northeast winds were the worst, since they came in from the ocean, bringing rough seas. We left a disappointed Ronni Gilligan waving to us from the dock. As it turned out, she missed one of the best diving days out on the wreck.

Empress 2003 group picture. Kneeling: Matt Robinson. Front row, left to right: Gary Gilligan, Jean-Pierre Bouillon, Dan Crowell, Kevin McMurray. Back row, left to right: Will Allen, Matts Kulisek, Gary Kulisek. *Courtesy of Edie Summey.*

The big winds never materialized, and there was no current to contend with. Gary Gilligan and Matt Robinson splashed in with me, with Dan Crowell following us with his underwater video camera. Kulisek entered with Edie Summey. Visibility down on the wreck was close to fifty feet. Being the more experienced *Empress* diver in my group, I led the way, swimming forward from amidships along the port rail. An exploration of the forward deck and bow was the best introduction to the *Empress*. In this area of the wreck, the narrowing of the ship to the bow gave a diver a good perspective on its size and the angle at which it sat on the bottom. To find your way back to the anchor line was just a matter of swimming up to the high side of the wreck and keeping the angled deck to your left. The temperature on the bottom was a relatively warm thirty-seven degrees.

Everyone was excited by the dive. They had all been warned that conditions on the wreck could be poor. The problems of cold water, five feet of visibility, and swift currents didn't materialize. Having optimum conditions on the first dive was a stroke of good luck. Kulisek and I felt sorry about leaving Ronni Gilligan behind. Since she couldn't make the dive, she had decided to visit some friends in Matane, so we knew we couldn't get her aboard for an afternoon dive. As luck would have it, the afternoon dive was as good as the morning one.

Tuesday morning was shaping up to be a marginal weather day, so we had Gilligan wait once again. The rest of us went out, and again we had good conditions out over the wreck. We cursed our judgment, and Kulisek and I resolved to get Gilligan out on the *Empress* the next day.

Kulisek and I asked Ronni Gilligan if she was up to attempting a dive on Wednesday morning. Without hesitation, she said she was. In flat seas, clear skies, and warming sun, Ronni Gilligan sat on the transom on the ride out. Sitting down next to her, I asked if this all brought back memories of her dives so long ago. She told the story of André Ménard's ridiculous little sighting device, made of a wood block and screws, that he used for lining up landmarks to determine the *Empress*'s location. She studied the Pointe-au-Père lighthouse as we passed it. I could see she was lost in thought. I felt good about my part in helping to bring about her reunion

Ronni Gilligan, August 2003. © *Dan Crowell.*

with the *Empress*, and I was sure her old dive buddy Pete Perrault would have approved.

Arriving at the dive site, we moored to the amidships anchor line. Gary Gilligan, Robinson, and I geared up to splash in first, clearing the deck for Ronni Gilligan to get into her drysuit and tanks. Crowell would be staying behind to film Gilligan entering the water with Will Allen. If conditions were poor on the bottom, I was to surface immediately and cancel her dive. Visibility on the wreck was good, about twenty feet, and there was no appreciable current. We proceeded with our dive plans, and the three of us went our separate ways once we were on the wreck.

I wanted to see the grand staircase, so I tied off my penetration line, dropped into the explosion hole, and swam down into the blackness. About a hundred feet into the wreck I came upon the anchoring post for the banister and the last remaining bottom step of the staircase. It's a sad sight, these pathetic remains of the ornate Edwardian ship. In the darkness I did a 360-degree turn. It was as if I were in a tomb. I reeled in my line and headed for the faint glow of sunlight that was visible through the distant explosion hole above me.

On my way up the anchor line to my first decompression stop, I encountered Will Allen and Ronni Gilligan descending. Gilligan waved to me, and I could see her smiling widely behind her faceplate. She looked like a young girl on her way to the fair. Ronni Gilligan, pioneer *Empress* diver, was back on the *Empress*.

Back aboard the boat, Crowell was hurrying to get into the water and catch up to Gilligan and Allen on the wreck. I was sitting on the transom, stripped of my gear, catching my breath and trying to get warm when Bouillon hollered that Gilligan and Allen were up.

Allen was pulling Gilligan by her tank's manifold, and he shook his head when we shouted to ask if everything was all right. From the dive platform on the stern of the boat I could see that Gilligan, still in the water, was in distress. Allen said her suit was flooded. It took Kulisek, Crowell, and me several attempts to pull Gilligan on board.

Allen then told us that Gilligan had become inverted near the bottom, and all the air in her suit had rushed to her feet so she couldn't right herself. Allen was afraid he'd lose her, so he had stabbed a hole in her suit at the ankle so the air would escape. With all the water that entered her suit, it was a herculean effort to pull her up off the bottom. Allen was exhausted. Gilligan was responsive, but the freezing water had her near to hypothermia. Luckily they had had little bottom time, so there had been no decompression penalty.

We helped Gilligan strip off her drysuit and quickly wrapped her in blankets. Shivering from the cold, she still managed to smile and say, "I did it."

I tried to warm her by rubbing her vigorously. Through chattering teeth, Gilligan told how she and Allen had swum along the hull and made it over to the explosion hole. It was when she dropped into the hole that her problems began. Gilligan was used to wearing wetsuits and swimming down headfirst, something she shouldn't have attempted in a drysuit, given her inexperience in them. She couldn't compensate for her suddenly inflated legs, and that's when Allen had to stab the hole in her suit. I was amazed to hear that despite the problems, she was ecstatic that she had gotten to see the *Empress* one more time.

We reached Rimouski in record time, since Bouillon opened the throttle, and I whisked Gilligan up to the hot showers in the marina. I kept thinking how lucky we'd been. Apparently Gary Kulisek was thinking the same thing when we met after Gilligan had warmed up and dressed. Puffing on a cigarette and shaking his head, he said, "We were good and we were lucky. We'll be good again, but we might not be lucky. That was her last dive."

I had to agree, since I was not about to encourage her to go back in harm's way. I wondered if my dream of reuniting her with the *Empress* had been foolish. We had all wanted her to see the wreck again and had glossed over the dangers. "Was it worth it?" I asked myself. I got my answer later that day back at the hotel, where I found Gilligan sitting outside her room cradling a tumbler of scotch.

She told me how special it was seeing the *Empress* again and how it brought back all the wonderful memories of expeditions in 1968, 1969, and 1970. She choked up a little when she spoke of Pete Perrault. Incredibly, she wanted to try to dive the *Empress* again. I knew there was little chance of that after Kulisek's assessment. I also knew Bouillon would be against bringing her back out. There was also the problem of the drysuit. It was doubtful that it could be repaired properly in time, but I didn't want to rob her of her good feeling, so I said nothing.

Canadian Television, CTV, had gotten wind of the story, and they were sending up a reporter and cameraman the next day to shoot the story of Gilligan's return to the *Empress*. As it turned out, it was a good day for it. The wind started blowing that evening, and it would be worse the next day. Bouillon had already scrapped the dives for Thursday.

The CTV news crew and their star reporter, John Grant, wound up staying the whole day with us, filming interviews and reviewing the underwater footage of the wreck Dan Crowell had shot. Ronni Gilligan's interview was emotional and poignant. Grant listened entranced as she recounted how special the return had been. I was caught up in the emotion too, but I couldn't shake the feeling of how badly it could have gone. This could have easily been a tragic tale.

Ronni Gilligan was proof that the power of the *Empress*—the passion she evokes—is not something that passes with time. Gary Gentile, David Bright, Philippe Beaudry, John Reekie, and Jean-Pierre Bouillon had all spoken about that power. Every one of them, given the opportunity, would accept the challenge and dive her again. The thrill of the experience simply makes one beg for more.

Gilligan accepted Kulisek and Bouillon's decision reluctantly. She had made her one dive down to the wreck and was happy for it. She wished the dive had gone better, but she was proud that after three decades she had made her emotional return and survived. The rest of us made one last farewell dive on the *Empress* Friday. We almost didn't make it back.

The weather forecast was dicey, but as always the pressure was on

Bouillon and Kulisek to get the dives in. Bouillon thought it could be done, but we'd have to hurry to beat another nasty front that was bearing down on us from the west. Out of Rimouski Marina I looked behind us to see a gathering storm moving downriver. The seas were picking up, and it looked as if we might have a rough time of it out over the wreck. Kulisek told me later that had we left fifteen minutes later, Bouillon would have turned the boat around outside the marina's breakwater.

Out over the wreck, the skies to the west looked ominous and angry. We all knew this was our last chance to dive. We tied into the stern moorings and found less than accommodating conditions below. Visibility was under ten feet, and a stiff current buffeted the wreck. Since I had been the last one in, I was the last one back on the surface.

It was tough coming up the anchor line in the suddenly fast current. I struggled to keep a grip on the line during my decompression stops. Pulling myself along the trail line to the boat took almost all my strength. When I made it to the dive platform, I needed help from Matt Robinson and Gary Gilligan to get aboard. I couldn't take my tanks off on the dive platform or on the transom, since the boat was now tossing violently in the swells. I flopped like a fish on the aft deck, where I got help stripping off my gear.

Bouillon was quick to release the mooring line and wasted no time in pointing his bow back to Rimouski. We headed right into the system. Rain poured down, and the seas were huge. Like everyone else, I kept my drysuit on. Bouillon, of course, didn't have one, and Will Allen was aboard as a deckhand and hadn't brought his drysuit. The boat was making little headway; we couldn't have been going faster than a few knots. There was little distance between the waves that were washing over us. At one point it seemed we were going backward.

With the spire of the church in Sainte-Luce visible, Kulisek and Bouillon conferred excitedly in French. Bouillon pulled out his tidal charts and pored over them with Kulisek. I knew something was seriously wrong when Kulisek consulted Dan Crowell, another licensed boat captain. We were about four miles from Sainte-Luce when Kulisek came over and said that Bouillon didn't think we could make it to Rimouski and was considering running the *Marie A.B.* aground at the closest point of land. Now I understood why they were studying the tidal charts. With the tide out, Bouillon knew he could never make it over the shoals to shore. He had hoped the tide was going in, giving him enough depth to reach the mudflats, but that wasn't the case.

Bouillon hugged the coast as closely as he could, at least two miles out. If the boat capsized, the divers in their drysuits could swim to shore. It was a different scenario for him and Will Allen. Kulisek told me that if the boat went down he'd stay with the crippled Bouillon. Bouillon would never make it to shore in the frigid water with his handicap, but Kulisek thought he might be able to save him if a rescue boat arrived. Allen, young and strong at twenty-one years, would have to stay close to one of us.

The seas reached eight to ten feet high. The bow constantly plunged deep into the waves, sometimes becoming totally immersed. Water poured over the bridge canopy, and the boat was pitching like a toy in the ferocious seas. We were able to get in the lee of the point at Pointe-au-Père for some respite from the raging Gulf. The seas seemed a bit calmer in the bay between the point and Rimouski. Bouillon decided to make a run for it. We entered the protected marina two and a half hours after leaving the wreck site. The trip usually took only thirty minutes.

The harrowing trip was another reminder to take nothing for granted when diving the *Empress*. I had finally become completely comfortable on the wreck and didn't particularly worry about my safety while I was down on it, but then the Gulf threw me another curve. Thanks to Bouillon's skillful handling of the boat, we narrowly made it back to shore. It was a sobering experience. Once again I had been humbled, not by the wreck, but by the sea that cradled it. I'd come to realize that there were no givens when diving the *Empress of Ireland*. The challenge of the *Empress* is unrelenting.

EPILOGUE

Empress Alumni

It's never the conclusions, it's the story, the experience.

—Jim Harrison, author of *Off to the Side*

Almost forty years ago, sport divers made the first dark descent to the wreckage of the *Empress of Ireland*. It was a daring feat, and not just in an adventurous sense. The tenacity of their research on the lost ship and the navigational trials and errors used in locating the grave of the Canadian Pacific Railway ship is as inspiring as was the courage to go where no one had been in fifty years. This team of amateur divers from Montreal, led by André Ménard, accomplished a truly impressive feat. Divers who visit this shipwreck today owe these first divers a huge debt of thanks, as does society at large, for reviving the tragic story of one of the greatest maritime disasters in world history.

André Ménard, the man who had made diving the *Empress of Ireland* a standard in extreme diving, died on April 1, 1978. Two serious car accidents forced him into early retirement, and he was only fifty-five when he succumbed to a heart attack. At the time of writing this book, the two Villeneuve brothers, Claude, sixty-six, and Robert, sixty-nine, were still living in the Montreal area. Jean-Paul Fournier, who first helped to locate and dive the wreck back in 1964, was eighty-six and lived in Hull, Quebec. Fernand Bergeron, living an active life at seventy-two, never left Rimouski after the famous 1964 and 1965 expeditions to the wreck of the Canadian Pacific Railway ship. Mario Lavoie, the original *Empress* charter dive captain and the man responsible for finding the *Empress*, was in hospice care in Montreal, dying of cancer at sixty-nine. Harold Smyth, the cameraman for the 1965 expedition and the film *Empress of Ireland*, was a healthy sixty-four-year-old in Trois-Pistoles, Quebec, thirty miles up-river from Rimouski. Donal Tremblay left the Marine Institute in Rimouski in 1983, and at sixty-five, retired to Quebec City.

Philippe Beaudry, the most experienced of all *Empress* divers, fittingly called the 1964 and 1965 team of French Canadians the "best divers of their time." Sadly, none of the men have any of the artifacts they recovered from the wreck. They turned all of them over to Aubert Brillant, the backer of the expeditions, who subsequently lost them in bankruptcy proceedings. The artifacts wound up at the Musée Maritime du Québec in L'Islet-sur-Mer, where they remain on display. None of the divers from those two expeditions, or even its backer, Brillant, are credited with the recoveries and donations. Brillant, at seventy-six, lived in Montreal.

Pioneer wreck diver Peter Perrault, the man who planted the seed of my *Empress* passion, died on July 27, 2000, at age seventy-two in Syracuse, New York, from complications from Parkinson's disease and cancer. A researcher and engineer to the end, Perrault left instructions that he wanted no memorial service and wished to donate his body to the SUNY Upstate Medical Center in Syracuse.

Perrault had been the inspiration and the leader to a group of dedicated divers who first penetrated deep into the wreck of the *Empress of Ireland*. Ronni Gilligan was amazed at what they were able to accomplish with the gear and diving techniques they had back then. Spending week after week in a strange country with little money, they had dived a virtually unexplored wreck in frigid water using only the most rudimentary diving equipment. In a time before GPS navigation, buoyancy-compensator devices, drysuits, mixed breathing gas, caving techniques, and dive computers, they helped open up a whole new world of underwater exploration. French Canadian André Ménard, a pioneer in his own right, best summed up what the Syracuse group accomplished up on the St. Lawrence when he said in his uniquely Gallic way, "The *Empress* was a virgin until the Anglo-Saxon Americans arrived."

AFTER THEIR last dive on the *Empress* in 1972, Ron and Diane Strong moved to Guam so Ron could pursue a master's degree in marine science.

As Diane told me, "We found paradise and never left." But in 1996 Diane lost her husband and dive buddy of twenty-six years to cancer. Already retired, she discovered that with her beloved husband's death she also lost part of her identity. With the help of old friends, scuba, and great memories of diving the *Empress*, she forged a new one.

Diane, now fifty-six, returned to diving a few years back with a new passion. She took advanced scuba courses and plunged back into the sport with a succession of dive adventures in the South Pacific. But another old friend was calling. She found out about the dedication of the new museum building at Pointe-au-Père, Quebec, scheduled for June 1, 2000. As she later said, "A light went on in my head." She thought about the *Empress*'s compass and binnacle, which she and Ron had recovered in 1970. She knew she had to do the "right thing." Rather than have the artifacts languish in a private home in Florida, she thought these proud pieces of history belonged within eyeshot of the *Empress of Ireland*'s grave.

Catching a last-minute plane from Guam to Tokyo and then a flight to New York, she managed a rendezvous with diving friend Rob Betz in Connecticut. In a complicated relay, the compass and binnacle had been carted up from the Florida residence of a family friend (where it was housed for safekeeping) with the help of old diving buddy, Evelyn Dudas, who was in nearby Ginnie Springs. After Strong underwent the bureaucratic delay in customs at the Canadian border and a 670-mile drive, the compass and binnacle finally arrived home in Pointe-au-Père, where she presented them to the museum's curator in a small ceremony, also attended by John Reekie and underwater filmmaker Terry German, in Pointe-au-Père during the new building's dedication.

It was an emotional moment for Strong. The artifact and Pointe-au-Père brought back memories of her husband and the adventures they had shared. Now she was parting with the treasure, but she was happy to do it. "It belonged there for the public to see," she would later tell me, "and not in a private collection." There would be one more poignant day ahead for Diane Strong on the waters above the *Empress*.

The day after the dedication and the presentation of the *Empress*'s compass and binnacle, Strong rented a Zodiac and sped out to the grave of the sunken ship with Rob Betz and Chris Cadieux. Cadieux is the Canadian cofounder of LostLiners, an organization for those who share a passion for "the Golden Age of Ocean Travel," the heyday of ocean liners such as the *Empress*.

Diane Strong was pleased to see three other inflatables moored over the wreck with drysuited divers ready to make the plunge. She eased the boat into neutral and took a film canister from her bag. Opening the little urn, she checked the wind direction, poured some of the ashes into the water, and said: "Here's to my lifetime buddy and favorite *Empress* diver."

Strong told me that spreading Ron's ashes was a ritual she had performed at several places in the world where the couple had shared special moments. She said some of Ron belonged in the waters over the *Empress*, for it had meant so much to them both in life.

Philippe Beaudry

I looked forward to meeting Philippe Beaudry in person, since all our conversations had been over the phone and by e-mail. Our long-delayed meeting, after my return to the *Empress*, would help me understand the lost ocean liner's place in history, and especially the role of politics and international law when it came to her artifacts. Everyone I talked to about Beaudry had either extremely negative or extremely positive feelings toward the man. But no one could deny Beaudry his *Empress* dive experience: over six hundred dives on her over the course of twenty-five years, more than any other human being.

He'd graciously offered to put me up in his home, adding that his wife was a very good cook. I had accepted, thinking there was no better way to get to know a man than staying at his home, except perhaps diving with him.

Phil Beaudry met me in September 2002 at Dorval Airport in Montreal after I passed through Canadian customs. Even without his trademark full beard, he was immediately recognizable as the man others had described to me. He was wearing a T-shirt, shorts, and a pair of worn leather sandals. His prominent Gallic nose reminded me that Ronni Gilligan had called him Hook. I now knew she wasn't referring to the pirate, although given his piles of booty from the *Empress* that would have been understandable. Phil Beaudry looked every bit of his fifty-six years, a man of considerable life experience, adventure, and hard living.

Beaudry lived across the St. Lawrence River from Montreal in the suburb of Longueuil, where he ran his accounting business out of his spacious ranch house. Pulling up in front, Beaudry pointed out the place where he'd found a paper bag containing dynamite, most likely a warning from an *Empress* salvor in Rimouski whose job was made difficult by Beaudry's efforts to preserve the wreck. Beaudry smiled, stared at the spot for a moment, and added as an afterthought, "But it didn't scare

Philippe Beaudry at Rimouski Marina, 2003.

me." I made a mental note to pursue the question when I had my tape recorder running.

Despite finally winning government protection for the *Empress*, Phil Beaudry had been soured by the whole experience. He felt he'd been a "hostage of the system," since he'd had to shoulder all the legal costs and had received no offers from the provincial or federal governments to underwrite an exhibition or offer fair payment for the collection.

Euchariste Morin, a heritage agent for the province's Ministry of Culture and Communication in Rimouski, told me they couldn't give Beaudry money even though the collection has "a great deal of cultural value." Historians and archaeologists for the ministry, he said, couldn't place a commercial value on recovered artifacts, since it would only increase the demand and encourage looting of historic shipwrecks. The Ministry of Culture and Communication, Morin said, adhered to the United Nations

Educational, Scientific, and Cultural Organization (UNESCO) pronouncement that individuals should not profit from the cultural heritage of a nation.

In the course of five years, from 1993 to 1998, Phil Beaudry claimed to have spent $250,000 seeking protection of the wreck and exhibiting his artifacts in public shows in Quebec City and Montreal. Beaudry had in his possession five hundred prized artifacts that he and divers from his *Empress of Ireland* Historical Society had pulled from the wreck and over six hundred supporting archival pieces, including the original 1965 documentary and all the stock footage that was shot. From the beginning his dream was to house his collection in a museum in Quebec, and that dream had cost him plenty.

In February 2000, Phil Beaudry met with Odette Duplessis, the Quebec assistant minister of culture and communication. Inspired by the traveling *Titanic* exhibition, Beaudry proposed a traveling exhibition of the *Empress of Ireland* that would visit major Canadian cities and a few cities in the United States. He requested $100,000 as seed money to get the exhibition started in conjunction with the Quebec Maritime Museum in L'Islet-sur-Mer. Beaudry's proposal would allow him to recoup his expenses and profit from the exhibition's income. The ministry denied the request, saying they had received a negative report on his proposal from a group in Rimouski. Beaudry guessed where that report came from—the Musée de la Mer and the Marine Institute.

That was the end of patience for Phil Beaudry. He remembered thinking, "I'm going to sell the whole collection." Thus began another odyssey for the veteran *Empress* diver. Beaudry had a standing offer of $1.5 million U.S. for the entire collection from an American collector in Florida. It was time for Phil Beaudry to collect on thirty years of work. A month later he applied for an export license from the Canadian federal government.

The government quickly refused to issue the export license, backed by Robert Grenier, the chief of underwater archaeology for Parks Canada and president of the International Scientific Committee for Underwater Archaeology for UNESCO. Grenier told me he has known Phil Beaudry for thirty-five years, and for most of those years, he added with a laugh, they were friends. "It was determined that the province of Quebec had ownership of the wreck, since the bottom where the *Empress* rests is their jurisdiction, and Quebec declared that the *Empress* was a 'cultural entity' that was to be protected."

Beaudry told me that since the wreck was now protected, thanks to his efforts, then so was the collection, and therefore it could not leave Canada. Grenier told me he was not at liberty to discuss the issue, since it was a legal matter in the hands of another Canadian ministry.

Beaudry appealed to the Review Board in Toronto, outlining all the work he had done and how little support the federal and provincial governments had provided. The Review Board appeared to be sympathetic. They issued a moratorium on the sale of the collection for six months but stipulated that if within that time Beaudry hadn't received from the Canadian government or Quebec an offer equal to the $1.5 million offer he already had, then he was free to export the collection to the United States.

All museums across Canada were warned by the government of the pending sale. A public relations spokesman for the Musée de la Mer at Pointe-au-Père officially proclaimed on public television that the museum would block Beaudry's export license and the sale of the artifacts. Shortly afterward, the provincial government asked Beaudry if he was willing to have the collection valued by another independent estimator. He agreed.

The estimate came in at $2.7 million Canadian, or $2 million U.S., thirty days before the end of the moratorium. According to Beaudry, the Pointe-au-Père museum knew the estimate and still offered only $325,000 Canadian for the collection. The museum claimed that since many of the artifacts in the collection were duplicates of ones they had, that was all they were worth. Beaudry refused the offer. The museum appealed to the provincial government for still another valuation, but this time from marine experts in Halifax.

Beaudry was leery since he'd learned that one of the "experts" was not a certified estimator and the other was certified only for estimating household valuables. In the meantime, the six-month moratorium had passed. The second estimation of the value of the collection eventually came in at $1.5 million Canadian, better than the $325,000 but still 40 percent lower than the American collector's offer. The federal government stepped in and told Beaudry he would have to accept it or wait two more years before he could reapply for the export license. Beaudry was outraged. He claimed that the Pointe-au-Père museum was working with the Quebec government to block his export license. Beaudry refused the offer as "completely unacceptable." One thing he had was time; another, as a deep-wreck diver, was perseverance. He would wait them out once again.

The two-year wait came to an end in May 2002. Beaudry reapplied for the export license. The Federal Ministry of Canadian Heritage, Beaudry claimed, tried to block the export license based on a UNESCO proclamation that the underwater heritage of one of its signature nations couldn't be sold for profit by any individual. Beaudry countered by noting that the UNESCO agreement did not have the force of law, since the required twenty country signatures had not yet been obtained. Further, Canada wasn't among those that had signed. The Review Board issued another six-month moratorium on the sale, to end on December 19, 2002.

On the advice of a well-placed friend in the Canadian government, Beaudry, before the deadline, wrote to the Quebec minister of culture and communication and asked for a meeting to hammer out an agreement. It took three months to receive an answer. The letter referred the matter to a minor functionary totally unfamiliar with the situation or its history.

By September 2002, Phil Beaudry almost didn't care where the collection ended up, as long as he received fair compensation. He was tired of the fight and blamed the legal battle for the pacemaker now implanted in his chest.

Finally, on December 24, 2002, Beaudry received a Christmas present. The Canadian government issued him his export license; the tenacious French-Canadian had finally won.

But one last effort to keep the collection in Canada materialized. Beaudry was approached by a group of western Canadians who were descendants of immigrants who had crossed the Atlantic to Canada aboard the *Empress of Ireland*. The group had formed the *Empress of Ireland* Artifacts Committee in Czar, Alberta, and they were intent on keeping this part of their heritage in their country. They offered to match the American offer. Beaudry had always claimed that he wanted to keep the collection in Canada, so he agreed to wait. He gave the artifacts committee until October 2003 to raise the money. Beaudry even lowered his price, asking $1.5 million Canadian (30 percent less today because of currency fluctuations), to make it more feasible for the Alberta group. By the deadline, however, the money raised was far short of the price—just $20,000. Today the collection of *Empress* artifacts remains in a warehouse in Montreal awaiting export.

Philippe Beaudry was apprised, along with other principals in this book, of all descriptions and explanations on *Empress* dives made by David Bright, Gary Gentile, John Reekie, and Serge Lavoie, and the legal difficulties regarding the wreck as described in this book. Beaudry insists he never misled Canadian or American divers, nor did he obstruct them—in any way—in their efforts to dive the wreck or even in their efforts to retrieve artifacts as long as they were reported to the proper authorities. He also told me he never notified authorities that resulted in any legal action taken against said individuals by Transport Canada or the receiver of wreck. I saw fit, nevertheless, to include their observations since they were the opinions of divers who were there and had visited the *Empress* during those turbulent and exciting times of the late 1980s and early 1990s when Philippe Beaudry was such a prominent protector of the wreck of the *Empress of Ireland.*

Philippe Beaudry is, without question, a controversial figure in Rimouski. What cannot be denied is his influence in deep wreck diving because of his 600 dives on the wreck and his contribution to the preservation and protection of the *Empress of Ireland* to which the North American dive community and those concerned with Canadian heritage owe him a great debt of gratitude.

Gary Gentile

"Definitely in the top six," Gary Gentile told me. He was talking about where the *Empress of Ireland* ranked among his all-time favorite shipwrecks. He placed it up there, in no particular order, with the infamous

Andrea Doria; the Civil War ironclad *Monitor*; the World War I USS *San Diego*; the German World War I warship *Ostfriesland*, at 380 feet deep; and the *Lusitania*. Impressive company, especially when you consider who ranked it there: Gary Gentile was probably the most famous wreck diver in the world. He had also been on more sunken ships than anybody else in the world. His dozens of shipwreck guidebooks were testament to his expertise and passion.

Gary Gentile had not been back to the *Empress* since 1993. The "hassles" from Canadian authorities and Philippe Beaudry over the artifacts he recovered from the wreck, along with John Reekie's canceled charters, soured him on the experience. If he ever had any thought of returning to Rimouski, it was quashed when the *Empress* received permanent official protection status in 1999. If he couldn't recover artifacts from the wreck, he wasn't interested in diving her again. Gary Gentile had already logged forty dives on the *Empress*, and he saw no reason to return if he had to come away empty-handed.

When I caught up with him in July 2003, Gentile was living in his boyhood home in north Philadelphia, which he inherited from his parents. He

said he was looking at some property in rural Pennsylvania and laughed when I remarked that he would have to hire a moving van just for all the artifacts he had recovered from shipwrecks around the world. His thirty years of diving had produced an impressive collection.

Gentile's focus lately had been shipwrecks in the American Great Lakes, an area where he was spending more and more time, yet he

Gary Gentile in 2002 with his *Empress* artifacts.

sounded nostalgic when recalling his years diving the *Empress of Ireland.* "I had some tremendous adventures and memories that will live with me forever. But there's such a thing as gilding a lily. That isn't to say I wouldn't go back. After all, it's a fun wreck to explore."

It was a recurring theme among veteran *Empress* divers who swore off diving the wreck for good. In retrospect, I discovered they couldn't quite close the door on making a return visit to the wreck. It spoke of the power of the ship's story and the passion she evoked. I would later sense that even John Reekie would return if given the opportunity.

John Reekie

John Reekie's dive career ended, by his account, deep inside the wreck of the *Andrea Doria* in the summer of 1993 when he was thirty-nine years old. Famed *Doria* explorer John Moyer, a good friend of Reekie's, had chartered Steve Bielenda's RV *Wahoo* out of Long Island, New York, for the expedition.

That summer Moyer had enlisted Reekie and his dive buddy Kim Martin to take on one of the most daring and dangerous penetrations of the deep-residing wreck yet attempted. Reekie and Martin had impressed their American dive friends with the skills they had honed in the hundreds of cave dives they'd logged in the claustrophobic caverns of Ginnie Springs, Florida. Their experience diving the cold-water wrecks of the Great Lakes and the St. Lawrence, particularly the wreck of the *Empress of Ireland*, made them the ideal divers for the job.

A ship's bell and its helm remain the most prized artifacts from any sunken ship. Given the notoriety of the *Doria*, the Italian ocean liner that had sunk in 1956, the bell would be a prize worth thousands of dollars. Moyer had determined, from previous explorations of the forward deck of the *Doria* and the sandy bottom around it, that the bell could not have been in its usual mount on the deck or they would have found it. He'd learned through research that deckhands often removed the bell from its mount once the ship put to sea and stored it in the paint locker, two levels below the forward deck.

According to their dive plan, John Moyer, Gary Gentile, and the rest of the Americans were busy as two-man teams amidships in the first-class bar area, freeing the ceramic artwork by Italian artist Guido Gambone from the walls. Meanwhile, Reekie was negotiating an underwater labyrinth inside the wreck in pitch blackness. After dropping down to 220 feet, into the small paint locker, he began to dig for the bell. American Bart Malone was his safety diver, hovering over the entry point and shining his light down into the room while Reekie dug through the muck. Kim Martin led the second tag-team diving for the bell, with fellow Canadian Terry German as his safety diver.

Reekie, his mask in the muck and his fins above him, would immerse himself up to his waist in the sediment and dig with his arms for the brass prize. But Reekie did not realize that the cramped locker still held a toxic sludge of lead paint and paint thinner. Reekie thought that the ocean had long ago corroded away the paint and swept the poisons from the ship. But the thick sediment on the bottom of the room was permeated with them.

Both bell retrieval teams complained of feeling nauseated after their dives but attributed it to the air pumped into their tanks by the *Wahoo*'s compressor. But none of the other divers experienced any nausea.

Reekie and Martin each made three dives down into the paint locker and finally determined that had the bell been there, they would have found it. The ascent from that last dive was pure hell for the big Canadian. After leaving the wreck at 190 feet on the port side, Reekie suddenly felt an agonizing pain in his head, as if his skull would explode. He realized something inside the paint locker might be toxic but thought the poison was just in his regulator. He switched to his back-up regulator but found no relief. He thought, "That's it; it's over. I'm gonna die."

Bart Malone, by this time, was already above him; he hadn't accrued as much decompression time since he had not been as deep as Reekie. Reekie began to ascend the anchor line in three-foot increments. After each effort he would stop and scream in pain. Finally, at his twenty-foot stop, he scribbled on a slate, "Danger, Poison" and sent it up on a lift bag. The divers aboard the *Wahoo* sent down an oxygen bottle and regulator for him to use. Still, Reekie had no relief from the unbearable pain that had him crying into his dive mask. He now realized that the corrosives weren't in his regulators; they were in his body. Reekie had absorbed the contaminants through his head and hands, protected only by his wetsuit hood and gloves.

Back aboard the boat, alive but still in horrible pain, Reekie shocked everyone when he removed his gloves and hood: his skin had turned black. Once ashore, the discoloration of his skin disappeared, but he still was suffering headaches. Reekie drove straight back to Canada from Massachusetts without seeking medical help. When he arrived home, he found that all the parts inside his regulator's second stage (the mouthpiece) had fused from exposure to the corrosives inside the *Doria*'s paint locker. He could only guess what was happening to his insides.

For months after the *Doria* expedition he was sick. Kim Martin had initially suffered from the contamination as well, but his symptoms quickly disappeared. Doctors told Reekie there was nothing they could do for him; he had been poisoned. Other health problems, likely related to the poisoning, soon followed. Persistent viral pneumonia and allergies plagued him. By 1995, said Reekie, "Things started to get weird."

During dives he would have problems with his lungs, and after emerging from the water he found it hard to breathe. He soon knew he couldn't dive anymore. It was a devastating realization. Diving had been his life. John Reekie told me that he'd already had his retirement and fun. Now he'd just be working for the rest of his life—a short one, he guessed, given his condition.

I visited John Reekie in September 2002, in the small rural community where he lived, halfway between Toronto and Kingston on the shores of Lake Ontario. He and his wife, Susan, owned an attractive rambling ranch house high on a hill just off a narrow country road. They lived comfortably on the income from his dive equipment business and Susan's government job. Reekie distributed dive equipment in Canada for the American manufacturer Dive-Rite. He had established his reputation in Canada as a technical deep diver years before, and his company, Alternative Dive Products, was a direct outgrowth of that active career. Now he rarely left his home and did business by phone, fax, and e-mail. He told me he had everything there that he needed.

John Reekie put a videotape in his VCR. He wanted me to see the kind of diver he used to be. While we viewed the tape, full of footage from his dives on the *Empress* and inside the cave systems of Florida, especially in Ginnie Springs, he told me those were the best days of his life. The diving he did, and the friends he made, were unforgettable. I watched in amazement as this large man who now sat beside me wiggled and squirmed on screen through the tightest of rocky openings, often with his tank pushed in front of him. "Fat bends," he said with a laugh, "but muscle doesn't."

Some of Reekie's penetrations took place hundreds of feet underwater and thousands of yards from the entry point. Three to five hours of decompression hangs weren't outside the norm for him. He said the hangs were never a problem, since he had "his tunes"—his underwater sound system—and some paperbacks to read, tearing off the sodden pages as he decompressed. Then he left the room, leaving me to watch the tape alone for the next hour.

I finally joined him beside his pool. Sitting under an umbrella in the uncommonly hot autumn sun, smoking a cigarette and sipping some dark Jamaican rum, John Reekie was lost in thought. He finally confessed that it was always difficult for him to watch those videos of himself diving. "Thinking about diving really upsets me," he said quietly. "I try hard to put those things behind me and not think about it, because diving meant so much to me. It was my whole life. All I did was go diving. When I realized my dive career had come to an end, it was hard to take. What was I going to do now?"

Reekie had realized he must make some life changes. He said he'd never made a dime from all those years running trips out to the *Empress*. Now he had to make a living. The only other alternative, he said, was "to hang out on a corner in Toronto with a cup and his set of 104s [double scuba tanks] and beg."

Making a living in the dive business in Canada hadn't been easy. The dive season was short, the water cold, and the weather unpredictable, and dive sites were remote and hard to get to. And this was in a country with just a tenth of the population of the United States to market to, spread over a larger land mass. John Reekie admitted that he also had to contend with the famous "frugality" of his fellow Canadians. "Cheap bastards, really," he said with a smile.

In his basement, Reekie kept a six-hundred-gallon freshwater aquarium and peripheral tanks. It had taken him three years and thousands of dollars to build. He designed the entire system—tanks, filtration, refrigeration, underwater landscaping, and back-up power—and selected each type of fish to inhabit it. It was a wonder. I'd never before seen so large an artificial underwater ecosystem with such a huge selection of fish outside a public aquarium.

He told me he spent hours staring into the miniature watery world, alive with color. Reekie was in a somber mood but brightened up as he explained all the nuances of his hobby: the various species of fish that inhabited his underwater ecosystem, how they interacted, and which foods they preferred.

But the *Empress of Ireland* seemed never far from his mind. There was still a lot of resentment in the Canadian dive community because he'd introduced so many Americans to the wreck. That they "were getting more booty" than the locals was particularly galling to them. Some Canadians felt the wreck was theirs and that the Americans had no right to come up and take their historical artifacts.

John Reekie felt differently. He'd spent a lot of time down in the States diving with Americans, especially in his beloved Ginnie Springs. The Americans were always generous and accommodating to him, so he saw no reason why he couldn't reciprocate when they were in Canada. "Anyway," he said, "instead of bitching and griping, Canadian divers should have been getting their skill level up so they could do the same."

The American divers had taught Reekie a lot. To him, the bow had always been the "pointy end" and the stern the "blunt end." He'd marveled at how the American divers would pore over ship plans and plot their entry and exit points. It was no wonder these guys were so successful. But Reekie felt Canadians had one advantage had over Americans: they were used to the cold.

He had to laugh remembering how his American dive friends always bitched about the cold when diving on wrecks like the *Doria*, where it was "only forty-five degrees." To Reekie, that was warm. He and his Canadian dive buddies were used to diving in deep water in thermoclines, abrupt temperature gradients in layers of water, that never rose above thirty-nine degrees. On the North Shore of the St. Lawrence, just across the Gulf from the *Empress*, Reekie once dived in water that was twenty-eight degrees, not frozen because of the currents. Now that, he said, was cold-water diving.

Politics and his 1993 expedition, even more than his accident, killed diving on the *Empress* for John Reekie. He could remember arguing with friends from the museum at Pointe-au-Père about Quebec's place in the federation. According to Reekie, the Canadian government sent a disproportionate amount of money to Quebec to "calm them from their French woes," and the rest of Canada was resentful.

For all the problems that "Big John" had with the Quebecois, and with Phil Beaudry in particular, ironically it had been the Toronto resident Reekie who'd blown the whistle on Michel Tadros and his team of salvors in 1993 when they were stripping the wreck of teak. Reekie had been diving the wreck with Gary Gentile, John Moyer, and Bart Malone from the Ontario dive boat *M R Duks* when Tadros's *Gesmere* was over the wreck. Reekie alerted his dive buddy Steve Brooks, who in turn spoke with lawyer and diver Mark Reynolds. Thus it was Reekie who indirectly started the legal ball—and Phil Beaudry—rolling against Tadros, which ultimately led to official protection of the wreck.

The way he was treated by the Quebec authorities finished off his *Empress* diving. Reekie's reward for his work was having his chartered boat confiscated and losing four precious weeks out on the wreck and most of his clients. The partially lost *Empress* season cost him more than $40,000. After four years and fifty dives on the Canadian Pacific Railway ship, it was over for John Reekie. He would never have tired of diving the wreck; it was a special place to him. But all the politics and "lawyer bullshit" ruined it for him.

On his dangerous penetrations into the *Empress*, when he wasn't sure he'd make it back out, John Reekie never felt more alive. Like other deep divers of his caliber, during those dives every nerve in his body awoke, and he felt a natural high that could never be produced artificially. Because the average person never gets to experience that high, John Reekie felt like a lucky man.

Jean-Pierre Bouillon

In an interview with me at his home in August 2002, Jean-Pierre Bouillon reflected on the 1991 diving accident on the *Empress* that crippled him. He told me he has learned to "take a wider view of things" and let the "little pleasures in life" become more important to him. He and his wife, Eve, had a son, Charles-Étienne, and he has taken an active role in the boy's rearing. He'd missed that opportunity with his two sons, now grown, from a previous relationship. At forty-nine, he didn't want to repeat that mistake.

Although Bouillon was still somewhat bitter that he hadn't been treated as long as he thinks he should have been in the Montreal recompression chamber, he was grateful to those who helped in his rehabilitation. The Province of Quebec also provided him, through a government-subsidized program, with the latest addition to his family, Pernod, to aid in his daily activities. The big friendly black Labrador retriever was Bouillon's constant companion. He proudly ran the dog through his gamut of skills. Pernod fetched his cane, picked up a dime from the wooden floor, and steadied his master over uneven terrain, all on voice commands. In a sense Pernod had become Jean-Pierre's legs, helping him extend his reach beyond the physical limitations of his DCS-ravaged body.

On board his boat the *Marie A.B.*, Bouillon seemed to find a nimbleness that belied his handicap. Perhaps his passion for the *Empress* helped him overcome his disability to some degree. For that passion, and for his knowledge of the wreck, divers intent on visiting the *Empress* would continue to seek him out.

Like most extreme divers who dived the *Empress*, the handsome Quebecois often thought about her. On a clear day he could see the buoy over the wreck from his back porch, a reminder to maintain his vigilance lest the wreck fall into the hands of the wrong people.

Jean-Pierre Bouillon and Pernod
aboard the *Nipigon*, 2002.
Courtesy of J.-P. Bouillon.

In 2003 there was still a question about who would have jurisdiction over the *Empress*, a sticky problem wrapped up in Quebec politics. The Musée de la Mer in Pointe-au-Père, said Bouillon, was eager to take control of it. If any community is entitled to the *Empress*, Bouillon believed it should be the place nearest to the wreck—Sainte-Luce—and not the Pointe-au-Père museum. His community pride aside, he had what he believed was a better idea.

Bouillon had been actively lobbying the Quebec government for five years—the Ministries of Culture and Transportation, in particular—to have the organization he formed, the Société des Récifs Artificiels de l'Estuaire du Québec (RAEQ), the Artificial Reef Society, assume control over the *Empress of Ireland*.

Bouillon stressed to me that in his plan the RAEQ wouldn't own the wreck but would simply have the authority to protect it. Because the Society represented multiple interests, including Canadian and Quebec ministries and local community governments, control would be exercised in the interests of all. Bouillon, like his friend Philippe Beaudry, never had a problem with a diver retrieving a porthole or a dish from the wreck as a souvenir. What he feared were the "big blasters," the commercial salvors like Michel Tadros. Getting the government to protect the wreck had been an "all-or-nothing deal," he said, "and the lesser of two evils." To prevent the *Empress* from being reduced to a pile of junk by big salvors, they had to be willing to prohibit artifact retrieval of any kind.

In Bouillon's plan, the RAEQ would also be responsible for putting moorings on the wreck and issuing permits for diving. Along with the old Canadian Navy destroyer *Nipigon*, sunk near the *Empress* on July 26, 2003, Bouillon hoped the *Empress* would make the waters of the St. Lawrence a world-class diving destination. Bouillon might not be able to dive the *Empress* again himself, but he could have the satisfaction of making it available and safe for divers from around the world. At the time of this writing, as an intermediate step, the RAEQ has stewardship over the *Empress of Ireland.*

Serge Lavoie and the Musée de la Mer

Gary Kulisek arranged for me to meet Serge Lavoie for a late dinner on August 19, 2003, in a busy restaurant in downtown Rimouski. Kulisek sat in, just in case translation was necessary. The bespectacled Lavoie, head of the commercial diving program of Rimouski's Marine Institute and chairman of the board of directors of the Musée de la Mer, is an unassuming man, soft-spoken, with a professorial air. It was easier to imagine him in front of a class than as a hard-bitten commercial diver and one of the early divers on the *Empress*. His English is good enough that he could express himself clearly, although he occasionally asked Kulisek for a word he had difficulty coming up with.

Despite his difficulties with Philippe Beaudry, he wasn't eager to intensify the vitriol between them by venting to a journalist. Serge Lavoie, as I found out, was not combative by nature. He was more at ease talking about his diving career, the Institute, and the museum he headed than the controversies swirling around the *Empress* and the death of his good friend Hector Moissan.

The battle between the museum and Beaudry for ownership of the *Empress* artifact collection and the dispute over whether Bouillon's RAEQ or the museum controlled access to the wreck had all started, according to Lavoie, with the power struggle between Donal Tremblay and Philippe Beaudry. As a result, lines had been drawn and sides taken.

The bad blood continued. On August 10, 2002, Lavoie had been doing recreational scuba certification dives with his students at the wharf at Pointe-au-Père. During a training exercise they found a porthole from the *Empress* at the base of one of the wharf pilings. Lavoie guessed it was an illegal removal from the wreck by a diver who planned to reclaim it after dark. Lavoie immediately deposited the artifact at the nearby museum and notified the Quebec Provincial Police. Days later, Lavoie was shocked when he heard Beaudry on the radio claiming that Lavoie had stolen the porthole and was keeping it for himself—illegally. Lavoie claimed he had become the target for Beaudry's displeasure with the "Rimouski crowd."

Lavoie had succeeded his friend Donal Tremblay as the museum's chairman, while Jean-Pierre Bouillon and the RAEQ succeeded Phil Beaudry as the guardians of the *Empress*. The ill will was passed along as well.

Serge Lavoie was amazed when told that Jean-Pierre Bouillon claimed the museum wanted control over the *Empress*. According to Lavoie, the museum had no desire, and neither the time nor the money, to control access to the wreck. As a matter of fact, claimed Lavoie, the museum had turned down a request by the Ministry of Culture and Communication and the Ministry of Transportation to take control of the *Empress*.

Lavoie thought that Bouillon wanted the RAEQ to have control so that he could monopolize charters out to the *Empress*. If there had been any doubt of that, said Lavoie, Bouillon had proved it true when he tried to prevent Lavoie from diving the wreck.

Lavoie's September 6, 1999, dive on the *Empress* turned out to be his last. Dany St-Cyr was also out over the wreck that day. St-Cyr, a business partner and good friend of Bouillon's, motored over to Lavoie's boat and asked if he had permission from Bouillon to dive. Lavoie told him he didn't need anyone's permission to dive the *Empress*. St-Cyr made a cell phone call to Bouillon, who was waiting at the dock when Lavoie returned. Lavoie told me that Bouillon had made a scene, accusing him of using one of the mooring buoys that Bouillon had owned and placed there without his authorization. Lavoie had had enough. He confessed to me that he was "very tired about all these troubles" and had stopped diving the wreck.

The Musée de la Mer now welcomes over forty thousand visitors a year to its riverside location near the old Pointe-au-Père Lighthouse. That, and its successful partnership with Parks Canada, is satisfaction enough for Serge Lavoie. He insisted that the museum doesn't want the headache of controlling the wreck and dealing with the politics that continue to surround it.

Dany St-Cyr

When I talked with Dany St-Cyr at a diving trade show in New Jersey in March 2003, he told me he wanted to spend the rest of his life diving the *Empress*, but that he wasn't jealous about her. Diving the wreck with clients was a labor of love for him, and making other divers' *Empress* experiences unforgettable was a job he found truly rewarding. He might be called "king of the *Empress*," but it was a realm he wanted to share with the rest of the world.

St-Cyr told me that he made little money shepherding divers down to the wreck during the summer, and that he could make "a ton of money" driving a tractor-trailer full time instead. But there were other reasons for his frequent visits to the decomposing ship. He and his dive buddy Pierre Lepage had a history together there. It was there that he could ponder the fate of his friend—and no doubt his own.

That the cause of Pierre Lepage's death remained inconclusive in St-Cyr's mind, despite the coroner's report declaring it a "multiple gas embolism," still rankled. Lepage's death had had a profound effect on him. Every day he thought of his friend and the terrible day he died, but his death hadn't permanently tainted the *Empress* for St-Cyr. He still returned, intent as ever on exploring her mysteries. To him the *Empress* wasn't inherently dangerous; it just happened to be dangerous for Pierre Lepage on that day.

Simon Pelletier (left) and Dany St-Cyr.
Courtesy of Dany St-Cyr.

During our 2002 expedition to the *Empress*, Gary Kulisek had told me he thought one day he'd get the call saying that his friend St-Cyr had not returned from an *Empress* dive. The man, Kulisek said, was obsessed with exploring the wreck and took incredible risks deep inside her. Like many of the visitors to this hallowed site, I was coming to understand why.

Diving the *Empress of Ireland* was a way of becoming part of her dramatic story, from grande dame of the sea to tragic figure in a golden age of ocean travel. It was like climbing into a time machine and heading back to 1914. Truly comprehending the majesty of the ship, and in turn understanding her place in history, wouldn't come until you actually saw her, ran your fingers along the rails her passengers had clutched, swam along the decks they had strolled, and explored the rooms that once housed hundreds of people with dreams and aspirations.

I had touched her anchor and read the big brass letters spelling out her name across her now-silent hull. Diving the wreck was a difficult, dangerous challenge, but if it were easy, it would be a mere tourist attraction. Meeting that challenge and succeeding made diving her an experience that was both humbling and exciting, and that's something I can't get enough of. It's a passion that *Empress* divers all share.

In MARCH 2003 I had the chance to meet with Quebecois diver Jean Philippe Ewart, who talked with me in his hotel room in New Jersey at the Beneath the Sea Exposition, where he was manning the Alp-Maritimes Sports booth with his partner, Gary Kulisek. Ewart and Kulisek have been partners for twenty-five years. I wanted to augment what I had already learned from my research and hoped that, as a native Quebecois, he could explain to me the unique culture of Quebec. The droll and meticulous Ewart, a prominent lawyer in Montreal, is politically well connected, a student of French Canadian history, and of course an accomplished wreck diver. He seemed eager to educate me about the intricacies of what English-speaking Canadian John Reekie called "the French woes." He was also a dyed-in-the-wool federalist ("Don't take away my Rocky Mountains," he told me, claiming that the mountains are his, too, as a Canadian).

Historically, the minority Anglophones had always controlled the economic levers in Quebec, on both the federal and provincial levels. After France was defeated by the British, France signed the Treaty of Paris in 1763, officially ceding North America to English dominance. The French-speaking majority in Quebec nevertheless maintained strong emotional and cultural ties to France and Catholicism. To them, the English language and Anglicanism were the tongue and religion of their oppressors.

It was not until the late 1950s and early 1960s that a French-speaking class of decision makers and business owners of any significance emerged. Thus began the "quiet revolution" in Quebec, with the popular slogan of "Let us be masters in our own home." A power shift with enormous consequences followed.

Resistance ensued among the Quebec population to the continuing encroachment by English-speaking Canadians on their language, culture, and politics. French-speaking Quebecois focused on protecting the French character of the province and also entertained the dream of independence from the rest of Canada. Over the past decade, however, the desire for independence has become diluted by the realization that the present federalist arrangement has benefited Quebec economically. As it so often does, economic necessity rules.

Tourism is one of the major cogs in the economic machinery that generates a large portion of Quebec's income. But tourists looking for a relaxing vacation typically seek out politically stable environments. The remote Rimouski area, unlike the more populous, cosmopolitan western section of the province, is predominantly French, with few Anglophones. In the past it was a part of Quebec that Anglophones were hesitant to visit, primarily because the tourist infrastructure, such as hotels, restaurants, telephone operators, and dive operators, was (and still is) unilingual in an officially bilingual country. It is also a political stronghold of the Quebec separatist movement and therefore assumed to be anti-Anglophone. According to Jean Philippe Ewart, that is a misperception. With the creation of a diving mecca that includes the *Empress of Ireland* and the recently sunk destroyer *Nipigon*, the Quebec Maritimes are eager to be seen as friendly to tourists. "The region has realized," Ewart told me, "that tourism will be linked to language and to the diversity of services in both languages."

My three trips there all held lessons in the reality of French-speaking Canada. The Quebecois I met were friendly, kind, and generous. Their rich culture is a joy to experience. Diving the *Empress of Ireland*, for many of the American and Canadian divers who have taken part in her history, has been its own unique experiment in cross-cultural empathy, community, and exchange.

ON FEBRUARY 7, 2002, Minister Richard Legendre of Quebec Sports Safety (Ministre responsable de la Jeunesse, du Tourisme, du Loisir et du Sport et Ministre responsable de la Faune et des Parcs) signed a decree that would establish new regulations for sport diving in the province. The decree was the result of a series of reports that had been issued by the Quebec coroner, Denis Boudrias, in which he had analyzed the "sad situation" responsible for the thirteen most recent deaths of scuba divers in Quebec's waters. The ministry had delegated decision-making authority to the Fédération Québécoise des Activités Subaquatiques (FQAS). The nonprofit FQAS, which groups under its leadership "all the people and organizations in the Quebec diving community," had been asked to come up with a set of governing guidelines for the sport of scuba diving in Quebec.

Minister Legendre announced the decision: a complex set of regulations to rank the experience and training of sport divers, categories that would determine when, where, and how deep an individual diver might go. The new regulations were designed to ensure that divers would "benefit from safe diving courses, adapted to the diving conditions found in Québec."

To outsiders, especially divers from the United States, it smacked of government intrusion into the realm of sport diving. The diving community on both sides of the border, not surprisingly, wasn't happy with the government's stepping in. Neither was I, but Gary Kulisek explained to me the reality of the newly issued diving regulations. He sat on the board of directors of the FQAS.

Kulisek told me that Canada, and Quebec in particular, is a "very socialist country," and "hence the government feels it has to protect its people, even from themselves." This paternalistic tendency puts the Canadian sporting community at constant loggerheads with its government leaders. Kulisek gave me another example. Several years ago, after a government study on snow skiing accidents, the ministry decided to install traffic lights on its slopes. The ski industry strongly protested the ridiculous suggestion. A standoff resulted, and fortunately for skiers the plan withered away.

Government intrusion into sport, Kulisek told me, had a history of noble desires to correct what was wrong and dangerous; but, he added, "the regulation process was then handed over to the bureaucrats to implement, and they turned it into something that was insane."

The dive community was terrified that the same bureaucratic process might begin to develop in its waters. Motivated by the dive community's fear of being regulated out of business, the FQAS, as a concerned party, stepped in with more practical suggestions and forced a compromise of sorts.

The regulations, which Gary Kulisek insisted do make sense, are now in place, but nowhere near ready to be implemented. Kulisek, like other Rimouski dive operators, does little to help this implementation along. It's a form of benign neglect, I deduced, that will ensure that the *Empress of Ireland* remains accessible to divers.

Compounding the problem of the new regulations is the issue of policing them. The government has never determined who would enforce them. The FQAS has no policing mandate. Even if the practicalities of issuing the appropriate new dive cards were in place in Quebec, Americans, at least officially, would have to prove they had had the necessary stateside training to be issued temporary FQAS cards.

But as Kulisek somewhat indelicately puts it, "Since the mechanics for issuing the cards are not in place, we can't issue the cards. So you can't be at fault for not having one because where the fuck would you get it?"

The newly proposed FQAS regulations may die a slow death. The only danger in that, according to Kulisek, is if some other Quebec agency stepped in and did something "really stupid." I'm sure that when he told me that he was thinking of the traffic lights on the ski slopes.

As it stands today, the practicalities of diving in Quebec remain unchanged because of regulation and likely will continue that way for some time. The Ministry of Tourism, a powerful force in Quebec, remains eager to smooth over any rough spots in the way of tourist dollars; the ministry wants to see the Quebec Maritimes flourish economically, and diving has always helped. Diving access to the *Empress of Ireland*, it appears, will not be affected in the near future.

As noble as the government's intentions toward diving safety are, in my estimation the bureaucratic intrusion only confuses matters and incenses divers. The dive operators in Rimouski already have legitimate concerns about who dives the *Empress*. A diving death in the Gulf of St. Lawrence is bad for everyone, so they already screen divers before taking them to the wreck. Certainly diving accidents out on the *Empress* will continue to occur, since the danger is part of its appeal. But deep-wreck diving can be reasonably safe if a diver's credentials are adequately checked. You can't put a cop out on the *Empress* any more than you could on the ski slopes. Most divers, including me, don't think the government should be in the position of determining who belongs out there. Concern for safety by the wreck-diving community and operators, as imperfect as it may be, is still the best way to keep the sport safe.

The politics and cultural history surrounding the *Empress of Ireland* will probably never go away. I wholeheartedly agree that divers should no longer remove artifacts, since that lessens the historical significance of the wreck and diminishes the cultural heritage of Quebec for the benefit of a few individuals. I don't believe most wreck divers would want to accept the challenge of diving the *Empress* only to find a vacant shell of what she once was. It would be like visiting an empty museum. Time capsules are meant to remain intact.

IN MY DREAMS I sometimes still see the *Empress of Ireland* ablaze in its Edwardian splendor, steaming down the St. Lawrence toward her fate. I can picture her this way only because I have seen and known her as she is now, resting on the bottom of the Gulf, still a tomb to hundreds of souls. Her ghostly image, in reality as in the imagination, evokes wonder, excitement, fear, and sorrow. For me, knowing the *Empress* has been a way of connecting to the past, and the past is part of who we are.

Diving Guidelines

Wreck of the *Empress of Ireland*: A Protected Cultural Resource

The following is provided by the Québec Ministère de la Culture et des Communications (Quebec Ministry of Culture and Communications) and the Récifs Artificiels de l'Estuaire du Québec–RAEQ (Artificial Reef Society of Quebec Estuary).

THE WRECK OF the *Empress of Ireland*, classified an historical and archaeological monument on April 15, 1999, by the Culture and Communications Department of Quebec, represents a major cultural and tourist attraction in the Lower St. Lawrence region. In order to protect this unique heritage and further its promotion, some rules have been set out to prevent damages that might be caused to the wreck and ensure the safety of divers.

Two Laws to Protect the Wreck

The wreck of the *Empress of Ireland* stands now under the protection of two complementary laws. As far as the Canadian government is concerned, the wreck of the *Empress of Ireland* stands under the responsibility of the Receiver of Wreck pursuant to part VI of the *Canada Shipping Act*. This act provides that the discoverer of a wreck has the obligation to deliver it to the Receiver of Wreck. According to this act, a wreck can be a ship or any other boat, a part of a ship, her cargo, or the personal belongings of the crew or the passengers.

For being classified an historical and archaeological monument, the wreck stands under the provision of the *Cultural Property Act of Quebec*. In the case of the wreck of the *Empress of Ireland*, that means that **the removal of objects or deeds that might cause damages to the wreck is now prohibited**, except within an archaeological research authorized by the Ministère de la Culture et des Communications. Thus, in consultation with the concerned parties in the region, **diving the wreck is always authorized** and no permit from the Ministère de la Culture et des Communications is needed **as long as the provisions of the *Cultural Property Act* are adhered to.**

Access to the Wreck

- An information buoy installed by the Canadian Coast Guard over the wreck states that is a protected historical wreck.
- The wreck lies at 42 meters (140 feet) depth on her starboard side at 6.5 nautical miles northeast from the Pointe-au-Père pier and 4.5 nautical miles off Sainte-Luce and within the territory of this municipality. At latitude 48 37′30″ N, and longitude 68 24′30″ W (approximately).
- Any removal or displacement of objects as well as any deed likely to alter the wreck is strictly prohibited under the provision of the *Cultural Property Act*. Is guilty of an offense and liable to a fine any person who contravenes the provisions of the law, as well as any person who, by performing or failing to perform an act, assists another person in committing such offense.
- Divers must use any of the three private mooring buoys installed by the Société des Récifs Artificiels de l'Estuaire du Québec (Artificial Reef Society of Quebec Estuary—RAEQ). These buoys, which adhere to the *Private Buoys Regulations* of the *Canadian Shipping Act*, have been authorized by the Ministère de la Culture et des Communications in keeping with the *Cultural Property Act*.
- The wreck of the *Empress of Ireland* is accessible until October 1, when the buoys will be removed. The ships mooring at said buoys must be less than 5 tons with a length overall not exceeding 30 feet.
- The Société des Récifs Artificiels de l'Estuaire du Québec (Artificial Reef Society of Quebec Estuary—RAEQ) releases itself from any liability as to the use of these buoys or any activity over the wreck of the *Empress of Ireland*.
- For safety reasons, no other buoy shall be tolerated over the wreck.
- **As these are private buoys, it is mandatory for the divers to register at the head office of the RAEQ (22, route du Fleur Ouest, Sainte-Luce, phone 418-739-5271) or at de Rimouski-la marina (418-723-0202). Registration will contribute to a better management of the site and increased safety for the divers.**

Safety Recommendations

The location of the wreck of the *Empress of Ireland* is considered to be a challenging diving site that could involve a few risks. Divers have to take into account the depth, which will make the dive tables necessary, occasionally strong currents, poor visibility at times, cold waters, sometimes adverse sea conditions, distance (4.5 nautical miles offshore) and the wreck herself, the structure of which can trap even experienced divers. These conditions demand the greatest prudence and respect of scuba diving safety rules.

- Acknowledged experience and technical certification in scuba diving.
- Never leave a boat unoccupied on the surface.
- Have a marine or any other efficient communicating system.
- Respect laws and regulations pertaining to navigation.
- Check weather conditions (temperature, tides, wind, etc.) before every dive.
- In view of the risks for the divers' safety and the damages that might be caused to the wreck, it is recommended not to penetrate into the wreck.
- No mooring ropes or any other equipment must be left abandoned on the wreck by the divers.
- Divers are responsible for their own safety. The Ministère de la Culture et des Communications du Québec releases itself from any liability and therefore cannot be held liable for the safety of people diving on the wreck.

In Case of Emergency

- Divers must report all their dive trips prior to the departure and when they are back.
- In case of an emergency, call immediately the Coast Guard: channel 16 VHS, *16 cellular telephone.
- Diving Emergency: (418) 723-7851.
- Centre hospitalier de Rimouski (Hospital)—Emergency: (418) 724-8554.
- Police and ambulance: 911.

For Further Information

For further information about the protection of the wreck, please contact:

Ministère de la Culture et des Communications
Bas-Saint-Laurent Regional Office
337 Moreault
1st floor, Room 12
Rimouski, QC
G5L 1P4
Phone: (418) 727-3650
Fax: (418) 727-3824
drbsl@mcc.gouv.qc.ca

Michel Demers, Receiver of Wreck
Fisheries and Oceans Canada
Navigable Waters Protection
101 Champlain Blvd.
Quebec City, QC
G1K 7Y7
Phone: (418) 648-5403
Fax: (418) 648-7640
demersm@dfo-mpo.gc.ca

The wreck of the *Empress of Ireland* belongs to our heritage; help us protect her. Your co-operation is essential to protect this historical treasure and to ensure your own safety and the safety of other divers.

Data Sheet of the *Empress of Ireland*

Architect:	Francis Elgar
Shipbuilder:	Fairfield Shipbuilding and Engineering
Length:	548 feet (168 meters)
Breadth:	65 feet (20 meters)
Gross tonnage:	14,500 tons
Displacement:	26,000 tons
Draught:	27 feet (8 meters)
Propulsion:	Quadruple-expansion reciprocating steam engines
Horsepower:	18,000
Top speed:	20 knots
Watertight bulkheads:	10
Watertight compartments:	11
Maximum capacity:	1,550 passengers, including 420 crew members
Lifeboats:	16 steel, 20 Englehart collapsibles, 20 Berthon collapsibles
Quebec to Liverpool:	6 days, including 4 for crossing the Atlantic

Waiver of Risk for Diving the *Empress of Ireland*

All diving charter operations require divers to sign waivers of risk due to the inherent danger in sport diving. Because of increasing litigation resulting from diving accidents charter operators have become more specific about the risks that a diver will be taking on any specific dive. The following waiver from Alp-Maritimes Sports is the one a diver intent on diving the wreck of the *Empress of Ireland* must sign before boarding the dive boat.

RELEASE OF LIABILITY, WAIVER OF CLAIMS, ASSUMPTION OF RISKS AND INDEMNITY AGREEMENT

BY CHOOSING TO SIGN THIS DOCUMENT YOU WILL WAIVE CERTAIN LEGAL RIGHTS

PLEASE READ CAREFULLY!

Name of participant_____

Address:_____

_____ City:_____

Prov/State:_____ Postal Code_____

Telephone: (_____) _____

To: ALP-MARITIMES SPORTS INC. and its subcontractors, the vessel owners, charterers and operators, the sponsors and their respective directors, officers, employees, agents, representatives and volunteers (collectively, the "Released Parties")

ASSUMPTION OF RISKS

I, THE UNDERSIGNED, _____,

HEREBY DECLARE THE FOLLOWING:

I am aware that participating in the activities offered by or associated with the Released Parties, including the use of equipment and facilities, exposes me to many inherent risks, dangers and hazards. By engaging in any activities offered by or associated with the Released Parties, I freely accept and fully assume all inherent risks, dangers, and hazards, including the risk and possibility of personal injury, death, property damage or loss resulting therefrom. _____ (initials).

I expressly understand and agree that the Released Parties assume no responsibility or liability for service, transportation or equipment made available by any travel company or travel agency, equipment manufacturer, distributor or rental agency, resort, hotel or other such entity, as to availability or safety, quality or condition, nor for the acts of any employee or agent of any such entity. I understand and agree that the Released Parties do not accept or assume any responsibility or liability for my safety, freedom from accident or injury that may arise or result, directly or indirectly, while participating in the activities offered by or associated with the Released Parties.

LIABILITY RELEASE, WAIVER OF CLAIMS & INDEMNITY AGREEMENT

I, THE UNDERSIGNED DECLARE THAT:

In consideration of the Released Parties permitting me to participate in their activities, permitting me the use of equipment and facilities, I hereby agree as follows:

TO WAIVE ANY AND ALL CLAIMS that I have now or in the future against any of the Released Parties; _____ (initials)

TO RELEASE suffer or that my legal representatives may suffer due to any cause whatsoever including negligence, breach of each of the Released Parties from any and all liability for any loss, damage, injury, or expense that I may contract, breach of duty of care, product liability, strict liability, unseaworthiness of vessel, or fault of any of the Released Parties, notwithstanding any statutory provisions to the contrary; _____ (initials)

TO HOLD HARMLESS, DEFEND AND INDEMNIFY the Released Parties from any and all claim or liability for any property damage, loss, personal injury or death to any third party, resulting from my activities and my participation in the activities, and use of equipment and facilities, offered by or associated with Released Parties. _____ (initials).

I further understand that remoteness of the area, local custom and prevailing weather conditions may cause substitution of facilities and/or equipment, and inconvenience or modification to portions of the activities and the Released Parties reserve the right to modify and/or cancel arrangements due to unfavorable weather conditions and the right to substitute facilities and equipment. In the event of equipment failure of the vessel, unavailability of labor or equipment due to strikes, lockouts, political or labor disturbances or the like, or passenger bookings which are in the sole discretion of the Released Parties insufficient to permit a charter or the conduct of any proposed activity, the Released Parties reserve the right to cancel the charter or any proposed activity and to refund all deposits. Notwithstanding anything contained herein to the contrary, no refunds shall be made for cancelled diving arrangements due to adverse weather, or for substitution of facilities and/or equipment.

IN ADDITION TO THE FOREGOING, I, THE UNDERSIGNED DECLARE THAT:

I am a capable swimmer in good health, and have no medical condition that could affect my corporal integrity. I am aware that the activities may require vigorous physical effort and stamina.

I am not impaired or influenced by alcohol or drugs and will not partake of the same during the activity. I have read and responded truthfully to the medical questionnaire attached hereto and understand and agree that the Released Parties accept no responsibility for determining my physical fitness to engage in any of the activities offered by or associated with the Released Parties.

I authorize the Released Parties to produce pictures of videos containing my image for sale or publicity without compensation, and I authorize the use of my name for mailing list purposes.

I HAVE READ AND UNDERSTOOD THIS AGREEMENT prior to signing it.

I am aware that by signing this agreement I am waiving certain legal rights that I or my heirs, legal representatives, executors, administrators and assigns may have against the Released Parties. It is my intention that this Agreement may be used in any claim, suit or litigation that may be brought against any of the Released Parties and that it shall constitute a complete defense.

This agreement shall be effecting and binding upon my heirs, legal representatives, executors, administrators and assigns. I understand and agree that, in the event that one or more of the provisions of this agreement, for any reason, is held by a court of competent jurisdiction to be invalid or unenforceable in any respect, such invalidity or unenforceability shall not affect any other provision hereof, and this agreement shall be construed as if such invalid or unenforceable provision had never been contained herein.

I hereby declare that I am of legal age and am competent to sign this Agreement or, if not, that my parent or legal guardian shall sign on my behalf, and that my parent or legal guardian is in complete understanding and concurrence with this Agreement.

I HAVE READ THIS AGREEMENT, I UNDERSTAND IT, I AGREE TO BE BOUND BY IT.

SIGNATURE OF PARTICIPANT_____ Date_____

WITNESS (Name)_____

SIGNATURE_____ Date_____

SIGNATURE OF PARENT OR GUARDIAN IF PARTICIPANT IS MINOR, and by their signature they, on my behalf release all claims that both they and I have.

_____ Date_____
(Parent Signature if participant is a minor)

WAIVER REAFFIRMATION
I HAVE READ THIS AGREEMENT, I UNDERSTAND IT, I AGREE TO BE BOUND BY IT.

SIGNATURE OF PARTICIPANT_____ Date_____

WITNESS (Name)_____

SIGNATURE_____ Date_____

SIGNATURE OF PARENT OR GUARDIAN IF PARTICIPANT IS MINOR, and by their signature they, on my behalf release all claims that both they and I have.

_____ Date_____
(Parent Signature if participant is a minor)

Diving Fatalities
on the *Empress of Ireland*

June 21, 1914: Edward Cossaboom, American commercial diver

June 24, 1981: Hector Moissan, Canadian commercial and sport diver

September 28, 1996: Lise Parent, Canadian sport diver

September 28, 1996: Xavier Roblain, Canadian sport diver

July 24, 2001: Pierre Lepage, Canadian sport diver

August 6, 2002: Serge Cournoyer, Canadian sport diver

Notes

Preface

xv **proof of that.** The *Mary Celeste* was the legendary ghost ship discovered-without a crew and cast adrift off the Azores in 1872. Cussler later found its wreckage on the Rochelais Reef in Haiti.

The *Lexington*, a ferry in transit between New York and Stonington, Connecticut, sank after a fire that killed nearly all of its passengers and crew in 1840. Cussler found what was left of the *Lexington* on the bottom of Long Island Sound near Port Jefferson, New York.

In 1864, the CSS *Hunley* became the first submarine in history to sink an enemy ship. Cussler found the Confederate submarine in the depths of Charleston's harbor in South Carolina.

The *Carpathia* was the ocean liner that rushed to the aid of the *Titanic* and arrived first on the scene. She was later torpedoed by a German U-boat during World War I off the coast of southern Ireland.

xv **torpedoed ship *Lusitania*** The *Lusitania* was the British ocean liner that was torpedoed by a German U-boat off the coast of southeast Ireland in 1915. The outcry over the sinking of the unarmed passenger ship led to the United States' entry into World War I.

xvi **the overall average.** Divers Alert Network 2001 dataset.

Chapter One. Fourteen Minutes

11 **events and gallant deeds.”** Marshall, *Tragic Story of the “Empress of Ireland,”* 166.

11 **down to the sea in ships.** Marshall, *Tragic Story of the “Empress of Ireland,”* 165.

13 **other part of the world.”** Croall, *Fourteen Minutes*, 42.

13 **Papa & Mama** Creighton, *Losing the “Empress.”*

21 **together in the distance.”** Wood, *Till We Meet Again.*

21 **pulled on their trousers.** Zeni, *Forgotten Empress*, 103.

21 **do anything for them.”** Marshall, *Tragic Story of the “Empress of Ireland,”* 48.

22 **so many monkeys.”** Croall, *Fourteen Minutes*, 105.

264 NOTES TO PAGES 24-77

24 *Storstad* **picked him up.** Marshall, *Tragic Story of the "Empress of Ireland."*
25 **you all the same."** Marshall, *Tragic Story of the "Empress of Ireland,"* 67.
29 **finish it is too."** Zeni, *Forgotten Empress,* 114.
29 **higher than the last."** Croall, *Fourteen Minutes,* 78.
30 **pluck and courage needed."** Marshall, *Tragic Story of the "Empress of Ireland,"* 69.
31 **weird moans of terror."** Marshall, *Tragic Story of the "Empress of Ireland,"* 73.
31 **had been exhausted."** Croall, *Fourteen Minutes,* 137.
34 **imminent danger of sinking.** "Women and children first" was law until rescinded in 1990.
34 **a hog in a ditch."** Zeni, *Forgotten Empress,* 122.
35 **reckless of the consequences."** Croall, *Fourteen Minutes,* 179.
39 **solution of the difficulty."** *Report and Evidence of the Commission of Inquiry into the Loss of the British Steamship "Empress of Ireland" of Liverpool through Collision with the Norwegian Steamship "Storstad"* (Quebec, June 1914).
41 **force of the impact."** *Report and Evidence of the Commission of Inquiry.*
41 **fog coming on.** *Report and Evidence of the Commission of Inquiry.*

Chapter Two. Brave Pioneers

46 **blown-out tire.** Ellsberg, *On the Bottom.*
47 **dangling canvas tentacles."** Zeni, *Forgotten Empress,* 171.
47 **release to the surface."** Zeni, *Forgotten Empress,* 172.
52 **only "Mae West"** The "Mae West" was the horse-collar CO_2 type of inflation vest first developed by the U.S. Navy in World War II for aviators and named after the busty film star Mae West.
53 **U.S. Navy Dive Tables** The United States Navy Dive Tables were first published in 1953 and to this day remain the standard for decompression diving.
53 **found the *Empress of Ireland."*** *Star Weekly* (Toronto), July 10, 1965.
59 **invaded their wetsuits.** Drysuits were first developed in 1958 as a result of a joint venture of the Poseidon Company and the Swedish navy. The perfecting of a gas-tight zipper (thanks to high-altitude flights in the 1950s) made drysuits practical. The first commercially marketed drysuit, the Poseidon Unisuit, which would not become available in North America until 1975, was a constant-volume suit, complete with a dry hood that incorporated a mask. But Ménard and his 1965 expedition crew used prototypes.
77 **twenty years away.** Loran-C, standing for LOng RAnge Navigation, is a radio navigation system developed by the U.S. Department of Defense

in the 1950s and maintained in North America by the U.S. Coast Guard. Loran-C provides precise marine navigation by vessels reading shore transmitters.

79 **stuck it in his own.** A second regulator, an octopus regulator, rigged to the first stage of the diver's regulator apparatus, was an innovation not yet widely implemented in the early 1980s. The second regulator would later make buddy breathing easier during emergencies, obviating the need to share the same mouthpiece.

82 **have safety standards."** *Summary Report (No. 213) of the Investigation into the Circumstances Surrounding the Loss of Life from a Diving Accident off Pointe-au-Père on 24 June, 1981* (Ottawa, November 1981).

Chapter Three. Extreme Diving

89 **"Beaudry lied to us."** Philippe Beaudry denied to me that he ever said the wreck lay in 180 to 195 feet of water. He claimed he had always said that it was 165 feet to the bottom off the bow, 145 feet to the bottom near the lifeboats, and less at the stern.

90 **books he had written.** Until recently nobody had more dives on the *Andrea Doria* than Gary Gentile. His record of 170 dives on the wreck was eclipsed in 2000 by Captain Dan Crowell of the dive boat *Seeker*. Gentile's dives on the deep-residing *Lusitania*, the famous ocean liner sunk by a German U-boat in World War I, were chronicled in his books *The Lusitania Controversies I* and *The Lusitania Controversies II*.

93 **copies for Gentile.** Ed Suarez ran his own trips to the *Empress* with dive buddies from his Maryland home area from 1990 to 1992. He was killed while diving deep in the Bakerston Mine, Harpers Ferry, West Virginia, on July 17, 1994.

93 **German warship *Ostfriesland*.** The USS *Monitor* lies off Cape Hatteras, and the German *Ostfriesland* is off the Virginia coast.

103 **diving the *Kolkhosnik*** The *Kolkhosnik* was a Soviet ship that had left Boston for Halifax to pick up cargo for Archangel, USSR, but sank when it ran aground on Sambro Shoal in Nova Scotia on January 16, 1942.

116 **Beaudry wasn't aboard.** According to Phil Beaudry, he would eventually lose in court in his effort to stop Michel Tadros from stripping teak from the wreck, but the legal action had already soured Tadros's investors, who were upset by the huge costs he had accumulated. The money dried up, and Tadros and his dive team quietly left Rimouski with only minimal damage done to the wreck.

Chapter Four. More Fatalities

128 **many seasonal moorings** In 1996 there were not yet permanent seasonal moorings. Local divers maintained their own until 1998, when the permanents went in.

129 **fatal gas embolism.** An arterial gas embolism is a major cause of death in diving that is most often caused by the expansion of respiratory gases while holding one's breath during ascent. Gas bubbles can occlude arteries, causing heart attack or stroke.

Chapter Five. Planning the 2002 Expedition

147 *Losing the "Empress": A Personal Journey.* Creighton, *Losing the "Empress,"* 120.

148 **the "Sally Ann"** "Sally Ann" was a nickname for the Salvation Army.

152 **memories of that night.** Grace Hanagan's story was told in Creighton, *Losing the "Empress."*

153 **this ghastly tragedy,"** Creighton, taped interview.

155 **Youth, Recreation, and Sports.** The Ministry for Youth, Recreation, and Sports was formerly known by the acronym RSSQ (Régie de la Sécurité dans les Sports du Québec).

164 **of progressive penetration.** Both independent twin-tank configurations and progressive penetration techniques had lost favor among wreck divers by the mid-1990s. The safer manifold-connected tanks with isolator valves and penetrations done with penetration reels had become accepted practice when diving deep wrecks.

169 **technically against the law,** The wreck of the *Empress of Ireland* was classified as a historical and archaeological monument on April 15, 1999, and protected by law from salvage or artifact removal.

Chapter Six. Adventure

173 **a factor in DCS.** According to R. W. Hamilton, cold reduces circulation, and this reduces gas transport, so that the body is further impaired in its ability to off-gas any toxic gases, increasing the chance that bubbles will form in the blood. This effect seems to be influenced by the phase of the dive where it occurs. On the bottom (gas uptake phase), this is not especially detrimental to decompression. Cold during decompression (outgas phase) is likely to increase risk, which may be why DCS is more likely the closer a diver ascends to the surface.

173 **sign expedition waivers** See Appendix Three.

174 **torso more closely.** The low-pressure hose from the first stage of a regulator connects to the second stage, the breathing mouthpiece. Low-pressure hoses also connect from the first stage to power inflators for the drysuit and buoyancy control devices. A high-pressure hose, from the first stage, connects to an air pressure gauge.

178 **back in 1914,** River pilots are now dropped off by outgoing ships and picked up by incoming ships at Les Escoumins, on the North Shore and thirty miles upriver (southeast) of Pointe-au-Père.

178 **but an estuary.** According to the Institute of Oceanographic Science at Rimouski (part of the University of Quebec), the waters off Rimouski are officially listed as Estuaire Maritime, or Maritime Estuary. Not quite river, not quite gulf.

194 **Weinke in 1995,** A handful of deep scuba divers were experimenting with deep decompression stops as early as the 1980s, but NAUI Technical Diving Operations didn't use a full-phase model based on Bruce Weinke's research at the Los Alamos National Laboratory until 1997.

Chapter Seven. Return to the *Empress of Ireland*

209 **submarine the *U-853*** The German *U-853* became trapped in Block Island Sound seven miles off Point Judith, Rhode Island. On May 6, 1945, the U.S. Navy depth-charged her, and she sank with all hands on board.

210 **breathing mix as needed.** The partial pressure of oxygen in the gas phase is the fraction of the total gas pressure that can be contributed to oxygen. For example, if air contains 21 percent oxygen, then the partial pressure of oxygen at one atmosphere (sea level) is 0.21 atmosphere.

210 **buoyancy compensator wings.** "Wings" have largely replaced the vest type of buoyancy compensators in deep diving. The wings are buoyancy air bladders mounted behind the diver on a back plate that secures the tanks or the rebreather unit to the diver's harness.

Epilogue

252 **individual diver might go.** See Appendix One.

Bibliography

Ballard, Robert D., and Rick Archbold. *Lost Liners*. New York: Hyperion, 1997.

Brown, David G. *The Last Log of the "Titanic."* Camden, Maine: International Marine, 2001.

Creighton, David. *Losing the "Empress": A Personal Journey: The "Empress of Ireland"'s Enduring Shadow*. Toronto: Dundurn Press, 2000.

Croall, James. *Fourteen Minutes: The Last Voyage of the "Empress of Ireland."* New York: Stein & Day, 1979, c1978.

Cussler, Clive. *Night Probe!* Boston: G. K. Hall, 1982.

Cussler, Clive, and Craig Dirgo. *The Sea Hunters: True Adventures with Famous Shipwrecks*. New York: Pocket Star Books, 2003.

———. *The Sea Hunters II*. New York: G. P. Putnam's Sons, 2002.

Ellsberg, Commander Edward. *On the Bottom*. New York: Dodd, Mead, 1929.

Grout, Derek. *"Empress of Ireland": The Story of an Edwardian Liner*. Charleston, South Carolina: Arcadia; Stroud, Gloucestershire: Tempus, 1998.

Marshall, Logan. *The Tragic Story of the "Empress of Ireland": An Authentic Account of the Most Horrible Disaster in Canadian History Constructed from the Real Facts Obtained from Those on Board Who Survived and Other Great Sea Disasters*. Philadelphia: John C. Winston, 1914. Reprint edited by W. H. Tantum, London: Patrick Stephens, 1972.

Wood, Herbert P. *Till We Meet Again: The Sinking of the "Empress of Ireland."* Toronto: Image, 1982.

Zeni, David. *Forgotten Empress: The "Empress of Ireland" Story*. Fredericton, New Brunswick: Goose Lane, 1998.

Acknowledgments

In writing a book of this nature I had to come to rely on dozens of people for their expertise, knowledge, and skills. One person who embodies all those talents and whose help was invaluable was Gary Kulisek of Alp-Maritimes Sports. Simply put, this book could not have been written without his help. His diving and organizing skills and his knowledge of the wreck, its history, and the people associated with it made this book possible. His grasp of the historical importance of the wreck and his knowledge of Quebec history and its people was of immense help. His command of French and English made him the ideal translator. The assistance of his sons Matts and Stefan and employees Tyler Bradford and Will Allen are much appreciated.

The Musée de la Mer in Pointe-au-Père, Quebec, and the George Scott Railton Heritage Centre in Toronto were great assets in forging the historical links to the *Empress of Ireland*. Heartfelt thanks to David Creighton for his help in putting a human face on one of the greatest maritime disasters in North American history. Clive Cussler was kind enough to allot me some time from his own writing to relive his history with the *Empress*. His contributions were essential to the telling of the story of the Canadian ocean liner.

Men and women long associated with the diving history of the *Empress*, much of it tragic, were generous with their time and patience. Philippe Beaudry, Jean-Pierre Bouillon, Veronica "Ronni" Gilligan, John Reekie, Diane Strong, David Bright, Bart Malone, Gary Gentile, Serge Lavoie, Marc Hardenne, Jean Philippe Ewart, and Dany St-Cyr need special thanks not only for sharing their memories of diving the *Empress* but also reliving for me some of the painful moments when the stories often ended in the death of friends and loved ones.

Sharing the experience of diving the *Empress* was an important ingredient to *Dark Descent*, and I would be remiss if I didn't thank my dive buddies for their participation and the stories of their dives. Thank you Peter Piemonte, Colin McRavey, M. Darryl Johnson, Tyler Bradford, Gary Gilligan, Dan Crowell, Matt Robinson, Gary Kulisek, Matts Kulisek, Jan and Hal Watts, Steve Brooks, and Will Allen.

Thanks must also be given to the piloting skills of Jean-Pierre Bouillon, Eric Boulanger, Simon Pelletier, and Jacques Tardis, who got us divers out and back to the wreck safely often in fog-shrouded and wind-tossed seas.

Photographs that liberally illustrate this book were supplied by Don Carroll, Philippe Beaudry, David Creighton, Ronni Gilligan, Diane Strong, Jean-Pierre Bouillon, Dany St-Cyr, Serge Lavoie, John Reekie, David Bright, Marc Hardenne, Gary Gentile, Gary Kulisek, Dan Crowell, Edie Summey, John McNally, and the George Scott Railton Heritage Centre, and to them I owe a debt of gratitude. Many thanks to Myron Stern for his mastery of Photoshop and the help he gave me.

Technical diving advice and diving physiology was generously provided by NAUI Director of Technical Operations Tim O'Leary, Dr. R. W. "Bill" Hamilton, and Dr. Robert Jackson, MD. Their thoughtful insights added to the depth of this book.

I must thank my editors Tris Coburn and Rebecca Taylor for their editing skills and for making this a measurably improved tome. My agents Jane Dystel and Miriam Goderich of Dystel & Goderich Literary Management made this book possible by expertly navigating me through the shoals of publishing. Special thanks go out to my wife Vicki, and daughters Kelly and Kaitlyn for suffering my diving absences and the seclusion I needed to write the book. My wife was also a terrific sounding board besides being a partner and stabilizing influence in this writing adventure. I couldn't have finished this book without her help.